IN AND OUT OF
THE BOX

D0727314

Robert Dougall

IN AND OUT OF
THE BOX

An Autobiography

FONTANA/COLLINS

First published by Wm Collins and Harvill Press 1973
First issued in Fontana 1975

Copyright © Robert Dougall 1973

Made and printed in Great Britain by
William Collins Sons & Co. Ltd, Glasgow

TO NAN
If a man will begin with certainties,
he shall end in doubts; but if he
will be content to begin with doubts,
he shall end in certainties.
                              Francis Bacon
                              (1561-1626)

The author wishes to express his gratitude to The Bodley
Head Ltd for permission to quote from *The Third Floor
Front: A View of Broadcasting in the Sixties* by Sir Hugh
Greene; and British Broadcasting Corporation; Asso-
ciated Newspapers Ltd.; Royal Society for the Protection
of Birds (Anthony Clay); Bedford County Press; Home
Counties Newspapers Ltd.; *Radio Times*; Dog's Life;
for permission to use copyright photographs

Contents

'This is Your Life'

A PAPERBACK PREFACE

Ever since I left the trams, or rather the regular rota of BBC Television News, things have been fairly fizzing. For a start, in the very first week I was invited to a party at London's Europa Hotel. *In and Out of the Box* had been launched just two months before and the Chairman of Collins the Publishers, the great Sir William himself, was going to present me with a copy of the book specially bound in calf leather to mark its seventh printing. Just one thing puzzled me. It was a much bigger party than I had expected and there were television lights and cameras too. I thought perhaps they were going to film a few minutes as a tailpiece to the News, but soon I met so many old chums I forgot all about the cameras.

We were just getting nicely under way when I suddenly had the shock of my life. Sir William had handed over the splendid presentation copy, there had been some speechifying and I was leaning over a low coffee table signing some books for friends.

When I looked up I nearly turned a couple of somersaults: standing beside me, smiling all over his face, was Eamonn Andrews. Under his arm was a large red book. Up till that moment, like dying, I had always thought 'This is Your Life' was something that only happened to other people. From then on the evening passed like some extraordinary dream. I couldn't believe it was really happening.

First I was driven to the headquarters of Thames Television at Euston Centre. There I was shown into a dressing room and Eamonn said would I please not come out for an hour. People taking part in the programme were in other dressing rooms and it was obviously important that I shouldn't see them beforehand. So there I was feeling rather like a condemned man – all alone except for a large bottle of champagne and a box of cigars. As it happens I don't smoke, and it's just as well I didn't drink all that champagne, otherwise it would have been a pretty comic programme.

Every so often someone would pop in to see if I was all right. They don't have a chaplain at Euston Centre otherwise he would probably have come to pray for me too. Instead, Howard Thomas, the chairman of Thames, looked in. He was quite jumpy: 'was I all right?' And he explained that they didn't usually do the show 'live' so he was a bit anxious. I realized that it was also one of the most expensive of all their programmes and that many thousands of pounds were at stake.

Then, at long last, my time had come. There was a short walk along a corridor with people I had never seen before patting me on the back and wishing me good luck. The skids were under me now. Then – the studio, the lights, the audience, and Eamonn doing his stuff and looking like the archangel Gabriel. The funny thing was I suddenly found I was enjoying myself enormously. How could I help it? There were so many lovely people gathered together and so many fantastic surprises. Like when Norbert Okare, the African newsreader of The Voice of Kenya, materialized from Nairobi; or that American seaman Harold C. Hazard whom we'd picked up from the Arctic thirty years before walked in miraculously from New York. Then there were colleagues old and new, family and friends; and I was particularly glad to see most of the ITN Newcasters too. Everyone had a night to remember and none more so than three-year-old grandson Ben who fell heavily for Jimmy Savile.

Thanks again, Thames, for a lovely party, and congratulations on all the meticulous organization and research that must have gone on behind the scenes.

Incidentally, that show was what this book is all about – a behind the scenes account of my own life spanning amongst other things forty-one years with the dear old Beeb. As far as I was concerned reporting the events of the day to the nation had never palled, but I'd reached the magic age of sixty and that's when the BBC whistle blows. For months well-meant little homilies came through the office post from the BBC Welfare Department offering me all kinds of helpful advice. It was even suggested that it would be better to wear loose-fitting shoes as my feet would probably begin to swell. I really feel I must be very lucky because so far my feet feel much as they have always done and, if anyone's interested, what hair I have left is my own; so are my teeth – all except one.

The fact is I'd had a good innings on the News and no doubt it was high time I had a chance to do something else. For a start I have written this book. My idea was simply to put on paper some thoughts I'd had buzzing around in my head for many years; also it seemed a tidy way to wind up a career. I don't think it ever occurred to me that anyone would buy it, let alone that the book would take off from the word go and become a bestseller. And now here it is again – popping up in paperback! So I hope you'll find some interest and fun as you follow me 'In and Out of the Box'.

Author's Note

As may well be all too evident, I wrote this book myself, in my primitive way, with a pen and countless sheets of foolscap. My wife Nan has been heroic in putting up with me meanwhile and in making endless trips to libraries for research material. Especial thanks too to Mrs Nicolette Talbot for deciphering and then impeccably typing the manuscript.

My debt to numerous colleagues on the BBC staff past and present is total: much of this book is their story as well as mine. Television pioneer D. H. Munro even lent me his scrapbook. The BBC Reference Library, the BBC Photographic Library, and BBC Television News Information have also given invaluable help.

I should like to acknowledge a debt to three authors in particular whose works have guided me: Professor Asa Briggs, Maurice Gorham and Peter Black, all meticulous chroniclers of the BBC. My thanks too go to the Director of the Royal Society for the Protection of Birds, Peter Conder, and members of his staff, especially Dorothy Rook, the Society's Librarian. For the Naval passages I was aided principally by Vice-Admiral B. B. Schofield's authoritative account of the Russian convoys.

Lastly, of course, my gratitude to that admirable and peculiarly British institution the BBC for providing me with such varied, fascinating and congenial employment over so many years.

Hampstead, April 1973

1 Turning-Point

'Meet Bob Dougall – he's quite mad!'

The words and the bantering tone were those of my old friend Hugh Venables as he flung open my office door at Bush House in Aldwych – the headquarters of the BBC European Service. It was the middle of that desperately bleak winter of 1947. Standing beside him was a girl with fairish hair, the lightest blue eyes and a determined expression. She looked very English, very sane and, for some reason, totally out of place. I didn't know it, but life was giving me a lucky break.

Hugh, who had been a colleague of mine as an Announcer in the BBC Empire Service before the war, was now Head of the Presentation Department. He had done a great job at Bush House – once the Navy, which he had been so anxious to join, had turned him down because of his colour blindness. He had in the meantime acquired an odd mannerism of fixing a point about a yard to one's left and addressing all his remarks to that. I found this a trifle disconcerting. He went on, grinning at this same invisible spot, 'Bob – meet Nan Byam, she's joining us from Broadcasting House. Perhaps you could give her an audition?' I said that nothing would please me more, and fixed a time for that same afternoon.

I was quite glad to have the prospect of something to do. I wasn't finding it easy to get re-settled in a BBC which had expanded and changed greatly during my three years or so in the Navy. In my mind, I could still hear the cries of the seamen we'd had to leave to drown in the Arctic night. I could still see the zombie-like figures from Stalin's slave camps, as they stumbled through the snow; still smell the nauseous stench of bodies under the rubble that once had been Berlin.

The trouble was that I hadn't got any definite job. Officially, I was on attachment to the Presentation Department of the European Service, but with the exception of a few talks I had broadcast in German and Russian nothing much had come my way.

Bush House, it seemed to me, was a confusing place to work in. It had never been designed for broadcasting. The BBC

European Service had moved into the East Wing of this sprawling office block in 1940. It was shared with various commercial companies and a branch of the Air Ministry. The dozen or so studios were scattered about on various floors and I was always getting lost. But all the same one remembered it had been from these drab studios that De Gaulle had rallied the French Resistance, and Douglas Ritchie, as Colonel Britton, had headed that great team of broadcasters with the inspired call sign, based on the opening bars of Beethoven's Fifth, that kept occupied Europe's hopes alive in the darkest days of the war.

So, there I was that afternoon sitting at the Control Desk, looking through the glass panel, where the new candidate was settling in at the microphone. I had suggested she should read a short passage from *The Listener*. There was something about the tilt of her head and the way she handled the script that told me she was a beginner, but hell-bent on cracking this, to her, unfamiliar nut. She began rather jerkily, but in a voice of exceptional clarity and pleasing tone, except for some slightly flattened vowel sounds. Then, there was an extraordinary coincidence: a sentence cropped up with the word 'misled' in it. This came out as 'mizzled'. It was too much for me, because it so happened that I had mispronounced this very same word at one of my auditions many years before. I rolled about with laughter. I saw her look up, startled. It occurred to me she might think I *was* mad, so I pressed down the talk-back, and the ice was broken between us. Incidentally, I still think that the verb 'to mizzle' sounds as though it ought to mean 'to cheat or deceive'. Anyway, in my subsequent report I wrote that Nan Byam showed considerable promise.

Two months later, we got married and were soon to leave for Singapore. Nan and I had met at a time when for neither of us were things at their best. She was a widow with a two-year-old daughter and an overdraft, and as you've gathered I wasn't exactly flourishing.

All that was in 1947, but I first joined the BBC as long ago as January 1933. So, I've had just on forty years of Auntie or the Corp or the Beeb – call it what you will. It will give you an idea when I tell you my staff number is 1426, whereas today there are more than 25,000 of us. In that time, I've seen many changes, lived through much history and met many of the people, who've shaped events.

It's been my privilege almost all of that time to be a front man either as Announcer, Reporter, Commentator or News-reader on radio and television. A desk job has never appealed to me nor has the BBC power game. To organise and control other people doesn't amuse me. My business has always been that of direct communicator with the public. I have felt that as long as I could please the listeners or viewers, the BBC Heads would leave me pretty much alone.

If this sounds odd, I must explain that I don't like being swallowed up without trace by a big organisation however humane or beneficent it is. It may be something to do with my having fifty per cent Celtic blood. Whatever it is, I think I am a loner. There may be subsidiary reasons for this too. As a child, I was plagued with asthma and in consequence I spent a lot of my early years alone in bed fighting for breath. Then, in my teens I knew what it meant to be hard up. My friends always had very much more money that I had and this made me feel different from them. I am glad now it was so. I learnt to have an understanding of and sympathy for other people's troubles and this too gave me an incentive. I knew that if I was going to make anything of my life it was up to me – and to me alone.

It taught me to make the most of opportunities as they arose, although, heaven knows, over the years, I've missed more buses than I've caught. In many respects, working on the Programme side of the BBC is much more than a job. It becomes a way of life. This is so, not only because of the demanding and often absorbing nature of the work, but also because of the shift system, which frequently means working over weekends and on public holidays. During my forty years with the Corporation, there is not an hour of night or day that I haven't broadcast in one Service or another. Inevitably this means one becomes a slave of the clock. Every broadcaster knows what it is to wake in the night in a frenzy at dreaming he has missed a programme. It is a recurrent nightmare. Another variation is the dream when you can't find the studio where you are due to appear. The number of times I have chased along endless corridors and up endless staircases in a mad search for the studio that just isn't there . . . One consequence of all this is that most long-service BBC types have built-in clocks in their heads. Their lives have been ruled by the moving hand for so long that they're almost incapable of being late for an appointment.

Another aspect of the broadcaster's life is that he so often finds himself going against the tide. A normal social life is almost impossible. This is one of the reasons for the frequency of BBC inter-staff marriages. In this respect, I feel sure, the medical profession and the broadcasters must be at the top of the league.

On the credit side, on the other hand, there's a great deal to be said for missing out on rush-hour travel. Also for having days off during the week, when most people are at work. And what better time is there to sleep than after lunch?

So, I think I've been lucky all along the line. In getting into the BBC in the first place, in meeting my wife when I did, in making the change from radio to television, and also, most important this, in being able to acquire a country cottage about twenty years ago. It was in Suffolk on one of the most easterly parts of the coast and for this reason exceptionally rich in bird-life, being right on the migration route from Scandinavia to Spain and Africa. In watching and studying the birds over the years, I have gained a whole new interest, almost a new dimension. It was, I found, the perfect antidote to the hectic life and the bright lights of the television studio and I soon enrolled as a member of the Royal Society for the Protection of Birds.

This contact with wildlife and the countryside has been tremendously important to me over the years. It has helped me not only to keep reasonably fit, but also to keep things in perspective. It's so easy at the Television Centre building to think that the whole world revolves around it. But out on the reed-beds of Suffolk, watching a marsh harrier gliding low in search of his prey, there's a timelessness about the scene that makes present troubles seem remote and less important. I became all the more interested because a few miles down the coast at Minsmere was one of the largest bird reserves in the country. As the years went by, in one way and another, I found I got more and more engrossed with the important conservation work the RSPB was doing.

Nevertheless, I was totally unprepared for a certain telephone call which came to our Hampstead home at about ten o'clock one Saturday evening. It was from the Chairman of the RSPB, one of the most distinguished ornithologists in the country. I had never met him. To me he was just a name on their notepaper, but here he was saying: 'This is Stanley

Cramp speaking, would you allow me to put your name forward as President of the Society?'

I was so astonished I couldn't even reply. He must have thought I'd been cut off, because, in a moment, he was saying, 'Are you still there?' I asked him if he was serious. He assured me he was, so I said I would like time to think it over. We arranged to meet for lunch a few days later at Simpsons in the Strand.

When I got there, I found him sitting at a table together with the Director of the Society, Peter Conder, whom I had met before at Minsmere. As I went up to them, I remember saying, 'Don't worry, if you've changed your minds I shall quite understand.'

To my surprise they said they hadn't, and with a little arm-twisting and after the second dry Martini, I agreed to let my name go forward. And, marvellous to relate, at the subsequent Annual General Meeting I was duly elected. That is how I found myself the President of the largest conservation society in the country: the Royal Society for the Protection of Birds.

What could be a more complete contrast to the world of television? In my working life, the camera focuses on me, but in my private life I am the one who does the focusing on the fascinating birdlife of this and other lands, which I have been lucky enough to see.

2 Out of the Box

Come to think of it – I suppose I am rather a rare bird myself. I mean my head and shoulders have been appearing on the box in people's homes for so long that there has been speculation in some quarters as to whether I am ten feet or perhaps two feet tall or, indeed, as to whether I have legs at all. The result is that when I pop up in another setting, away from the box, people tend to clutch at me almost as though I were an escaped budgerigar. Television breeds a closeness and intimacy quite unlike that of any other medium. Your image is projected straight into people's homes. You become, as it were, a privileged guest at innumerable firesides. What is more a Newsreader is not playing a role, not appearing as another character, or in costume, but simply as himself. He therefore builds up over the years a special kind of rapport with the public.

Firstly, there is the recognition problem. This can take many different forms. In some cases it is only partial. The face is familiar, but where on earth has it been seen before? This can be trying if you are on the receiving end, because it sets up a curiosity that can break over you in waves. I may be in a restaurant, a pub, in a bus, a tube, on a beach, or almost anywhere in fact, when someone spots me ; and then the trouble begins. Let me give you an example. A classic case of partial recognition. One morning I was doing some shopping in Hampstead, where our family has its London headquarters. When not on duty at the Television Centre, out come old corduroys and polo-necked sweater, and, I suppose, sometimes, I do look a bit rugged.

This particular morning I was just coming out of a shop and about to cross the road, when an oldish lady, pulling one of those shopping trolley baskets on wheels, plonked herself in front of me and kept on staring into my face. I wasn't awfully pleased but, as she was blocking my way, I just had to stand there and try not to look too put out. When she had peered her fill, as you might say, she growled at me, 'Are you the Robert Dougall who gives the News on television?'

I thought I'd better own up, so I said, 'Yes,' hopefully, because I thought, well, you never know, she might say something nice, with which she promptly fired her second salvo.

'Oh! You look ever so much better on television! Ever so much better – whatever do they do to you?' There was no answer to that one. I just tried not to look too hurt and carried on my way with what little dignity I had left. I can only imagine that she thought the television boys must give me a re-spray or something every night before I was allowed on. In fact, we hardly use any make-up at all.

Then, there's a second kind of half recognition, which takes a different form. Here, the face is instantly spotted, but the spotter remains totally confused as to where he or she has seen it. This is perfectly the largest category of all. At one time or another I have been mistakenly identified and hailed, as a doctor, as a member of one of London's Clubs, or as someone who once stayed at a certain hotel. The worst aspect here is that the spotter gets so curious that a situation develops, even if nothing is said. Their friends are nudged and whisperings go on, until, sometimes, I can bear it no longer and bark at them: 'Yes, all right, I know, you've seen me on telly.'

A typical case of mistaken identity of this kind occurred one day as I was leaving the Westbury Hotel off London's Bond Street. No, I wasn't staying there, in fact I can't even afford to eat there very often but it so happens that Topper's, the Bond Street Barbers, who have cut my hair for about twenty years, have set up their establishment in the basement at the Westbury. I was leaving the opulent portals, having been smartened up by Henry at Toppers, when a shortish chap, wearing a nifty suit, and with a pink, English-looking face crowned by a bowler, approached me with arm outstretched. I tentatively shook his hand, as he exclaimed: 'Marvellous to see you, old boy – where have you been all this time? – Haven't seen you for ages – let's go and have a drink somewhere.' I continued looking pretty blank, so he eventually tumbled to it that I hadn't the remotest idea who he was. His smile began to fade as he asked me, 'You were the political candidate at High Wycombe, weren't you?' I hastily disabused him of any ideas of that kind and continued on my way.

Then, again, there's the form of recognition where you get called a name, but the wrong one. I was walking along Oxford Street one afternoon, it was raining, and a little old lady came at me with her umbrella at the charge. I was forced to take sudden avoiding action, just as she was about to poke me in the left eye. Thereupon, she lowered her umbrella and looked up at me roguishly, as she said, 'Excuse me – but I know you – Alvar Lidell, isn't it?' No, lady – actually I'm the Shah of Persia, I felt like replying.

Then there is another kind of challenge in this recognition game. Some viewers seem offended if I don't immediately hail them with a merry smile when I meet them in the street. One morning, when I had slipped out of Television Centre for a breather, which is a very necessary thing to do from time to time, I happened to see two ladies on the pavement. As I passed them, one turned to the other, saying, in a recriminatory tone which I felt I was meant to overhear: 'He doesn't recognise us when he's out!' This made me feel I had let the side down but, really, I can't go around all the time with a fixed grin on my face!

As always, it is the young who ask the most penetrating questions. When I get any spare time, which isn't very often, I love to slip along to Lords to watch some cricket. One day I was leaving the pavilion, which is rather like a mixture between a museum, a Victorian railway station and the Chamber of Horrors, when I was surrounded by a babble of small boys demanding my autograph. There were about eight of them. I was busy signing away and thinking what splendid little chaps they were, when I was chilled by a hoarse, rasping whisper from the back of the throng, as one of them turned to his chum and asked, 'OOwizee?'

Oh well, the young, of course, have always been devastating at cutting one down to size. I ought to know. I was walking in Regent's Park, near the Zoo, when I unexpectedly ran across an old friend and colleague. He had his small daughter with him – a charming child of about three, with beautiful, straight fair hair. She was clutching her father by the hand, and he, by way of introduction, said to her, 'This is Mr Dougall, you know, the man you see at home in the box.' Thereupon, she fixed me with her penetrating, cornflower blue eyes and, turning away, looked up at her father as she piped up, 'Daddy, how does he get out of the box?' A good question.

But, there is no doubt that television does seem to be a confusing medium for people of all ages. This could be told by the tone of the mail reaching our third floor office at Television

16

Centre. It is a pleasant room with a large desk, two office chairs, an armchair, and a television set, although the most important item of furniture is a nest of trays for correspondence.

The curious thing is that from reading some of the letters it becomes clear the writers have a shrewd suspicion that when reading the news we can in fact really see them. One lady even asked if we liked the colour of the new curtains she had put up in her sitting room. Mercifully the BBC has a Programme Correspondence Section which copes with queries about general points. These receive official Corporation answers which, while courteous and urbane to a degree, are not conducive to a lengthy correspondence. But for the most part, letters addressed to one of the Newsreaders require personal replies, This takes up a lot of our spare time between News programmes.

Some people seem to think we are exalted beings. One day I answered the office telephone and a rather blah male voice at the other end was asking, 'Is that Mr Dougall's private secretary?' It was a retired Naval Commander asking me to open a fête or something. As a matter of fact, we don't have secretaries, let alone a private one. So, if a viewer or listener writes in, he or she really does get a personal reply. This, it seems to me, is an important part of the job. The letters are incidentally a startling indication of the numbers of lonely people in our society today. For them, especially, the Newsreader appearing in their homes night after night over the years becomes, it would seem, almost a trusted friend. He regularly brings news and information, if not always good tidings. His dress and appearance are usually neat and mostly inoffensive. He never answers back, doesn't even smell, and smiles when he says good night. All that, judging by the letters, can add up to quite an important relationship. It does not seem to be confined to any age group, as I get many letters from school children (heaven knows they can be lonely too) ; also from teenagers, and frequently even from married couples.

Can it be that change of all kinds is so frequent and endemic in our life today that a television Newsreader can become a reliable symbol of permanence and continuity? After all, under present conditions, the family doctor, as we used to know him, has almost ceased to exist. The local vicar doesn't quite fill the role he used to either, and in many cases, even the small shop-keeper has given way to an impersonal supermarket. In these conditions, perhaps it is not so surprising that lonely people

17

will look even to an electronic image for reassurance. Some letters make me feel very humble, indeed almost all of them make me feel my job is, in a sense, a privilege. For example, when someone writes to say how much I have helped them at a difficult time in their life, I am inclined to be incredulous. How can you help a person by just giving out the News on television? But this has happened so many times I can only think it is because they can at least rely on my being there.

Letters often come from people when they move house or go on holiday. They say how pleased they were when they reached the new, unfamiliar surroundings to find I was on the box there too. Some of the most interesting letters of this kind have come from as far away as Australia when, to inaugurate the opening of the Pacific Satellite in 1970, a fifteen-minute News programme read by me was televised live from Television Centre in London across the length and breadth of Australia.

But there is no doubt that of all the thousands of letters I've received from viewers in the past fifteen years or so my favourite came from an old lady who lived somewhere in Hertfordshire. I think I ought to have it framed. She wrote to me, in a spidery hand, to say that she was a little deaf, so she did like to sit right close up to her machine, as she called it, when I was giving the News. But, if this put me off in any way, she would quite understand and move further back. Really, the height of consideration. Recently at a function, a dear old lady caused some raised eyebrows. She came up to me confidingly and then piped up at the top of her voice: 'There's one thing about you Mr Dougall – you're the nicest man I know to go to bed with!' She then explained that she had recently installed a TV set in her bedroom.

As stated, it is evident that a lot of people seem to think I can see them. There was a letter from Scotland, which came from a crofter's cottage in the Highlands. They were living in pretty close quarters there and a member of the family wrote to say that Grannie was preparing for bed when the News was switched on. They were tickled to find that Grannie got very upset and kept tugging her gown across her chest, as she said, 'I dinna want him tae see me like this!' Another letter, written to a Sunday paper, came from a good lady who used to take her portable television set with her when she was having a bath! Everything was going swimmingly until I came on to give the

News. At that point, she let out a yell, scrambled out of the bath, rushed to the set and covered it with a towel! Then, I was told of an old-age pensioner in Harrogate. Every time she drew her pension, it seems, she would come home and hide it in a tobacco jar on the mantelpiece. But, before doing so, she took great care to make sure the television set was well and truly covered up, just in case I was looking.

The young obviously get confused too. There was a letter, also published in a Sunday paper, from a lady with eighteen-month-old twins. She wrote that every time I appeared on the screen to give the News the twins toddled across the sitting-room floor, right up to the set, to offer me a biscuit.

There is another aspect of the Newsreader's relationship with the public and a very important one it is. From all I have been saying about his being regarded as a sort of family friend, it follows that he is also in great demand as an Opener of fêtes, 'Autumn Fayres' and Christmas bazaars. That is to say nothing of schools, exhibitions and flower shows; and once I was even asked to open some squash courts. The News-readers or other television personalities, whatever that expression means, are 'naturals' as Openers, because of their curiosity value. People want to see what they look like away from the box. Then, they are also, as near as possible, classless and politically neutral. Unfortunately, the hazards can be numerous. For some reason, the organisers of these functions seldom seem to think it necessary to provide adequate briefing. When notes are provided and a short speech is prepared, it is all too often only to find to one's dismay that the chairman, or whoever is chosen to introduce you, has been given the same notes. He will then proceed to say everything you were going to say, which leaves you floundering.

Even before you begin, as soon as you have set foot on a frequently rickety platform, there is the ordeal by floral tribute. This invariably takes the form of a diminutive figure, male or female, which clambers up, and quite often, having arrived, proceeds timorously, to hand the buttonhole to the wrong person. The audience love this bit. Then, eventually, the bearer of the buttonhole is steered, falteringly, in one's own direction. A loving pat on the head; and I am left holding a somewhat battered pink carnation esconced in asparagus fern. Much injury has been done to it with wire and silver paper. There are three choices: but, in no case, can you win. If you try to

19

plant it on some other platform figure, or simply lay it reverently on table or chair, you appear horribly ungracious. The alternative is to try to stuff it into your reluctant buttonhole. However, even if you should succeed, it is to find that not only does it look ridiculous, but the asparagus fern maddeningly tickles you under the chin. I recommend choice number three, although for this great sang-froid is required. The technique consists of rapid dismemberment: first the asparagus fern must be firmly plucked and if possible removed. The silver paper is unwound and what remains of the bloom can then be inserted masterfully in the buttonhole, even though it may look all askew. You might even get a round of applause.

There is, too, the ordeal by microphone. In general, unless you should be speaking in somewhere like the Albert Hall, mechanical aids are best avoided. For a start, you never know whether the beastly thing is working properly. It very often isn't. There are crackles and booms and it is disconcerting not to know for certain whether you can be heard. As an Opener's words should only be few, it's better by far just to stand there and bellow.

Then follows the ordeal by autograph. The best plan here is to suggest to the organisers that a table and chair be provided. You can then sit in reasonable comfort and at least write legibly. If it is a charity, make a small charge. The alternative is chaos.

Other public functions at which a Newsreader will almost certainly be asked to appear are school prizegivings. In this case, I personally feel in a slightly false position, as, when I was at school, I only once won a prize and that was at the age of ten. They presented me with Chaucer's *Canterbury Tales*, heavily expurgated I presume. Thereafter, I must have run out of steam. The difficulty about giving an address on these occasions is that your audience consists of three disparate sections. Pupils, parents, governors and staff. Whichever section you aim your remarks at, you are bound to bore the pants off the other two. Then there is the interminable shaking of hands to cope with, and the problem of finding something jolly to say to each and every child. How do the Royals do it? It's depressing too to find that most schools have three or four young geniuses, who walk off with all the prizes.

In some ways more demanding, but at least more cut and dried, are the talks given to women's organisations. There's the Women's Institute, the Townswomen's Guild, the Business and Professional Women's Association, the Ladies' Circles, and the numerous Ladies' Luncheon Clubs on the lecture circuit. The main problem with these engagements is that when you leave London for Scunthorpe, or Solihull or Southsea, or wherever it is, you never know what kind of function you will find at the other end. The place you had always imagined to be an industrial slum may well turn out to be more like a country spa, full of retired Generals' wives. This kind of travel is, however, most instructive, and I nearly always enjoy myself immensely. It seems to me a mistake to spend all one's time in London. A visit away from the capital in these confusing days can do much to restore one's faith in the country. In the provincial centres, the old values and virtues seem more in evidence. There is not quite the same apparent mania, so prevalent in London, of change for change's sake.

There are invitations to all sorts of other functions too. An interesting and successful experiment was the 'Television and Radio Weekend' held at the Imperial Hotel, Torquay. Cyril Fletcher invited me to join Lady Barnet, Wendy Craig and Sheridan Morley in entertaining the guests. I was booked to give a forty-five-minute talk with questions, and to take part on the panel of a Quiz Show. I found it slightly alarming to have to give one's talk not only to the fairly high-powered guests at the hotel, but also in front of fellow professionals. Isobel Barnet was as suave and entertaining as ever. Wendy Craig, fresh from her 'Not in Front of the Children' success, whom I was meeting for the first time, was every bit as charming as I had imagined from seeing her on the screen. Sheridan got off to a bad start by arriving for the weekend minus a dinner jacket, but survived the situation and carried it off with great aplomb. He spoke wittily and with a flow of reminiscence about his life, his father Robert Morley, his glamorous grandmother Gladys Cooper, and also recounted many anecdotes of the Master, Noël Coward, whose biography he had recently completed.

Cyril was the evening high-spot, when he gave one of his polished cabaret turns in the ballroom. What a great professional he is. His charming wife Betty Astell was with him.

From the Imperial, Torquay to the village Women's Institute may seem a far cry. But as a Newsreader one is greatly privileged in feeling among friends at one place or the other.

In any case, the WI is not just the jam-making, flower arranging, feudal set-up it is so often thought to be. The National Chairman of the organisation, Sylvia Gray, has not that kind of image at all. She is a highly competent, dynamic business-woman in her early fifties. For some years she has run with great success the Bay Tree Hotel at Burford in Oxford-shire.

I greatly enjoyed her company in the train in the spring of 1970 when we returned together from Hereford after a meeting of the County Federation of WI's, where I had been the speaker. As we drank our Scotch and dry ginger in the buffet car, our conversation covered a whole range of world affairs. To her delight she has now seen the WI vote at its National Conference at the Albert Hall to include the discussion of politics and religion in its deliberations.

So, it is a highly organised and forward-looking movement that Sylvia Gray is so efficiently steering through the seventies.

There is one WI talk I know I shall always remember. The invitation came in a modest envelope with the familiar initials on it. A Mrs Annison, the branch secretary, was writing to ask me if I would give a talk to the village WI at West Newton on the Sandringham estate.

She made a passing reference to the fact that the Queen Mother was the President and that, if her other engagements allowed, Her Majesty might possibly attend.

It so happened that Nan and I had arranged to spend a week in our Suffolk cottage at that time, so there would be no great difficulty in our making the pleasant drive over to San-dringham and I accordingly agreed. We had to be at West Newton Village Hall at 2 p.m. on 21 January, 1970. Neither of us thought there was the slightest likelihood of the Queen Mother's being there and had, in fact, completely dismissed it from our minds. I was wearing a shabby old country overcoat and Nan was in tweeds. We stopped at a pub for a snack lunch. When we arrived at the tiny hall, we could hardly see it for cameramen. It was evident that something was up. I jumped out of the car, feeling rather silly, and jauntily asked the nearest cameraman what was going on, saying I didn't know I was that important. 'Oh! haven't you heard?' he said. 'The Queen and the Queen Mother are coming.' I felt, instantly, hollow inside, but managed to totter into the Hall. I couldn't believe what was happening.

We waited inside and, in a few minutes, the Royal party arrived. The Queen Mother led the way. She was wearing a bright blue coat and a very beautiful feathered hat. She also wore magnificent pearl necklaces and a brooch, bracelets and rings of diamonds and other precious stones. The Queen followed, wearing a quieter shade of blue and scarcely any jewellery. Then came their ladies-in-waiting. With very little fuss, the Queen Mother, as President, took her place at a trestle table facing the audience, which consisted of about thirty wives of workers from the Estate. The Queen herself was sitting in the front row. After some remarks in general terms, I heard myself being introduced. Then, the Queen Mother walked away from the table and sat down next to the Queen. The floor was mine. By this time, not only was I feeling hollow inside, but my feet had turned to lead as well. Somehow, I managed to stumble over to the table and the speaker's position, which was about three yards from the front row. I bowed and opened my talk with the unlikely sounding preamble, 'Your Majesties, Madam Chairman and Ladies.'

Not having dreamt for a moment that this situation would ever arise, I had not prepared a special talk. So, for the most part, I gave my usual one (lasting about forty minutes) except that I had to edit it as I went along, because some of the anecdotes seemed unsuitable. But I felt the best thing to do was to carry on as normally as possible. The fact was that I couldn't really believe this afternoon was happening and this helped me to be less nervous than I might otherwise have been.

After my talk, there were some questions. I remember the Queen asking if at times it wasn't rather chaotic in the News studio, and I said there were occasions when it was really necessary to have something of the temperament of a police horse. Then, Nan and I were presented to Their Majesties and we chatted informally for about five minutes. We talked about the war years and I remember the Queen Mother saying that it was a good thing Hitler hadn't had a WI in Germany or he might have won the war! After that we all had tea and Their Majesties walked round the stalls, laden with village handicrafts. Finally, we resumed our seats, and the members put on a fifteen-minute series of sketches, played in costume on a tiny stage. During some of these, the Queen laughed so much that she was quite doubled up. As all the performers would be well known to her as gardeners' wives, or other members of the staff, it was natural and charming that she should be so especially amused. Then it was all over.

Not all WI meetings are as decorous as this. Shortly afterwards, I was invited to be the speaker at a big County Federation meeting at Winsford, outside Chester. There were over 1,000 members packed into a large hall on a new housing estate. Nan came with me and so, when we arrived, she was able to chat to the WI officials for a few moments while I slipped off to the Gents. It was an hilarious meeting. Never have I known one go so well. All my stories went like a bomb and it was just chuckles all the way. I was glad I'd worn my new suit.

As we left the hall, it was clear that Nan for some reason was not sharing my elation. All she would say drily was: 'Next time, see you're properly zipped up in front!'

3 Beginning

At the start of my life, for nine no doubt blissful months, I lived in the Golden Age before the First World War. I was born on 27 November 1913 in South Croydon and the house was called 'Braemar'. My father was a Scot. He had come south from Glasgow in his early twenties, met my mother, married her, and they had settled in Surrey at the turn of the century. In those days, unbelievable as it seems now, Croydon still retained something of the character of a market town on the edge of the Surrey countryside. My two sisters and I, at intervals of five years, were born there. First Nell, then Moira, then me. My father was a charming, gentle, essentially simple man, who might perhaps have made a good village school teacher. Instead, he had been seduced by the big city life of high finance for which, by reason of his trusting nature, he was totally unsuited. My mother was, by far, the stronger character with endless resource and capability. Heaven knows, even she was driven to her wit's end in her struggle to keep us fed and clothed in the lean years which were to come.

For some reason, mainly financial I suspect, we were always on the move in Croydon. When I was about eighteen months, we moved from 'Braemar' – a few streets away to 'Dalwhinnie', the Scottish influence in house names still prevailing. This was a fairly spacious house, standing at the top of a steep hill, which incidentally, was very nearly my undoing. My sister Moira, then aged seven, had been bidden to mind me in my pram at the front gate, while mother went into the house for a moment. Moira, distracted by a puppy, let go of the pram handle and leant down to fondle it. The pram, with me all unsuspecting in it, began to roll off and gather speed with my little sister in frantic, terrified pursuit. It careered madly down the hill, lurched across a kerb, across another road at the bottom, and finished with an almighty crash into the side of a stationary coal cart! They picked me out, unhurt. That was my first of many lucky breaks.

The house itself was white, rough-cast and had a large balcony. The first memory I have is of standing on this balcony at the age of about three and a half and being scared out of my life by a new and, to me, terrifying sound. A donkey had been moved into a neighbouring field and it was the first time I had heard it bray. I rushed back into the house and, promptly, fell headlong down a flight of stairs. A favourite aunt, who was incidentally soon to die, then gathered me up, placed me on a sofa and plied me with chocolates. I must have been a stupid, timid little twit.

The next early memory I have was of a dog called Billy. He was a wild, black and tan, mongrel terrier, but I loved him dearly. Especially was I fascinated to watch him eat and hear the gulping, slurp-slurp sound he made, as he did so. He had a voracious appetite, which one day stood me in good stead. They were very much more formal times than nowadays and, for Sunday churchgoing, my mother bought me a grey tweed coat with cap to match. I loathed this headpiece with a deadly, unreasoning hate. Billy was always game to try something new, and so when I, surreptitiously, fed it to him, he obliged and promptly ate it.

For children's parties and other special occasions I usually wore the kilt, and my sister Moira and I would sometimes dashingly assay the Highland Fling. People always said how very alike we were, which pleased me enormously because I adored my sister and thought her at that time the most beautiful person I had ever seen. We both had large brown eyes with long dark lashes and fairly high colouring.

Once at a party I was horrified to hear a rather mean-minded mother say in an aside, 'I'm sure those children are made up.' I was reminded of this recently when sitting in a London theatre with my wife. Someone in the row in front spotted me and said to his neighbour, 'There's Robert Dougall – he's even got his make-up on!'

When I was about four, at another children's party, a red-haired girl called Marjorie Sloane, aged seven, said suddenly, 'Let's play barber's shop!' With which she sat me in a chair, draped a towel round my shoulders, and producing an enormous pair of scissors proceeded to cut off my eyelashes. It didn't worry me too much but, when I got home, Mother nearly hit the ceiling, and I believe diplomatic relations were broken off with the Sloane family.

I can just remember the Great War – the first air-raids and being plucked warm and protesting from bed in the middle of the night. Mother telling me there was a thunderstorm and taking me downstairs to place me under the seeming safety of the dining-room table. The view from there was of trouser legs, some khaki and some blue. It was all strangely exciting. I also remember the black treacle we had instead of sugar. Then in 1917, at four and a half, I went to my first school.

For some time Mother had been preparing me for this step by telling me what fun it was all going to be. All the same, when I came to the day, she had to drag me unwillingly down the hill, as I kept on repeating, no doubt in a persistent whine, 'I don't think I want to go to school after all.'

St John's School, as it was called, was housed just near where I'd hit the coal cart. It had only been going for about two years – and was run by three generations of Polleys. Grandpa Polley was ninety-nine, then came Mr and Mrs Polley in their seventies and their daughter Miss Polley, aged about thirty, who was the headmistress. She wore ankle-length skirts, nipped in at the waist; her hair was parted in the middle and brought forward in two charming pre-Raphaelite loops on either side. Her skirts impeded her not at all as she rushed nimbly up and down the field teaching us the rudiments of hockey and football.

A short time ago I had a letter from her to say that the school had finally closed in March 1972. Economic circumstances had defeated it but nothing else. She said she always remembered me as the little boy in the kilt. Now, nearer ninety than eighty, Miss Polley was sad at the closure: she felt she had many more active years ahead.

Over the decades more than seven hundred boys had worn the dark green caps with a light blue eagle on the front, but when I first went there in 1917 there were only four of us. The result was that we had a lot of individual attention and I was able to read quite fluently by the time I was five. My prize at the end of that first year was a children's Shakespeare. I didn't think much of it and, on the sly, tried to swop it with the boy who'd won the second prize, consisting of chocolates. I must have been a squalid little beast – and it ended in tears.

Another unfortunate episode at Miss Polley's was when I was dared to tip my pot of paint-water out of the upstairs classroom window, just as Mrs Polley was passing by in the garden below. No one would believe I hadn't done it on purpose – more tears.

We didn't see much of Grandpa Polley. He was a bonfire

27

fanatic. Such an enthusiast was he that often, when lunchtime came round, he refused to leave his fire and so he stayed, crouched on his upright kitchen chair at the bottom of the garden for many a summer and autumn day, munching the sandwiches sent down to him. It was a happy time and I shall always be glad I went to St John's School where I stayed until I was eight. However, before that time, we had moved house yet again, to Birdhurst Road, some four miles away. Malcolm Muggeridge was living in the next street, but I didn't know him then. In all weathers, I walked the four miles or so to school. This included crossing the busy Brighton Road. I don't suppose many parents would let their six-year-olds do that today.

If it hadn't been for one thing, I'd have had no complaints. Unfortunately, as a child, I was a chronic asthmatic. I came to dread the cold, wet winters and especially the freezing fogs. There were no smokeless zones then. The family doctor recommended sea air, so my worried parents decide to take the plunge and we were on the move again, this time to Brighton.

There, we rented a furnished first-floor flat in Brunswick Road, at the Hove end of Brighton. On health grounds, I was excused school and so began, perhaps, the most perfect six months of my life. Brighton I adored. The front, the lawns, the wrought-iron shelters and the grandeur of the West and Palace Piers.

The West Pier was the nearer of the two. It was smaller than the Palace Pier and being at the Hove end rather more refined. At the very end of it were wrought-iron staircases leading down to the landing stages for the paddle steamers. What a delight they were with their great wheels churning and threshing the water, as they manoeuvred to come alongside. This was a magical sort of place from which you could see the mysterious dark underneath of the pier. The intricate supporting iron work encrusted with barnacles and green slime. The hungry sucking noise the sea made as it heaved and slopped about underneath. A place beloved by anglers and small boys.

Mother wasn't keen on my going to the other pier, the Palace, which was rather more raffish. It had more of everything, especially of machines. These were a constant delight, although some of them were a trifle macabre. One I used to like particularly was of an execution. You put your two pennies in and the great grey prison doors opened to reveal a victim on the scaffold. A priest popped up with his open bible. A bell

28

tolled. The masked executioner pulled a lever, the floor opened, and the prisoner fell to his doom. Marvellous. But it was all rather expensive.

Once a young friend called Peter was staying with me. I naturally wanted to show him the best of Brighton, so off we went to the Palace Pier. As it was rather frowned on at home, this naturally made it all the more exciting. Peter and I soon used up all our pennies, but a kind white-haired old gentleman, seeing our obvious disappointment, came up and said he had a whole lot of coins, which were only weighing down his pocket, and would we like to use them? In fact, he said, we would really be doing him a favour. This was too good to be true and Peter and I had a marvellous time.

Afterwards, we sat on a seat with the old man and he said would we mind doing a little thing for him? He did so like to be tickled. He had already unbuttoned his waistcoat and shirt. Inside, it looked very white, and there were a lot of grey hairs on his chest. He took my hand and guided it in. I didn't let it stay there long, because it felt clammy and cold. Then, he asked Peter to do the same. We didn't really mind, especially as he'd been so kind giving us all those pennies. We said goodbye and arranged to meet him the next afternoon. When we got home, I mentioned this casually to Mother who nearly had a fit. After that, the Palace Pier was positively out of bounds, but I could never really understand why.

Perhaps most of all I loved the baroque bandstand. Every afternoon in the spring and summer, the military bands would play. I was entranced by the music, the glitter of the uniforms and perhaps most of all by the conductors. Their smartness was superb. Slim, graceful and ram-rod straight and some had waxed moustaches. They had no more faithful supporter. On cold days, and even when it was wet, I would still sit enraptured, sometimes with rows of empty chairs all round, hoping the band would break into Suppé's *Light Cavalry* overture, my favourite piece.

In the winter, with a fourpenny bag of sticky bull's eyes in my mac pocket, I'd walk for miles, a solitary figure along the front. I liked it best when it was rough and the waves crashed over the top and I could stand there getting drenched through with spray. In the hot, endless summer days Mother and I would take a sandwich lunch down to the beach. A deckchair for her and a rug for me in the lea of a stone groyne. Bliss, but it had soon to end. My father and elder sister found the daily journey to work in London too much for them, so for me a fateful decision was made. The family would return to yet another house in South Croydon and I would be left behind at a boarding school. It was a red-brick barracks of a place and I loathed every minute I spent there. Incredibly enough, Aubrey Beardsley had once been a pupil. Perhaps the flowering of his effete, exquisite artistry was partly in revulsion at the Spartan life which obtained. It was certainly the most miserable time of my life. Homesickness when very young is hell. In my case it seemed the worse, because my prison was in the very place I loved, and where, for the last six months, I'd run completely free. Apart from the aching emptiness of life without Mother and the family, I loathed the mass living. In the dormitories up to twenty or so iron bedsteads with tiny lockers beside them. Acres of shiny brown linoleum, washing in cold water, stripped to the waist. The only place one could find to be alone was in the 'bogs'. I would sit there and pray to be taken away, as I had never prayed before. Then, that winter, asthma and bronchitis attacked me again and for weeks I wheezed away miserably in the sick-bay. It was a tough school and the sheltered, solitary kind of life I'd led till then had done nothing to prepare me for it.

Ragging was endemic and almost everyone, at one time or another, became a victim of it. One wet Sunday afternoon, to my astonishment, I even found myself in the unaccustomed role of leader of the pack. About eight of us set off in hot, murderous pursuit of a pale, weedy boy with protuberant eyes. His name was Beale. I had no great enthusiasm for the hunt, but at least it made a change from being chased oneself. Finally, we ran him to ground in a music room. Triumphantly we hurled open the door. At first, the room seemed empty: bare floor and walls, but in the far corner, was an upright piano. Beale was sitting on a straight-backed chair at the keyboard. He looked desperately alone, his face now the palest shade of green. As temporary, acting leader, I was expected to decide his fate. So abject did he look, that I had no stomach for further persecution and told him he could go. This unforgivable weakness cost me dear. The pack, baulked of its kill, soon turned on me.

On fine Sunday afternoons we processed two by two, in crocodile, along Brighton front to Black Rock over the very same ground where, a short time before, I had run so free. One Sunday, a friend and I, having been marched to the Rock, felt we couldn't face the regimented march back again. We slipped away from the column and daringly nipped on to a bus, which would return us to the school. Caps stuffed deep in overcoat pockets, we sat near the conductor and facing the inside. It had all been so simple we couldn't think why we hadn't tried the dodge before. Casually, I looked across at the occupants of the opposite seat and my stomach promptly fell through the floor. There, incredibly, looming larger than life, sat the Headmaster. He was a big burly man with a red face and a shaggy, whitish-grey moustache. The awful thing was that he just sat there, smiling strangely, until, after what seemed an endless age, we reached the gates of the school. All he said, as he passed us to get off, was 'Come and see me in my study at seven.'

Hearts in mouths, we waited outside his door. We knew it meant a beating. I went in first. He didn't say much, except 'Bend over.' He gave me three strokes of the cane, but he wasn't really trying and hardly hurt me at all. I suppose he thought we'd been through enough for that day.

One way and another, at that school, bottoms were in a constant state of nervous twitch. In the dormitory it was the slap of slippers on shivering, pyjama-clad behinds. Even in the asphalted playgrounds bottoms were much in view. They were the end-product of a variety of catching games. If a catch were dropped, the victim would have to bend over against a wall, his tremulous posterior the target for tennis balls shied with deadly aim. In wet weather, when the ball was heavy, it hurt most.

A year went by and, for me, I think the worst was over. I was beginning, at last, to grow a thicker skin. But my earlier prayers had not gone unheeded and my parents had, unbeknown to me, arranged for me to return home and enter Whitgift Junior School, a day boy again, in Croydon.

Croydon had not yet been quite engulfed in suburban sprawl. There was still a cattle market every Thursday in Selsdon Road, near South Croydon Station and there were several farms quite near. On Sunday morning walks with my father and sisters, we would often call in at Fox's Farm in Ballards Way for a glass of creamy milk straight from the cow. It was about this time that I was given my first puppy. It came in the shape of a small, blackish-grey, irresistible object I at once named Bogey. He was two months old with the brightest of brown eyes. He also had a smooth, round, dark grey stomach with an absurd but endearing, wispy plume sprouting from his undercarriage.

I was a fairly solitary child and so we became the closest of friends. We shared the same interests, and both loved, more than anything, chasing a ball. We also liked playing hide and seek. I used to hurl a ball up the straight, seventy yard gravel path, leading from our house to the front gate and, while Bogey streaked after it, I would dash into the house and try to make myself as small as possible behind a chair or perhaps in a cupboard. I had to keep on ringing the changes, as he soon got to know all my hiding places, and while I crouched, holding my breath, I would hear Bogey panting round busily from one place to another in tireless search. Sometimes, he would keep it up for twenty minutes before he found me.

Bogey was also a brilliant retriever. There was a wall in the garden, against which for hours on end, as small boys will, I banged a ball with a tennis racket or sometimes a cricket bat. Understandably, Bogey found this frustrating, except that, every now and then, I, inevitably, knocked the ball over the wall. It then usually landed up somewhere on the other side in a yard, where cars were garaged. To get it back meant a tedious, two minute walk round some buildings. But all I had to do was just flop down on the grass and have a rest, while off shot Bogey, without a word from me, to appear a few minutes later, grinning all over, and triumphantly carrying the ball.

Every day, I used to groom his blackish-grey, wiry coat. On the top of his head, the hair was a softer, silvery grey, and, after brushing, had regular waves. There was longish, soft hair on either side of his muzzle too and, when combed, this gave him a silky, grey moustache. I could not have wished for a better companion.

Then – tragedy. It had already happened, when I came home for lunch from school. Unbeknown to me, Mother had put rat poison on a piece of bread and hidden it, as she thought, at the back of a cupboard in the room where I used to do my home-work, which we called the study. Bogey, for ever exploring, had found it. He was lying on his side by the skirting board and panting his life away. There was nothing the vet could do. In the corner of the room on the frayed carpet was an old tennis ball. I somehow felt if I bounced it he must surely leap up again. But I knew his inside was on fire and there was nothing I or anyone else could do about it. I buried him in the garden, and was desolate.

Whitgift Junior and Senior Schools, in stately Victorian gothic, with playing fields and five courts, occupied a splendid site in the very middle of the town. I enjoyed my time at Whitgift from the start. Brighton had toughened me up, so I sailed through the initiation ceremony at my new school of kissing the idol on a buttress of stone. I was just on ten when I started my first term in Form 1B. The form master was a kindly old Scotsman – a Mr Snell. His usual way of referring to us was as 'You horrible little worrrms!' To my amazement, I took the form prize at the end of the year.

My school career was not spectacular but I liked best French and German. Fortunately for me, Whitgift has always had a first class reputation for teaching languages and I took full advantage of it. One thing in particular for which I am still grateful is that we all had the phonetic system drummed into us. This made me for the first time conscious of the beauty of sound in language and gave me from this early age the ability to enunciate clearly and correctly in French and German. The drilling in phonetics was tedious at the time, but, in my opinion, it is as basic and important in learning a language as square-bashing in training for the Forces. It is, of course, equally valuable for the correct pronunciation of English too. This helped me when I came to work in the BBC some ten years later.

If languages I loved, mathematics I hated. Arithmetic, algebra, geometry, trigonometry were all totally incomprehensible to me, and, in spite of extra coaching, I made scarcely any progress.

There were beatings, of course. My first caning was when I was twelve. The reason was trivial enough. Another boy and I were, as we thought quite harmlessly, doing a bit of swopping at the back of the room. I was trading a penknife for two hardened conkers (one was a 'forty-niner'), when the form master, Mr Kitchener, pounced. 'Golly', as he was known throughout the school, by reason of his upswept hair, shining red face and rimless glasses, was an irascible man. We'd just picked the wrong afternoon for our trading.

He ordered us to wait for him downstairs. We knew what that meant. For at least twenty minutes we waited, not feeling

B

too good. Then Golly appeared briskly, gown billowing behind him. The execution room was off the assembly hall. It was quite small with bare walls. There was a cupboard and inside a whole selection of canes of different lengths. My friend, his name was Hill, went in first. There was a horrible silence. Then, three almighty, violent, thwacking noises and out he came, looking whiter than I had ever seen him and walking stiffly like a marionette. I was next. 'Touch your toes.' A ghastly nothing. Then, a sudden searing hurt and again and again. Back to the classroom, walking mechanically, conscious of looking ashen, but trying to grimace a smile. Eager faces looking up from desks: 'What was it like?' 'Did it hurt?' 'How many?' Then Golly returned and all went on as before, only very much quieter.

This was the first of several canings, but the worst were always from the Prefects. They could pick on you for any fairly minor indiscretion, such as running in the corridors. Their execution room was the Library. Each lunchtime, six or so shivering victims would wait outside the big, heavy doors, while inside the Prefects sat round the table in magisterial calm.

Once I cut a rugger practice and the Captain of the 1st XV, who was an enormous boy of about nineteen, damn nearly cut me in half. I was black and blue for weeks. But it never occurred to any of us to bear a grievance. It was just an accepted thing. I can't help feeling the school would have been a bit of a shambles without the use of this ultimate sanction.

Most boys from the age of thirteen served in the Officers' Training Corps. Our parade days were on Mondays. This meant most Sunday nights were reserved for cleaning equipment. As this was all leather and brass, it would take the best part of two hours. The BBC, every Sunday at 8 p.m., relayed Albert Sandler and the Palm Court Orchestra from the Grand Hotel, Eastbourne. So, to the sound of those saccharine strings playing *In a Monastery Garden* by Ketelby or some other choice offering, I would make with the polish. Tins of Oxblood and dark-tan mixed for the leather, Brasso for the rest. The fumes filled the room, until one felt sick.

Then, next morning, black boots shining, puttees tightly rolled over spindly legs, cap set rakishly and swagger stick under my arm, I would as likely as not run straight into Mrs Oliver. At that time, she used to help Mother with the cleaning once a week. She was red-faced, big-bosomed and wore enormous flowered hats. An expansive woman in every way. Her voice was loud too. When she saw me, her whole face would light up – 'Morning, Mr Bobby, off to play soldiers?' I hated her.

Although I quite enjoyed it all, especially the summer camps, the military life wasn't one I felt in tune with. I was short in officer-like qualities and after four years, I remained a private. All the same, I was to be glad of the square-bashing and arms drill experience when, later, the war came.

At games, I played cricket and rugger with reasonable success but, best of all, I liked rugby fives. We had some rather unorthodox, open-air, singles courts and I played the game by the hour. One frosty afternoon, I returned home late after a match. It wasn't until my foot began to thaw out in front of the fire that I felt any pain. On removing my sock, I found I'd worn a hole in the ball of my foot the size of half-a-crown. The result was a poisoned foot which took some weeks to recover.

Fives is played with a hard, white leather covered ball, which is struck against and around the walls of the court with the hands. Padded gloves are worn. I became Captain of School Fives, which meant playing a lot of House tournaments, as well as matches against other schools. My hands used to get bruised and, in order to be able to play at all, I sometimes put a piece of raw cooking steak inside my gloves. At the end of one season, I put my things away in a cupboard and forgot them. Six months later, when I took them out again, the smell was noisome and indescribable. I threw the gloves down, the steak fell out and our dog scoffed the lot. And stayed alive!

My great friend throughout these school-days was a slim dark-haired lad, Dick. We complemented each other – he helped me with my mathematics homework, I helped him with languages. We were both mad about fives and cricket. In the holidays, we'd set off to watch Surrey play at Kennington Oval. Plentifully armed with sandwiches and ginger beer, we'd board the tram at Croydon for the ride through the South London suburbs. Swaying, lurching ; now gliding, now rattling over the points, bell clanging, it was a stimulating ride, especially on the upper deck.

The Oval was almost always bliss. What a team Surrey had! The elegant, incomparable Jack Hobbs, Hobbs the Great.

35

I've never seen a batsman to touch him. Always unruffled and immaculate. A consummate stylist. His partner, Andy Sandham, was the perfect foil. Steady as a rock and unobtrusive. Then, was there ever a better Captain than Percy Fender? The wiliest tactician and, incidentally, one of the biggest hitters of the ball I have ever seen. There were stalwarts like Ducat and Shepherd, the nimble, sturdy little figure of Strudwick behind the stumps. The mighty Bill Hitch to tirelessly hurl the ball down and the indefatigable Peach. Heroes all. And at the lunch interval, when we were full of ginger pop, we'd take a ball out on to the sacred ground and gaze with awe at the roped off square in the middle. Those for me were cricket's greatest days.

Now, when I return to Croydon, I feel like a ghost. Everything has changed. Probably no place in the south of England has been more greatly transformed, except perhaps Plymouth. The school moved in 1931 to its splendid new site at Haling Park a few miles to the south along the Brighton Road, where Lord Howard of Effingham once lived. On the old field in the centre of the town where we played cricket, there now stands a twenty-two-storey block, and instead of Whitgift School, it is Whitgift Shopping Centre.

Throughout all my school-days things were difficult at home, as there was very little money coming in. This perhaps helped me mature rather earlier than some of my friends, but I hated seeing my parents so worried. My father had given up a secure job in a stockbroker's office, in order to operate as a freelance financial adviser. He had excellent contacts in the City but, as a go-between, he seldom seemed able to secure his own commission on deals he had arranged and, once he had brought the parties together, would invariably be excluded or by-passed. He was, in fact, altogether too trusting.

He often spoke of these deals to me and, in time, I began to put images to the foreign sounding names he was always mentioning. There were names like Rheitlinger, who I imagined with pince-nez, goatee beard and butterfly collar. Chevau I always saw in a dapper brown suit and I felt sure he had a pink face, a small waxed moustache and wore spats. Then there was Van Den Berg in black jacket, striped trousers and patent leather shoes; Veno, who looked short and seedy; and Father also spoke quite often of 'a clever little chap called Marples'. The brutal fact was clear to me that they were all a darn sight too clever for him by miles.

36

The trouble was that at home as far as money was concerned we never knew where we were. Great deals were spoken of which were going to make thousands. One of them my father considered as good as clinched, so the Dougalls packed excitedly for their first holiday across the Channel. It wasn't so easy in those days. We booked for a fortnight in a hotel at Knokke-Le-Zoute near Blankenberghe in Belgium.

I was fifteen and in the evening used to act as a male escort to my sisters. They were both older than I and also had a girl friend with them. Sitting at café and night-club tables I tried to look as old as I possibly could and daringly smoked my first cigarette in public. These high jinks soon came to a sobering end. A cable arrived from London – the deal was off and we were broke again, only worse than before. Fortunately my mother was endowed with exceptional resilience and resource. She was also devout, in a jolly sort of way. In fact, she was a warm-hearted wonderful person, who worked daily miracles in keeping our family afloat in tumultuous, financial seas.

About this time, I began to feel disenchantment with Sunday church-going. There was no Welfare State and social inequalities and hardships were great. The Church didn't seem to be doing much about it. To my eyes, the Bishop and the Vicar began to look smug and well-fed. The congregation was almost wholly middle-class; and I felt the Church had lost touch with life. My favourite writers were Arnold Bennett, H. G. Wells, Aldous Huxley, D. H. Lawrence, Henry Williamson and the greatest of the nature mystics Richard Jefferies whose *Story of My Heart* I loved. At no time did I cease to believe in the deity, but I couldn't feel near him in church. For me, God was in the woods and fields and changing seasons.

At Prayers in school one morning, one of my buddies asked me to go with him to a dance in a church hall in the neighbouring village of Selsdon. He knew a girl, who had a friend. I hated dancing, and still do, but I was keen to meet the girl. She was dark and slim with grey eyes; we soon left the hall. Some woods were near. We stopped and leant on a farm gate. I was then seventeen and she was the first girl I had ever kissed and my first kiss was frankly a disappointment. Later, it was more satisfactory. We found an empty barn and stretched out together in the straw. Neither of us knew anything about sex, so we just went on kissing. Irene, for that was her name, somehow managed to suck sweets at the same time. It was really rather exhausting.

So that was how I kissed my first girl, and what's more, just to show how corny life can be, Selsdon Wood is still to this day a bird sanctuary.

4 From Ledger to Microphone

By 1931 the country was in the middle of a monumental depression. The crash had come on Wall Street in 1929 and set off a chain reaction. Soon, we had the Lord Kylsant scandal and then the Clarence Hatry fiasco, which ruined thousands. There were over three million unemployed, and it was in September of that year I left school. Not wishing to add to their numbers, I was prepared to take almost any job. There was no system of university grants then. My qualifications? Matriculation in eight subjects, with distinctions, oral and written, in French and German. Luckily, my father's contacts in the City included a partner in the famous firm of Chartered Accountants and Auditors – Deloitte, Plender, Griffiths & Co. – now known simply as Deloittes. So, in spite of my dislike and ineptitude for mathematics, when offered a job as an audit-clerk, I took it. My salary was twenty-five shillings per week. Although not articled, as the fee in those days was five hundred guineas, I was treated on exactly the same footing as all the other junior clerks.

It was a fashionable firm. Among my colleagues, was a very smooth product of Eton, whom we all knew as Sidney.[1] Another of the many who wore the black tie with the pale blue stripe was Roderick Leveson-Gower. An eccentric character ; he became a good friend of mine. Deloittes, being a traditional, long-established firm, would have no truck with new-fangled adding machines, so we clerks did all the casting of endless columns of pounds, shillings and pence by hand. Roderick lived for horses and racing, with cricket as his second string. He had acquired the knack of breaking off in the middle of a column of figures and looking up to tell you what his fancy was for the '3.30' and then to pick up again with his adding at the exact point where he had left off. With his curly brimmed bowler, drainpipe trousers, hacking-style jacket and rolled umbrella, he represented a type of Englishman who seemed to disappear with the war.

Among the many big industrial enterprises and firms we

[1] Later became Lord De L'Isle and Dudley, V.C.

visited to carry out the annual audit were the large West End hotels. So it was that I became well acquainted with Claridges, the Savoy, and the Berkeley, then still in Piccadilly. From the ledgers there wafted up a smell, compounded of cigars, rare scents, and exotic food and wine.

At the Savoy, as a concession, Deloittes men were, at one time, allowed to attend the Tea-Dances, but as the privilege was abused, through too many girl friends being invited, that soon came to an end. From the Savoy, we would then cross the Strand to Joe Lyons for tea and a game of dominoes. For some reason, our audit HQ at the hotel was set up in a room next to the ballroom. We found it none too easy to concentrate on the ledgers with the resident dance band – Carroll Gibbons and the Savoy Hotel Orpheans – rehearsing next door. But not all our audits were as rarified as this. I also visited the Port of London Authority, Bryant and May at Bow, the NAAFI head-quarters at Kennington (nice and near the Oval for Test Matches), and there was even a steam laundry at Clapham. This latter assignment I used, especially, to dread. In order to get to the office, it was necessary to pass through the laundry itself. I was a shy youngster, quick to blush. The women opera-tors regarded this as a welcome diversion from their labours. My arrival was therefore greeted with derisive cat-calls and cheers, as I, scarlet to the roots of my hair, ran the gauntlet of the pink, overalled ladies swathed in steam.

Another of our audits was at the BBC. The Corporation had recently moved into its new premises at Broadcasting House, Langham Place from Savoy Hill in the Strand. I was very happy with the Deloittes crowd, because they were such a jolly nice lot, but at the back of my mind was the nagging thought of what on earth could the future hold. Accountancy had minimum appeal for me, and in any case, not being articled, I could never become a chartered accountant. Tom Pearce, the Deloittes man in charge of the BBC audit, realised my position and one afternoon stopped me in the corridor on the third floor of Broadcasting House and grinning all over his face fired the question at me, 'How much do you want to be earning at twenty-five?' I looked as composed as possible and replied, 'Five hundred a year.' (A tidy sum in those days.) With which Pearce grabbed me by the arm and propelled me into the office of the Head of BBC Purchase and Accounts Department. A job was offered to me at thirty shillings a week and I asked if I might think it over at the weekend. I had to weigh a socially agreeable existence, albeit with not much future, against the hard graft in a BBC accounts office. But then I remembered there were things going on other than accounts in Broadcasting House and, with a little luck, who knows, I might be able to work a transfer eventually to the Programme side.

There couldn't be any doubt of my decision, so in January 1933 I started my career on the BBC staff – I was just nineteen. The bowler hat and umbrella could be put away. My new colleagues were more down to earth than the socialites I had worked with at Deloittes. At first, they tended to eye me with suspicion. Coming from the auditors they thought perhaps I was being planted by the bosses to report on them. They needn't have worried. I was fully stretched trying to keep up. The thought occurred to me that perhaps a pair of horn-rimmed spectacles would make me look more efficient. Anyway, being desperate, I felt it a chance worth taking.

An optician in nearby Wigmore Street showed me into his testing room at the back of his shop. He sat me down in front of the usual chart of letters in diminishing sizes. On my nose rested metal frames, into the eyepieces of which he dropped a sequence of lenses of varying strengths. I peered earnestly through them, giving my opinion of each in turn. Suddenly, the letters came bang into focus. 'That's fine,' I said. For some reason, the optician wasn't looking too pleased, as he explained patiently, at that point, the eyepieces were empty. Anyway, I managed to talk him into giving me a pair of solemn-looking black frames into which he put – plain glass.

I had little opportunity of trying them out in the office as, within a fortnight of joining the BBC, I caught 'flu. Being young and over-keen, I went back to work before I had fully recovered. By lunchtime my head was bursting, so I was taken to the sick-bay to see the Broadcasting House Matron. She announced that my temperature was 102° and promptly sent me home. By this time, we had moved again and were now installed in Fairfield Road, East Croydon. There, I languished in bed for three weeks making no progress whatever, in fact my local doctor seemed completely baffled. My future brother-in-law Pat[1] was then a young doctor working as a Houseman in St Thomas's. He came down to see me ; took one look, ran

[1] Major-General M. H. P. Sayers, O.B.E., late R.A.M.C. (retd).

his stethoscope over my chest and, with the power of decision which was to take him to the top in the Army, announced that I undoubtedly had pneumonia and that hospital was the best place for me.

It was early February and snowing. I dimly remember being bundled in an eiderdown and carried up the long garden path to a waiting car. In St Thomas's, Pat arranged for me to have a corner bed in a public ward. At first my bed was surrounded with screens, I suppose I was rather ill. Before the days of antibiotics, pneumonia was quite a serious illness, and the only treatment seemed to be a local application of a grey, glutinous mixture called anti-phlogistine, which they plastered all over my chest. After some ten days, the crisis passed and I started looking round. Apart from the bedpans and bottles, I began to have a pretty good time. St Thomas's is the policemen's hospital and most of the beds in my ward were occupied by burly coppers, who nearly all suffered from duodenal ulcers ; their diet was mainly milk. This was particularly unfortunate for them, as I was told to eat as much as I could of everything to try and build up my strength. In the next bed to mine a great, ruddy-faced character went through agonies as he sniffed the roasts being offered to me, while he had to make do with his glass of milk.

In all, I was in St Thomas's for five weeks and, although I had only served on the staff for a fortnight, the BBC paid my salary and my boss, Geoffrey Strode, even sent me boxes of fruit and get well letters. The best part of being in hospital was that the nurses were exceptionally glamorous. In those days – the early thirties – middle-class girls very often stayed at home to help Mother do the flowers. Taxation had not yet levelled incomes down and there was often no necessity for them to go out to work. But, nursing was one of the approved things to do and so I was looked after by the most gorgeous bunch of girls. I was quite sorry to say goodbye.

Back home, I felt as weak as a flounder, but a fortnight's convalescence put me right, and when I returned to Broadcasting House, it was to find that I had been put in charge of the Stationery Store. This was on the second floor. I had a clerk to assist me and two storemen.

The chief storeman, Mr Crickett, was an ex-guardsman, immensely tall with a nutcracker face. He was aged about fifty and I think he must have been sans teeth, because his scimitar-like nose and jutting chin seemed to rush towards each other whenever he spoke. Crickett was not the easiest man to handle. For instance, if it were necessary to pack up a large order for, say, BBC Aberdeen, and the time was approaching 5.30, when we closed, I soon learnt there was only one way to put it to him.

'Crickett,' I would say, 'of course, there's not the slightest chance of your being able to get this off tonight, is there?'

'That's what you think,' he'd say. 'Give it here.' And in a brace of shakes the job would be done. But, ask direct, and it would be:

'What d'ye take me for? Pack that lot up at this time of night? Not bloody likely!'

At least, presiding over Stationery, I was in touch with all BBC departments. I became even more determined somehow to transfer to the broadcasting side.

During this time, as an escape, I always kept a French or German novel stuck in my pocket. At weekends I used to play cricket for the BBC Club at their sportsground at Motspur Park. Another member of the team was a middle-aged Scot – W. M. 'Joe' Shewen, who was on the Programme side. In the winter I played a lot of squash and again met Joe. During a BBC tournament, I was drawn against Sir Cecil Graves, who was then director of the recently formed Empire Service. I beat him as tactfully as possible, after all he was giving me nearly thirty-five years. Then in the changing-room afterwards I overheard him asking Joe Shewen who that young chap was – and where did I work? This displeased me not at all.

About this time, I happened to read a notice on the board at Broadcasting House, inviting staff who were interested to attend an audition for a production by the BBC Amateur Dramatic Society of Jerome K. Jerome's *The Passing of the Third Floor Back*. I turned up and was asked by the producer to read the lines of Christopher the young artist. To my amazement I got the part. It was not my favourite play. A sort of late Victorian, cabbage-water, morality play, but the standard of performance was fairly high. There was much professional broadcasting talent available. I had only once taken part in a stage production and that had been at Whitgift. So, I felt it was a challenge and, until the opening night, thought of scarcely anything else.

The play was produced on 14 and 15 May 1934 in St

George's Hall, which stood in those days almost opposite Broadcasting House. Once it had been the theatre where Maskeleyne, the great illusionist, used to hold audiences spellbound with his mysteries. It was there, in fact, as a small boy, that I had first seen a woman sawn in half. This time, it was my turn to suffer.

I was terrified, because in the audience was a good sprinkling of top brass, and there in the second row loomed the craggy figure of the Director-General, Sir John Reith himself. As for my time on stage, it seemed rather unreal ; like rushing through the night in the lighted compartment of a train, with the audience just a blurred landscape in the outer darkness.

But, in spite of this, I felt strangely at home. This was something that made sense to me, unlike those damn ledgers. After the final performance, as I was coming out of the theatre, still in a bit of a daze, Norman Shelley, the actor, who had made us up said to me out of the blue, 'You've got a good voice me boy, you ought to make use of it.'

I made my way to Victoria Station in a state of euphoria, only to find the last train had gone. As I had no luggage and must have looked a bit wild for those days (I'd grown my hair fairly long, for the part), perhaps it wasn't surprising that the small hotels near the station said they hadn't any rooms. So I walked around for a few hours and then stretched out for what was left of the night in the station waiting-room. A week or so later, the production was reviewed in *The Heterodyne*, as the BBC Club magazine then was known. Of me, it said I was 'a convincing, if slightly plummy juvenile'. I didn't even know what 'plummy' meant, and had to ask someone to find out.

Things seemed flat for the weeks after that, and the accounts made even less sense. About this time I used to badger the BBC Establishment Officer, who was in charge of all appointments. D. H. Clarke had once been in the Guards. A meticulous little man, with a neat moustache and glasses and not a hair or a thought out of place. He used to attempt to discourage my frequent knocks on his door by saying to me, 'You know, Dougall, you won't do yourself any good worrying me like this.'

All the same, I kept it up and one day he asked me to sit down in his office and then rapped at me, 'How's your French?' Saying this, he passed me a French newspaper and asked me to read it. This was right up my street. In those days, I was always reading French and German for my pleasure. He didn't say anything for a time and then came the question that nearly bowled me over: 'How'd you like an audition to be an Announcer?' These words from the Establishment Officer shook me but, eventually, I managed to say, 'Yes please, I would like an audition. Yes, I would very much.'

In 1934 broadcasting was still an awe-inspiring business. It had come a long way from the crystal sets and cat's whiskers of around 1920, when to hear any sound at all had the heady excitement of a miracle, but 'it's a wonderful thing, this wireless' was a phrase still constantly aired, especially by those who had lived most of their lives without it.

And then, the gleaming white temple, built to house the new medium was awe-inspiring too. Broadcasting House, all eight stories of it, loomed over Langham Place like a great, half completed ship, with Eric Gill's controversial 'Prospero and Ariel' at the prow. The juxtaposition of the sculptured figures aroused much ribaldry at the time and legend has it that one of the BBC Governors gave it as his opinion that the naked lad was 'uncommonly well hung'. Gill was accordingly requested to scale the offending object down to size. The building was officially opened in the spring of 1932. The massive bronze doors, the commissionaires with their spotless white gloves, and inside a huge Latin inscription, to intimidate still further, the first thing to catch the eye. By the reception desk on the right, as a concession, a plaque which in the tiniest of lettering offers the translation —

THIS TEMPLE OF THE ARTS AND MUSES IS DEDICATED
TO ALMIGHTY GOD
BY THE FIRST GOVERNORS
IN THE YEAR OF OUR LORD 1931
JOHN REITH BEING DIRECTOR-GENERAL
AND THEY PRAY THAT GOOD SEED SOWN
MAY BRING FORTH GOOD HARVEST
THAT ALL THINGS FOUL OR HOSTILE TO PEACE
MAY BE BANISHED HENCE
AND THAT THE PEOPLE INCLINING THEIR EAR
TO WHATSOEVER THINGS ARE LOVELY AND HONEST
WHATSOEVER THINGS ARE OF GOOD REPORT
MAY TREAD THE PATH OF VIRTUE.

Under the great Latin inscription in the centre of the entrance hall, another sculptured figure, 'The Sower', and beneath it DEUS INCREMENTUM DAT. As the BBC, in those days, were not big payers, wags on the staff took this to mean 'Your only hope of an increment is from God'.

The effect of all this splendour somehow made you feel you ought to straighten your tie before entering the building, let alone adjust your dress. Sir John's austere presence permeated the whole place from the moment the commissionaires leapt to attention and saluted him on arrival. As Maurice Gorham put it: 'When the lift doors closed behind him, a sort of sigh swept across the hall as everybody let his breath out and got to work again.' Yes, there was quite a lot of awe surrounding the BBC of 1934.

Soon after my talk with the Establishment Officer, a short, concise memo came to my 'In' tray in the Accounts Department. It arrived one foggy November afternoon, when the ledgers were even more intractable and incomprehensible than usual. All it said was: 'Will you please attend at Studio 4A at 3.15 this afternoon for an Announcer's microphone test.'

It should be remembered that Announcers then were very different from the jolly chaps we know today. They were regarded by Reith as 'custodians of the spoken word' and the general idea was that they should 'build up in the public mind a sense of the BBC's collective personality'. The Announcers were anonymous, indeed almost indistinguishable one from another, and they spoke what came to be known as standard, educated speech. It was the voice of the upper middle-class and the BBC's Adviser on Spoken English was A. Lloyd James, the Professor of Phonetics at London University. Accent and dress were required to be impeccably correct.

To my great relief, on arriving at the studio, I found my friend from the cricket field and the squash courts, 'Joe' Shewen, in charge. He was the kindliest and least pompous of men and made me feel the whole thing was really rather fun. Thanks to him, I wasn't unduly nervous, and strangely enough seemed quite at home as I sat facing the enormous bomb-like microphone in the tiny studio. Of course, I knew my audition would be heard by the BBC chiefs assembled for the purpose in one of the offices at Broadcasting House. First, came a News bulletin, which I coped with fairly happily. After that, I was asked to present programmes of classical music in French,

German and Italian. An Announcer, in those days, was expected to be a 'man of culture, experience and knowledge'. Unfortunately, having scant culture, little experience of music and no knowledge whatever of Italian, I made rather a dog's dinner of this part of the audition. But, at the end, Joe was still grinning and I was still very determined. For two reasons I had to get that job: I needed the money, as things were going from bad to worse at home; and I simply had to get away from Accounts.

For the next hurdle, I was taken to see the Professor himself. By this time I was beginning to quake. I was shown into a room, which contained little but a long table and Professor Lloyd James. He sat at the end of it, slumped in his chair. Thick-set, leonine headed, white hair and reddish face under beetle brows. He went on just sitting there. It seemed like half an hour. I kept thinking of the great names on the BBC Advisory Committee of Spoken English: Robert Bridges (Poet Laureate), Bernard Shaw, Rudyard Kipling, Professor Lascelles Abercrombie, Lord David Cecil and Kenneth Clark.[1] How could I hope to get by. Why, they had spent hours, in solemn conclave, deliberating on the correct pronunciations of words such as 'garage' and 'margarine'! It was enough to make a simpleton like me totally tongue-tied. These sombre thoughts were dispelled by a sudden snort from the chair. The Professor was obviously returning from a long distance. He was sitting up straighter now and, what's more, he was smiling: 'Oh, my dear fellow, Dougall, isn't it? – Yes, I heard your audition – not bad. A pity you have no Italian, but you can soon pick it up. Your French and German are very good.'

Again, he fell into silence. Then, he started up once more in his silvery voice of utmost clarity: 'Now, I want you to imagine that I am thousands of miles away, somewhere in the middle of the jungle, it is very hot and steamy, I am being plagued with flies, and my supply of Scotch has given out. You have to rivet my attention with the News from London.' Saying this, he passed me a News bulletin, slumped right down in his chair again, and this time, to my alarm, covered his face with his hands. I started off somehow and my voice at first seemed to be coming from a long way away. But then confidence began to come back. My preoccupation with languages and the study of phonetics over the years was helping me. Reading aloud

[1] Now Lord Clark.

47

after all was something I had been doing for my own pleasure for years. This helped me overcome the lack of a more advanced academic education.

As I finished, he rocked me with a remark worthy of Professor Higgins: 'I can tell that you have been reading aloud a lot of French lately.' He was absolutely right and had detected the rising intonation in my voice at the end of most clauses. We parted on good terms. He had taught me incidentally a lesson I have never forgotten. A broadcaster in sound or vision must always work hard to hold attention. He should always remember that he is at the mercy of a switch and it is his job to ensure that the viewer or listener does not use it.

So far, so good, but the third hurdle was going to be the worst. If Reith were an inspirer of awe, his Deputy, Admiral Carpendale, was no slouch either. This I knew would be the crucial interview. His sanctum was in the suite of offices on the third floor. A confrontation of this kind alarmed me very much more than any studio audition. I felt completely hollow inside. As I entered, 'Carps', as he was always known, was sitting at a large desk and yet seemed to tower above it, because his back was so straight. Also my chair was rather low. He had piercing blue eyes and his features might have been hewn out of rock. The Admiral wasn't looking pleased. He obviously didn't think much of my qualifications. I imagine that he had only heard of a dozen or so of the top public schools. Whitgift wasn't one of them so, in his eyes, I was a suspicious character right from the start.

'One of the new schools, I suppose?' said 'Carps'.

'No, Sir, it was founded in 1596 by Archbishop Whitgift.' I wasn't going to let him get away with that.

Then he barked another question at me: 'Why haven't you been to university?' There was only one answer, so I explained that it was necessary for me to earn my living. That didn't seem to satisfy him either and he snarled back at me: 'No other reason?'

Well, to be charitable, I suppose I was a rather unusual candidate with almost none of the orthodox qualifications. But, thanks to his icy manner, I came out of that interview in a bit of a rage and on the point of not caring whether I got the job or not. It wasn't as if I were aspiring to be Prime Minister.

Subsequently, as the years went by, I found him to be quite a kindly chap, and also realised that my experience at that initial interview was not unusual. Most old BBC hands tremble a bit when recalling their first interview with 'Carps'. Perhaps he enjoyed putting people through it.

One thing is certain, that he suffered from a distinct rigidity of mind. Years later one of the Corporation's most brilliant staff accompanists Cecil Dixon, or Sophie as we all knew her, told me of one of her confrontations with him. It was at a time when Sophie was being hopelessly overworked. The international artists she used to accompany at the piano were, of course, very exacting. Each broadcast required hours of practice at home, even before any studio rehearsal. Eventually, she could stand it no longer and asked to see the Admiral. Sophie explained to him at length, but was obviously only getting a frosty hearing. 'I can't understand it,' he said. 'If the typists can tap their keys for eight hours a day – why can't you?'

For the next week or so I seemed to be living in a sort of vacuum. Work in the Accounts Department became more unreal to me than ever. My colleagues there, who had always been tremendously helpful, were beginning to look on me with new eyes. They almost seemed to share my interest. Would I be able to cross the great divide between the Business and the Programme side? The Head of Department, Geoffrey Strode, who had taken me on from Deloittes, knew how important it was for me to have the opportunity of earning more money and put no difficulties in my way. He had always treated me with the greatest kindness, ever since I went down with pneumonia just after joining.

At home – guess what? We had moved yet again. This time to Grove House in Chatsworth Road, East Croydon, where the family had installed itself in a flat on the first floor. It was one of the two remaining Wren houses in the district. A retired schoolteacher, who was a spinster and a family friend, was living in the flat on the ground floor. I loved it there. The staircase was splendidly wide, the rooms spacious and the walls panelled in wood. Mother, with her invariable cheerfulness and courage had done marvels in rigging up curtains and carpets and we all helped paint the floor boards with a dark stain. The house had, at some time, been used as a kindergarten school and on most of the doors one could faintly make out the names of certain flowers, which, I suppose, had once designated the classrooms. The sitting-room had BLUEBELL dimly showing through the paintwork and on my bedroom door

49

was DAFFODIL. There were folding, wooden shutters on the inside of each window. It was a house with character, and a happy house.

As far as money was concerned, the breadwinners were my elder sister Nell, who was in the West End dress trade, and myself. My father's earnings were almost nil. The city then was at its most depressed. My sister Moira had only recently married Pat Sayers a young doctor at St Thomas's, who a couple of years before had diagnosed my pneumonia. By now, I was earning £3 per week, but that didn't go very far. So, this was really the situation that had steeled me into making the effort for something better. How important incentive is! If things had been easier at home, I don't suppose I would ever have had the drive and single-mindedness to badger the Establishment Officer to give me a break.

When ten days had gone by and I'd heard nothing, I began to feel despairing. It seemed obvious to me that I hadn't made the grade. Then, a small brown envelope found its way through the inter-office post to my 'In' tray. It just said:

'This is to inform you that you have been appointed Announcer, BBC Empire Service. You should report to Room 412 B.H. at 10.30 a.m. on November 27th to take up your duties.'

27 November 1934, as it happened, was also my 21st birthday.

5 Reith's Temple

I must have been not only the youngest Staff Announcer the BBC had ever had, but the only one to be recruited from such an unlikely quarter as the Accounts Department. In those days, there were no rigid salary grades, but each employee got the best terms he could. Salaries were a personal matter between an individual and his Departmental Head. There was not even a Staff Association and very few seemed to feel the need for one. In fact, a year later in 1935, when there was a free vote of all the staff on this issue, as many as eighty per cent opposed the idea and it wasn't until after the start of the war that the first BBC Staff Association was formed.

My salary? The princely sum of £260 p.a. It seemed riches to me then: a whole £110 p.a. increase. As a rough comparison, I should say it would be the equivalent of about £1,500 today. Not bad for a young man, just twenty-one. It meant I would be able to help out more at home and then have something left over for myself as well. But it wasn't only the money. From now on, I would have the chance of working at something which really made sense to me.

The Empire Department was then not quite two years old and there were only forty people in it. So I was in near the start of what was to become during the war the great BBC Overseas Service, now known as the World Service. Under its Director, Sir Cecil Graves, the key man in charge of Programmes and Planning was J. B. Clark, later to become Sir Beresford Clark.

The BBC at this time was getting no grant from the Government to run the new Service and it was therefore operated on a shoe-string budget. In fact, the cost was only one penny out of every ten shilling licence. This was particularly unfortunate, because Germany and Italy were heavily subsidising their world shortwave programmes. American and Russian broadcasts were also having great influence, especially in the Middle East. So Britain, in spite of her vast Empire and world wide interests, was lagging behind.

The Transmitter was at Daventry and the broadcasts in 1934 were divided into five Transmissions, each one covering a particular part of the Empire and aimed to reach its listeners in late afternoon or early evening. Later, a sixth Transmission was added to cover Western Canada, broadcast at the ungodly hour, for us, of approximately 2 a.m. to 4 a.m. GMT. So it meant that the programmes went on pretty well all round the clock.

The organisation was rather like a present-day Regional Station in that most of the programmes were taken from the two National networks, but we had our own separate News Section and specialised talks. The expansion was fairly rapid and soon we were to have a BBC Empire Orchestra and produce our own plays and variety shows for listeners overseas. Our call-sign had a stirring ring: 'This is London calling through the British Empire Broadcasting Station at Daventry.' Then followed the frequencies which were suitably labelled: GSA for Aerial, GSB for Broadcasting, GSC for Corporation, GSD for Daventry, GSE for Empire, GSF for Fortune, GSG for Greeting, GSH for Home, and so on.

Reception was of course a variable business throughout the Empire. There was interference of all kinds from static to sunspots, but increasingly, the Dominions and Colonies rebroadcast at least some part of the service from London, so that, wherever a listener might be, he stood a chance of keeping in touch with home.

I could not have wished for two more charming colleagues on the Announcing staff. Joe Shewen I already knew. He was about fifty, rather a David Niven type, with a small moustache, a legacy from his days as a Major with the Army in India.

Basil Gray had started his BBC career in Belfast. He was a gay, mercurial, complex character. Both were Scots. Both had a marvellous sense of humour and I was soon to find out what a necessary attribute that was.

For a few days, I just 'trailed' the other two. That is, I accompanied them on all their broadcasts and they patiently showed me the tricks of the trade.

Then the morning came when I was on my own, alone with the Empire in Studio 7A. Sitting in that tiny studio where I was to spend so many hours round the clock in the next few years, I was sweating with fear. That is how it used to take people in those days. The microphone itself was large and awe-inspiring: it was grey and shaped like a bomb. Even big-game hunters and photographers, like Cherry Kearton and Gandar

Dower, all said they would rather face a tiger in the jungle than a BBC microphone.

The current 'Pop' tune was Jerome Kern's 'Smoke gets in your eyes', and a very good one too, but as far as I was concerned the trouble was sweat running down my armpits. Not from heat, but sheer terror.

The fairly general fear of the microphone was something the designers of the twenty-two studios at Broadcasting House had borne very much in mind. For this reason, the décor and layout of each studio was intended, as far as possible, to make a performer feel he was on familiar ground. As an article in *The Listener* of those days put it: 'The musicians of the dance band, of the symphony orchestra, those who talk and play and sing, those who create "dramatic effects", must all feel – as nearly as possible continuously – at their best. Architecture must become an aid to well-being.'

How did it all work out? Well for a start the new Broadcasting House was too small. In no time, departments and staff were spilling out into neighbouring streets and into every available hall or hotel or office block that could be found.

The entrance hall was certainly impressive. A titled lady did the flowers, another charmer in black evening gown received the after-dinner speakers or musicians.

Down in the sub-basement: a small theatre for vaudeville, and, to give it the right atmosphere, a tiny stage with wings and spotlights, two rows of tip-up seats and a gesture of a gallery. This was Studio BA and it is no wonder that the true home of Variety soon became St George's Hall across the road. Also down there in the depths was BB, a plain, functional studio for hardened characters, who needed no cosseting, like the members of the BBC Dance Orchestra. Henry Hall was its Director and when I met him recently on the BBC 50th Anniversary Dinner at Guildhall he recalled George V and Queen Mary's tour of Broadcasting House at its opening in 1932. Henry, an erect, spry seventy-five-year-old told me that Their Majesties suffered that day from a surfeit of the National Anthem. The BBC Symphony Orchestra gave a splendid rendering when they visited the Concert Hall. The BBC Military Band blasted them with it in Studio 8A. By the time the King reached the Dance Orchestra studio it was clear he had had enough. 'Oh no, not again,' he growled to himself and sank wearily into a chair.

On the lower-ground floor was the *pièce de résistance* – the Concert Hall. Impressive, but too small. When first completed, it was found there was no entrance big enough to get a grand piano in. BBC folklore has it that the carpenters were then instructed to make a ply-wood piano and use that to check the size of doorway needed. Off they went and made a beauty – it looked just like a real piano – but they couldn't get it out of the workshop. The Symphony Orchestra had to use Queen's Hall, opposite.

Up on the third floor – the Chapel, Studio 3E. For religious services a cross was projected on to a white background in a white recess meant to convey an impression of infinite distance. The Director-General's sanctum was on this floor too. Also here was the 'Children's Hour' Studio, 3A, where Derek McCulloch, Uncle Mac, held sway. Just across the corridor, three Talks Studios 3B, 3C and 3D. This was where the nerves really needed soothing. Take 3D for instance. Just like a study in a play. A fireplace with a portrait of George Washington above it. The main chair was the one Arnold Bennett had used to write in. Round the walls luxurious, leather-bound volumes. Many of the distinguished old speakers went to clutch at these – but they turned out to be just phonies (the volumes, I mean).

Up on the sixth, plenty of tricks. This was the home of the Effects Studios. Thunder-sheet hanging against the wall, box of gravel for marching feet, big drum for guns, water tank for splashing noises and, of course, the famous coconuts for horses' hooves. This was Bryan Michie's domain, before he joined Jack Hylton. A chubby, red-cheeked giant, but nimble enough – during a production when, wearing his headphones, he would leap madly about the studio, picking things up, shaking them, opening and shutting doors, rattling the thunder – in fact if you hadn't known exactly where you were, you might have begun to wonder. His assistant was George Inns, frail and elfin, in complete contrast. George had a long way to go before he was able to pour all that enthusiasm of his into the Black and White Minstrel Shows.

Right at the top, on the eighth floor, Studio 8A – for the BBC Military Band, under the baton of genial B. Walton O'Donnell, 'Bandy' as everybody knew him. He was King George V's favourite.

The Control Room was just across the way – with all its

mysteries (to me anyway), and the finish here was in battleship grey with stainless steel fittings. In those days, one man had all the twenty-two studios under his control and even the switching on and off of the microphones took place up here. And this is where the six Greenwich Pips came from.

So that was the Broadcasting House of the early thirties and all the materials used were British – every blooming thing – the stone, brick, timber, metalwork and fittings, all were British or from the Empire. In every studio and along all the corridors were placed at intervals large gleaming buckets of copper and brass. Some people thought they were spittoons, as they had sand in the bottom, but those who knew better said they were ashtrays and probably from one of the Admiral's old battleships.

There is a famous BBC story, which gives the flavour of those times. It goes something like this. One night, at a later hour than usual, the Director-General, Sir John Reith, with the Admiral at his side, was stalking through the corridors of Broadcasting House. Rounding a corner, they came upon a young Announcer and a girl secretary in affectionate embrace. Sir John was furious and said the man must be got rid of at once. But the Admiral pleaded with him to sleep on it, to think it over, and give his answer in the morning. When the morning came, Sir John said: 'All right, I have thought about it. The man may stay – but he may never read the Epilogue!'

Even in Reith's day the Corporation frequently came under heavy fire. Whenever possible he replied to complaints himself. Once to his astonishment there was a broadside resulting from a talk on ornithology.

Somewhere in the shires a good lady on entering her drawing-room from the garden heard these words emanating from the loudspeaker: 'Great tits like coconuts.' That was enough for her! She rushed to the set, switched it off and sat down to write Reith a snorter. She accused him of polluting the ether with foul language and debasing womanhood and heaven knows what else. Reith's reply was short and to the point: 'Dear Madam, if you had only continued listening you would also have heard that rrobins like worrms!'

I personally never came in contact very much with Sir John, as he then was. But there's no doubt his presence made itself felt all right, and he was always popping up in the most unlikely places. One lunchtime I will always remember. I went

55

down to the canteen and was standing there quietly with my tray, when I felt a presence right beside me. Sir John was massive, about 6ft 5ins. I glanced out of the corner of my eye. No mistaking that craggy countenance with the deep scar, caused by a sniper's bullet in the First World War. I felt rather as Charlie Chaplin looks, when he finds himself alongside a big copper. To my astonishment, he peered down at me and said: 'Dougall, isn't it? Empire Service? Expanding rapidly.' Expanding? I was sinking through the floor.

The Announcer then, unlike today, wrote all his own material, chose his own records, put himself on and off the air and, generally, carried out duties later performed by a number of different people and departments. The most trying aspect of life in the Empire Service was the way the shift system worked. Six days on, three off and changing hours every two days, so that at the end of the six days one had worked all round the clock. This played hell with the digestion, and led to a certain amount of frayed nerves and irritability. It also meant a greatly restricted social life. And yet, in spite of all the snags, I loved it. Best of all we were left to our own devices to present the Empire programmes, as we thought fit.

I doubt if I should have survived the austere, impersonal, toffee-nosed approach the Announcers on the Home air were required to adopt – at that time. There were so many Speech and Presentation experts breathing down their necks that every time the poor chaps opened their mouths they were in danger of putting their foot in it.

Stuart Hibberd was the revered Chief Announcer. Golden-voiced, always immaculate, manners impeccable: a man of infinite charm and urbanity. So much so that I could never believe he was quite real.

At this time, when on duty after eight in the evening, Announcers were usually expected to wear a dinner jacket. There was nothing very extraordinary about this, as life was much more formal then. Dinner jackets were often worn in the best seats at the theatre, and as many artists and speakers coming to Broadcasting House would themselves be wearing evening dress, it was thought a simple matter of courtesy that Announcers should do likewise. But there were disadvantages. As Stuart wrote in his Diary:[1] 'It is not an ideal kit in which to

[1] *This is London* by Stuart Hibberd, published by Macdonald & Evans Ltd, 1950.

read the News – I myself hate having anything tight round my neck when broadcasting – and I remember that more than once the engineers said that my shirt-front creaked during the reading of the bulletin.'

Stuart's approach to his duties was very serious indeed. He was a great gargler and took the greatest care of his voice, in every way. In fact, I have known him decline to eat even a biscuit for up to an hour before he was due to read the News, in case a crumb should lodge in his throat.

Once in the Gents' Cloakroom, from behind one of the closed doors, he was heard to be intoning over and over again 'This is London'. After all, when you think about it, which is the right word to stress? You can say it in at least three different ways and, remember, Stuart was a perfectionist.

Yet, even he could fall from grace. Many eyebrows were raised when once he solemnly declared in the News that Queen Mary had just returned to Marlborough *Street*, instead of Marlborough House!

One of his colleagues, 'Ajax' Farrer, speaking in the News of a volcanic eruption in Turkey once astonished his listeners by informing them that: 'floods of molten lager are flowing down the mountainside.'

But, it was undoubtedly Stuart, in private the gentlest and kindest of men, who gave rise to the legendary image in the public's mind of the Olympian, omniscient, impeccable BBC Announcer (Mark I).

One night, when he had been kept late at Broadcasting House, he dashed to Charing Cross Station only to find that his last train to Chislehurst in Kent had already left, and what's more, from the wrong platform. Stuart wasn't best pleased. He called at the Inspector's office and made such an impression that a special train was run to get him home.

Freddie Grisewood was also a Staff Announcer at that time. Another great charmer, but somewhat more extrovert and with a splendid sense of humour. Once, Freddie very nearly exploded in the middle of the News. He was reading an item about the Police, who were then using motor bicycles with sidecars.

'This winter,' he read, 'the Police are changing their combinations – ' The visual image this conjured up was too much for Freddie – he got the giggles and had the greatest difficulty in finishing the sentence.

It's a funny thing this business of getting the giggles and it only seems to happen on radio. I've never known a case of it on television. I'm inclined to think that it is because in a radio studio you are to all intents and purposes alone. The whole performance is in a sense an act of faith.

One of my most hilarious experiences arose from the failure of a recording made between two professional footballers. It was a discussion between, I think, Charles Buchan of Arsenal and his opposite number of Spurs, in which they had been comparing their training methods. The quality of the recording was so bad that the programme director decided it should be scrapped and Basil Gray and I were asked to read the script 'live' from the studio, each taking a part. Unfortunately, there was only one copy of the script available, which didn't make it easy. With this between us on the desk, we started off solemnly enough. Then, when I heard Basil, whom I had never known to run even for a bus, saying in his somewhat pedantic voice: 'Well, Charlie, what I usually do is start with thirty press-ups, then take a run round the field four or five times –' the whole absurdity and improbability of the situation struck me with a bang. I let out an explosive snort and just managed to shoot my hand out and switch off the microphone, before collapsing in helpless laughter. Basil was similarly stricken and all we could do was pace up and down the studio, digging our finger nails into the palms of our hands in a desperate attempt to get control. After a minute, we started again, only even more grimly solemn. It was no good. In a few seconds we were hysterical again and the whole thing had to be abandoned. I only hope the Empire listeners put it down to sunspots.

It was round about this time that I was sitting in the Announcer's Room one day waiting to take over from Joe, when he finished his stint on the Empire Service. Joe, as I've already said, was a delightful chap with a marvellous sense of humour but, on the air, he used to speak very slowly and precisely and with the utmost deliberation, which in some ways was a good thing, because of all the static and interference on short-waves. On this occasion, he was ending his Transmission with a programme of light music. 'Ladies and Gentlemen,' Joe was saying, 'for the next half-hour, we are taking you over to hear a programme of light music played by the Bathroom Orchestra from Pump.'

I suppose all Announcers dread spoonerisms. Once I even

heard the national flag of the United States referred to as 'The Star-bangled Spanner'. Then there was a Peer of the realm, who when broadcasting during the Blitz days, talked of 'Dam bomage'. For some reason the weather forecasts used to be a minefield for unwary Announcers. I have heard talk of 'shattered scowers of sleet and rain', and on another occasion we were warned of 'Drain and rizzle'. Perhaps it's just as well that the weathermen now have to read their own forecasts. It also means that, at least, people can't now blame the BBC for the weather too. Incidentally it's good to know spoonerisms are still with us. On BBC television News recently I have heard with glee: 'Ugasian Andans' and 'Pie and Praces'.

Glancing through the programmes of those far-off days makes you realise we must have been made of sterner stuff, or at least that the listeners were. The Empire Service had three main sources. First, the offerings from our own small departments. Drama, where Howard Rose and the young poet John Pudney did marvels of production with only poor resources. Then there was Variety, Talks, News and so on. We even had our own BBC Empire Orchestra, under its Staff Conductor Eric Fogg. Eric also planned all the music programmes and I think he must have had a predilection for the cello.

He was married to a cellist at that time. It's not that I've got anything against the instrument, but, after a night on duty, one isn't in the mood. My memories of Transmission I to Australia at 7 a.m. conjure up the picture of a gawky, bespectacled female perched on a wooden rostrum in Studio 8A. Clutched between her knees, stretched to their utmost limit, a captive cello. An unnerving sight early in the morning and I used to wonder what I or the Empire had done to deserve it.

Eric was a bluff, forthright, North-country man with a tremendous sense of fun. A temperance brass band once complained bitterly to him that they were never booked for a broadcast in the Empire Service. He explained politely that they were not quite up to the required standard, and then must have rubbed salt into the wound by informing them that the next brass band concert would be given by the Friary Brewery Band with songs by Samuel Worthington (bass).

Light entertainment was in the hands of Cecil Madden. Cecil was essentially an impresario: he was always discovering someone. He had to, because his budget didn't run to using many established artists. His enthusiasm was unlimited – and everybody loved him. One of his many endearing qualities was his vagueness. Cecil would make a Bill of a number of his discoveries under the heading of 'Friends in Harmony'. This became a title to strike chill into any Announcer's heart. Having been up most of the night, I would go down to Studio BA at about 7 a.m. to find a mixed bag of artists limbering up. A seedy tenor in a fur coat gargling with port, a red-nosed comic, an Italian violinist and an impersonator of bird noises, all thinking they were the greatest, and waiting to be directed. Cecil, meantime, weaving about frantically rather like a demented grasshopper, roaring with laughter and slapping people on the back. The problem was, with about fifteen minutes to air time, to try to find out who was going to do what to whom and in what order.

Sometimes, when the budget would allow for a professional compère, a little man with glasses would appear. Arthur Askey was then on his way to the top and, never mind what the hour, he always managed to be full of bounce and livened up the dullest show.

On the music side Sir Walford Davies was one of the great broadcasters of the early thirties A fine musician and pianist, he also had the rare gift in those days of being able to chat in a friendly way with his listeners without the aid of a script. He was a big, benign man and so highly regarded that he alone was allowed to broadcast a secular programme from Studio 3E, the Chapel. But week after week, when Sir Walford was giving his talks on 'Music and the Ordinary Listener', the engineers would be mystified by inexplicable technical faults. These never occurred during religious programmes and the reason for them could seldom be traced. Perhaps there was an outraged Chapel ghost?

The real meat of the Empire programmes was the News and Talks. There was a regular series on 'World Affairs' with a distinguished panel of speakers – headed by H. Wickham Steed, former Editor of *The Times*. He had an almost Elizabethan look with his high forehead, parchment-like face and white goatee beard. He always seemed to be wearing a black jacket and striped trousers, and was as meticulous over his script and its delivery as he was over his attire. Microphones then were susceptible to blasting, and Wickham Steed, who had a somewhat explosive forceful style of speech, inevitably became known to us all as Suckem Steeth. Other speakers were

Sir Frederick Whyte and Vernon Bartlett, surely two of the best broadcasters of all time.

Then, on the home scene and playing strongly on a nostalgic note another great broadcaster in Howard Marshall. His talks 'Under Big Ben' had a tremendous following. I doubt if anyone has ever equalled the peculiar Englishness of Howard's voice, which held all the magic of the cricket field, the trout stream or the cathedral close. A. G. Street I also remember for the splendid earthiness of his delivery, which seemed to become more rustic with the years, and for his common sense strictures on the passing scene. The military outlook, none too rosy, was immaculately assessed by Cyril Falls, correspondent of *The Times*.

Apart from these programmes, especially planned and produced in the Empire Department, much of our output was shared with the two domestic networks, which were called the National and the Regional. Very often we would join a programme of music which was already in progress. This would mean sitting in 7A with headphones on and trying to identify the item of music being played while announcing as calmly as possible to the Empire: 'We are now joining listeners in this country for a programme of light music played by Fred Hartley and his Novelty Quintet.' If you felt like sticking your neck out, you might venture: 'they are playing as we join them – "I'll see you again".' As likely as not, just as we went over, they'd strike up 'In a Persian Market'. It was all very trying.

In addition to these shared broadcasts, there were, of course, the electrical recordings. The system in use in 1934 was the Blattnerphone. This was a clumsy process of recording on steel tapes, requiring large, cumbersome machines. Apart from changes in pitch, known as 'Wow', and a mysterious interference called 'Plop', the main trouble with the beastly Blattner was that the tape all too often broke. The engineers would then go quietly mad, trying to stick the two ends together again, while the Announcer apologised to listeners and played fill-up records. It was nothing to have to apologise as much as three times in a fifteen minute recorded talk.

There was another diabolical trick the Blattnerphone could play. It did it to me once, when, with a flourish of trumpets, I had announced a speech by His Royal Highness the Duke of Gloucester, and thereupon a noise ensued like the high-pitched chattering of monkeys at the Zoo. To my horror, I realised the tape was being played backwards. At least, I learnt to be a good apologiser, which served me well later, when television came along.

Generally speaking, the Empire Announcer had a solitary time of it on night duty. There was no other programme official in the building. As with a sea-captain, the log book recorded all his actions hour by hour. At one time, having said good night to listeners in North America at 1.30 a.m. GMT, we had to be on the air again at 6 a.m. for Australia and New Zealand. Sleeping quarters were provided in a converted office on the top floor of a house in Portland Place, where the BBC extension stands now. The system of calling was by telephone and there was an instrument close to the bed. To be in one's right mind and on the air at 6 a.m. meant a call at five. Sleep never comes easily in a room smelling of telephones and type-writers. There is something busy left vibrating in the air. As often as not, after a few hours tossing and turning, sleep would at last come, only to be shattered by the ringing of the bell. On one of these nightmarish occasions, I fumbled my arm out from under the sheets, grabbed the beastly thing, mumbled an acknowledgement, which must have sounded something like 'kewvairmuch'; and then, exhausted by the effort, crashed back on the pillow and was instantly asleep again.

At 6 a.m. the engineers duly flicked the red light in 7A, but answering buzz came there none. Panic stations, while listeners were treated to a record of Bow Bells. Ten whole minutes went by before I was roused. Then a dishevelled pyjama-clad figure, dressing-gown flying, I lurched through the endless corridors of Broadcasting House to tell Australia how sorry I was.

Afterwards, in the Announcers' Room I set about filling in the log. Miserably, I flicked over the page to look at the carbon copy of the previous day's happenings. Good grief! Basil Gray had done almost exactly the same thing. Mechanically, I turned back to the day before that and, fascinated, I read another profuse apology from Joe Shewen for, guess what? It was a hat-trick and, what's more, a totally unconnived at coincidence.

The sad part was that no one believed it; least of all our Director – J. B. Clark. He was convinced it was a conspiracy and instructed the Empire Executive, Commander Stride, RN retd, to call a meeting. At this, among other things, we were accused of mutiny, but once the dust had settled, we found we had done ourselves a good turn. J.B. agreed that a fourth Announcer should be appointed to relieve us.

6 The Thirties

One of the almost inescapable features of London society in the thirties was the 'Deb' dances. Heaven knows, it would have been difficult to find anyone less eligible than my impecunious self but, no matter, having attended one of those balls the invitations kept on coming. Perhaps my name had been put on some list or other. I loathed dancing, but there was a certain fascination in seeing how the other half lived. With hunger-marchers at one end of the scale and the Deb 'do's' at the other, the social scene was certainly not lacking in variety.

It so happened that I had been invited to one of these balls on a night when, for part of the time, I would have to be on duty at Broadcasting House. So I thought I would look in at the function, which was at the Hyde Park Hotel, then slip out for the broadcast and return later. That evening, in the North American Transmission, I was down to present a programme of Monckton Melodies for which Nelson Keys, then one of the big names of the London stage, was to act a compère. 'Bunch', as he was always known, was a chunky, spry little man, not much bigger than a jockey, but marvellously good company. That morning I met him for lunch in the Bolivar, as the present BBC Club bar used to be called. He was sitting arched up on a stool, and as we talked, double gin followed double gin, as he airily dismissed all my suggestions of solider fare. This, incidentally, was to present me with a problem when, later, I tried to recoup my expenses. To lunch with Nelson Keys – twelve double gins.

That evening, as arranged, I slipped away from the party at the Hyde Park for my programme at Broadcasting House. There I found Bunch in tremendous form. I steered him down to the concert hall and somehow guided him through the Monckton Melodies by sitting next to him and pointing with my pencil at the lines he had to speak. We got through it without any major disaster by about 12.30, but it left Bunch of course badly in need of a drink. All the pubs were closed, so, rashly, I mentioned I was going back to a marvellous party at the Hyde Park, and to my alarm he was all for coming along too. There wasn't much I could do about it. He just piled into the taxi after me. The only snag was that Bunch had a dinner jacket on, whereas the rig at the Hyde Park was tails. We got past the man at the door, who of course recognised him, then went into the ballroom and up to the bar at the far end. After a quick drink, I left him for a turn round the floor with an exceptionally delectable Deb. In fact, I was getting quite preoccupied, until I suddenly noticed a large circle of male, tailcoated backs near the bar. Every so often, the circle opened out to release a tremendous, explosive guffaw. More and more were crowding round and I realised that Bunch must be telling some of his racy stories. He was having himself a ball.

I teetered round, doing my ineffectual best to break it up, when my hostess, whom I hardly knew at all, bore down and, very reasonably, asked me to remove 'my friend in a dinner jacket' as he was emptying the dance floor!

One of the pleasanter things about Empire Announcer duties was that we wrote our own presentation material. The short-wave bands were so crowded that in order to hold your listeners' attention you had to go flat out all the time. No 'dead' air between programmes was allowed, so we used to fill-up by trailing future programmes, playing records or, if feeling in the mood, by personal chat. This might be about almost anything. The changing seasons were always good value. We had many a strong silent Britisher in fever-wracked jungle, or wherever, wiping his eye at the thought of, say, the first crocuses being seen in Regent's Park. In fact, judging by their letters, many listeners seemed to enjoy these off-the-cuff remarks rather more than some of the programmes.

One of my colleagues at that time started a saga about how he had been bitten by a horse-fly on his bottom. Only, of course, in those refined days, he described it as a sensitive place. Anyway, he recounted how he had swollen up exceedingly and was unable to sit down. Now, if there was one thing the Empire knew about more than another it was horse-flies. The remedies came flooding in by every post to give us one of our biggest mails ever. Howard Gee kept the story running until he was giving an almost nightly bulletin on his condition. That imperial horse-fly provided fill-up material for weeks.

Many of our listeners must have been stuck in totally isolated places, so that the regular, friendly voices from home be-

C

came an important link. The curious thing is that one came to sense this companionship, and always on entering the studio I too felt among friends.

Being alone in the building on duty at night, with the exception of the engineers, had its problems. Sometimes, with a ghastly sinking feeling, I would realise up in Studio 7A that I had left the script and details of the programme I had to announce next, down on my desk in the Announcers' office five floors below. There was only one thing to do. Put a record on the turntable and dash for the lift. While the Empire was listening to, say, the 'Flight of the Bumble Bee', I'd be speeding, heart thumping, to the office. A frantic search, a grab at the script and hell for leather back to the studio. Provided I didn't trip over one of the Admiral's spittoons and measure my length in the headlong rush, as happened once, I could make it down and back in three minutes flat. Any longer, and the ten-inch record would be at an end. The pick-up head rasping round and round as though in outraged indignation.

One of my most messy moments was when I had an unstoppable nose bleed just before the main News in Transmission V for North America, at about 1 a.m. our time. This presented quite a problem. There was no hope of the usual treatment – sitting down quietly, and tilting the head back, while holding a handkerchief delicately to the nostrils. I couldn't possibly read in that position, so I just had to let it rip. For the next ten minutes, I ploughed on while drops of blood dripped down heavily on to the sheets of paper and splodged all over the place. It must have been the snuffliest and goriest bulletin the BBC has ever broadcast.

The most trying chore over the weekend was reading innumerable Football Results. They had to be read in three separate Transmissions following one another, ending at about 3.30 a.m. for Western Canada. At that time I was at my lowest ebb and, on one occasion, the sound of my own voice intoning the results for the third time began to send me to sleep. I struggled to fight against it, but momentarily my head dropped down to the desk. By the time I had got to Div. III I was almost in a state of trance. Then, for a few seconds, my subconscious must have taken over because, instead of giving a result, I heard my voice say 'Brighton beat 'em up'. Then a short silence, and consciousness returned: 'Sorry about that – Brighton 3 Aldershot Nil.' And I was back on the rails again.

In May 1935 the country went Jubilee mad. The twenty-fifth anniversary of King George V's accession to the throne was as good an excuse as any for rejoicing. Life had been bleak enough at home with millions on the dole, while in Europe Hitler and Mussolini were ranting and raving. But here, at last, was an event we could almost feel happy about. On the eve of the celebrations, I went to a party at the Berkeley in Piccadilly which I had to leave, in order to be at Broadcasting House for the North American Transmission at 11 p.m. On my way through the West End, I saw that London was really letting its hair down. I'd never seen anything like it and I don't suppose anybody had since Mafeking Night. Floodlit buildings, Union Jacks blossoming everywhere, and the streets full of people who looked as if they hadn't a care in the world. Even at that time of night, newspapers were being spread out on the kerbs and positions taken up along the route of the procession.

When I eventually got into the newsroom, I found that in the bulletin they were only proposing to carry a factual report from the Agencies, as in those days we had no reporters of our own. I was so full of what I had seen that the News editor agreed to put me on to give an eye-witness acount. In the fifteen minutes before we went on the air, I hastily jotted down my impressions of the way Londoners were whooping it up in the streets outside. I hope my broadcast helped listeners over-seas to catch something of the spontaneous gaiety there was in the capital that night.

It was the Silver Jubilee broadcasts that first firmly estab-lished the Empire Service from London. Rapturous reports poured in from all quarters. From Ottawa we heard that even the clattering of the horses' hooves came over clearly, and there was great excitement in Sydney too, where their own Jubilee celebrations had been nearly washed out by rain.

These letters meant a great deal to us because they were almost the only reaction to our work we got. Christmas, of course, was the peak time for mail and it helped make up for the inevitable frustration of working in such a far-flung Ser-vice. One year, four large crates of grapefruit arrived from South Africa, one for each Announcer; bottles of whisky came from thousands of miles away too, as well as a colourful selection of socks and ties. Two of the more unusual gifts I had were an armadillo, carved in ebony, from Brazil and a table-size totem pole, shaped by the Red Indians, and sent from Vancouver.

One Christmas I shall always remember. An eccentric American millionaire from Philadelphia called at Broadcasting House and asked for the Empire Announcers. It seemed he was an avid listener to our programmes and, on arriving in London, felt he must call on his friends of the air. As he thoughtfully brought a case of whisky, we received him with open arms. Having shown him all over the studios, we proceeded to drink his health. The time passed with great speed until the sobering realisation that there was a News bulletin to be read. Hugh Venables, Dick Wessel and I drew lots. I got the short stick, but the bulletin seemed endlessly long.

Christmas also was the occasion for the big Empire Exchange programme produced by Laurence Gilliam on the new Dramatic Control Panel with fifteen knobs. D. H. Munro was at the controls in the hot seat. In fact, as Marsland Gander colourfully wrote in the *Daily Telegraph*:

> Mr Munro will sit like an organist at his instrument, but with half the world at his fingertips. A special seat has been constructed to enable him to slide rapidly from one end of the seven foot panel to the other. [He continued rapturously] The Programme swings backwards and forwards to Australia, India, back to London: to Rhodesia, New Zealand and then Liverpool: to Canada and (finally) South Africa, where natives thunder out a special salute and drums roll. Then comes the King's greeting to his subjects in all countries. Finally the National Anthem is sung round the Empire, verse by verse.

With all that seat sliding between Australia and London, D. H. must have felt red, white and blue all over at the end of it, and probably needed a draught of Empire wine or something stronger to revive him.

Among the Scotsmen on the staff the New Year could bring its problems too. On one New Year's Day, my relief was due to take over for the late night Transmission starting at 11 p.m. At 10.40, with a happy sigh, I closed Transmission IV and made my way down to the Announcers' Room on the second floor. I opened the door, and there was my relief – stretched flat-out on the large, brown leather settee. Shaking him brought

nothing but a sort of incoherent mumble. There was a powerful smell of whisky rising from him and, with a sinking heart, I
realised it was a clear case of chronic Hogmanay. Problem
number one – how to dispose of the body? I couldn't just leave
him lying there, perhaps for some other more official member
of the staff to find and put him on a charge. There was only
one thing to do – get him stowed away in one of the bedrooms – and take over his duties for the night. And there was
just a quarter of an hour to do it in.

I dragged him along the corridor, up two flights of stairs,
along another passageway, up more stairs, then, just as I was
within sight of the bedrooms, I lost my grip on him and he fell,
a dead weight, to the floor. In a panic by now, I glanced at my
watch to see it was five to eleven. Down in the concert hall of
Broadcasting House I knew the BBC Empire Orchestra with
its conductor Eric Fogg would be tuning-up for the special
New Year's Day Programme for North America.

At that second, a door opened and Freddie Grisewood
appeared. I'd never been more pleased to see anyone. He was
the most understanding of men, so I, gratefully, left him to
cope with the body and charged frenziedly back along the
corridors to arrive in the concert hall with thirty seconds to
go before the off. I got the programme launched somehow but,
after that, it seemed one of the longest nights of my life.

Meantime, things were getting rough in Europe. In October
1935 Mussolini invaded Abyssinia. Soon on a cinema newsreel,
we were to see Il Duce's aviator son getting out of his bomber
after a raid. His words struck a chill: 'I dropped an aerial
torpedo in the centre of a group of Abyssinian horsemen, and
the group spread like a flowering rose. It was most entertaining.'

About this time, my chief interest in the theatre was the
ballet. I had first been taken by my sisters, as a reluctant fifteen-
year-old, and to my astonishment fell in love with it at first
sight. But perhaps not so surprising, because the first dancer I
ever saw was Anna Pavlova. She must then have been over
fifty; it was one of her very last performances before her
death. At Streatham Hill Theatre in South London, I saw her
in the role she had made her own – 'The Swan'. It was magical
and her age was forgotten.

In the years that followed, I didn't see much ballet, except an occasional visit to Sadler's Wells, where there was an entrancing young dancer called Margot Fonteyn. But then in 1936 Colonel de Basil, a former Cossack officer who had become an impressario in Paris, brought his Ballet Russe to London for a season at Covent Garden.

It was a superb young company with Léonide Massine, who had worked with Diaghilev as chief choreographer. I managed to see all the productions, and always from the gallery. None of my friends at that time shared my interest in ballet so it was alone that I paid my half-a-crown and started the long climb. The seats were so steeply raked up there that at first you felt you were going to topple right forward down into the vast auditorium. But, once the house-lights were dimmed, there was the most marvellous view of the stage. For me, those visits to Covent Garden were a great theatrical experience and an escape into a whole new world of beauty. There were moments I shall never forget: Massine and the young Danilova in *La Boutique fantasque*, with its sparkling gaiety and wit; the excitement of the new Symphonic Ballets, especially the *Symphonie fantastique* of Berlioz, and the grace of the youthful trio Baronova, Toumanova and Riabouchinska. Ballet at its best is a marriage of the arts and the felicitous coming together of music, colour, design and dance made a deep impression on me. Night after night, I descended from the gods into the agreeably messy fruit market around Covent Garden: there were cabbage leaves scattered on the pavement, but to me they might have been rose petals, as I walked away in a heady dream.

Since then I have seen the finest companies in the world including the Bolshoi in Moscow, but none of them has recaptured for me the magic of that de Basil season I saw from the gallery. But then ballet is perhaps at its most potent for the young. As Herbert Farjeon put it:

> How we screamed and shrieked and hooted, how we
>   whooped and how we howled!
> We were ravished and uprooted! – we were frequently
>   disembowelled!
> You will never know the throb, the glow, the bliss that
>   we knew then,
> When Bolonsky danced 'Belushka in September 1910.[1]

[1] From the revue, *Nine Sharp*, Little Theatre, 1938.

Great Britain then was still one of the principals on the world stage, and anything that happened here was of immediate concern to the people of every land. Such a night was 20 January 1936. I had called in for the evening at the house of my old school friend Dick. The King had been ill for some time, but it came as a shock after the nine o'clock News, when we heard Stuart Hibberd announcing: 'The King's life is moving peacefully towards its close.' Then, all programmes were scrapped and nothing but the Bow Bells interval signal was broadcast.

We were feeling pretty glum, so thought a bottle of whisky might help. Every fifteen minutes the bells were faded down and, each time, it was just Stuart intoning the same words: 'The King's life is moving peacefully towards its close.'

The culmination came just before midnight when the gruff voice of Sir John Reith told us the King was dead. By then, we had finished the whisky and were feeling positively maudlin. It had been one of the most impressive broadcasts ever and yet could not have been simpler.

The funeral came just over a week later, during which the Press and the BBC carried little but news of arrangements for the ceremony and incidents from the King's life and long reign.

After a night on duty at Broadcasting House, I walked down to Oxford Circus. It must have been about 9.30 on a sad, grey winter morning. There were people swirling about in the streets and Oxford Circus itself seemed like a whirlpool. From there, I was swept along westwards, wedged in tight, no chance of pulling out, sometimes with my feet scarcely touching the ground. At Marble Arch, the crowd, like a great, muddy torrent, was surging north up Edgware Road, then to the left past Oxford and Cambridge Terrace, now renamed Sussex Gardens. It was there I managed to struggle out of the middle of the moving throng and anchor myself to some iron railings on the porch of a house. Even so I couldn't budge. The police had been caught by the vastness of the crowds and there was little they could do to control them. Trees, lamp-posts, anything that could be climbed had somebody hanging on to them. People were fainting and being passed over the solid mass of heads to improvised casualty stations in side streets. It was rather frightening and very smelly. A real, gutsy stench hung heavy all round.

Then came the awful, sobbing beat of martial music and about two hundred yards to my right I could just glimpse the head of the cortège. But, as soon as it was sighted, the great crowds on either side surged forward all over the road, so the procession was squeezed to a halt. After a few minutes of confusion, mounted police managed to clear a narrow path, and the coffin, on a gun-carriage drawn by sailors, passed on its way to Paddington Station and Windsor.

One unforgettable picture remains in the mind. That small, lost-looking figure walking behind the coffin ; the new King Edward – even his Naval greatcoat seemed too big for him.

The Empire shared the sorrow of the funeral, but there were lighter moments too. During the summer months, to cover the holiday period, we engaged relief Announcers. These were usually actors, who were apt to be rather at sea when required to say anything off the cuff. Two of the most regular helpers-out were Robert Mawdesley and Geoffrey Wincott. Geoffrey was especially good at bidding listeners good night. The drill was that at the end of transmission after the Announcer had said good night, Control Room would fade over to Big Ben and finally the Announcer would play the record of the National Anthem from the studio. On one occasion Geoffrey had done the good night bit 'Good night to you all – wherever you may be – Good night from London.' Having tucked them up so cosily for the night, Empire listeners were then startled to hear Geoffrey's voice adding 'the bloody fools!' and then, with even more feeling, 'Christ! the bloody fools!' The words were intended for the engineers only as Geoffrey had not heard Big Ben booming out through his headphones, but in cursing the engineers he forgot that his microphone was still 'live'. Bob, our other holiday relief, later became quite famous as the old rustic, Walter Gabriel in 'The Archers'.

Another Bob joined our Empire News Section from Canada. Bob Bowman was a big, jovial chap with an enormous sense of fun. His career in News came to an abrupt end, when in one of his bulletins, reporting the result of the trial of a South African financier, he pronounced him to be guilty instead of not guilty. The BBC weren't over pleased, as they had to fork out a few thousand pounds for the libel, but Bob was such a nice chap that, instead of sending him back to Canada, they had the good sense to transfer him to Outside Broadcasts.

It couldn't have been at a better time. The Ice Hockey

Olympics were due at Garmisch Partenkirchen in Bavaria. This was right up Bob's street. His first commentary made headlines in the popular Press. For the fastest game in the world the BBC, by good fortune, was able to come up with the fastest speaker. The British public was introduced to the quick-fire, transatlantic style commentary with colourful, vivid phrases like 'rib-roasting' and they loved it. Bob was not the first BBC man to shoot to overnight fame, after putting up a black. The British team turned up trumps too by beating Canada, who'd been champions for fifteen years.

One night, when he was giving a commentary on an ice hockey game in London, I went into the box with him and am still mystified as to how he kept up a non-stop flow of wise-cracks, without ever stopping to draw breath. Bob and I became good friends and some years later when he was back with the Canadian Broadcasting Company, he arranged for us to have a two-way transatlantic telephone conversation that was heard throughout Canada.

Soon from North America came the stories about Mrs Simpson and the King – ending in all the traumatic business of the Abdication and the Coronation of the new King, George VI, with his charming Queen. It was these great Royal events that had not only the Empire, but the whole world listening to London. In fact, at the time of the moving Abdication broadcast, New York reported one of the city's biggest telephone exchanges had been silent. There was not a single call.

Meantime, BBC Television, the first public service in the world, had started up in 1936 on London's northern heights at Alexandra Palace. For what was then a mysterious new medium, the BBC could scarcely have chosen a more fitting building. As for its location, Collie Knox, the Radio Correspondent of the *Daily Mail*, wrote in those early days: 'I arrived at Alexandra Palace after losing my way seven times – it really is an impossible place to get at.'

In fact, it's about seven miles north of London: a fantastic nightmare of Victorian architecture, surely one of the ugliest buildings in the world. It is set up high on a kind of plateau, which gives quite breath-taking views all round the northern suburbs especially if you have toiled up the hill from Wood Green Station – the nearest Underground, about a mile and a half away. It dates back to 1873, when it was opened in honour of Princess Alexandra, and then promptly burnt down. The citizens of North London, unable to take a hint, rebuilt it as a challenge to Crystal Palace in the south and it was re-opened on May Day 1875.

Gerald Cock, who had organised the Jubilee broadcasts, was the first Director and his office had the finest view of any in the BBC with enormous bay windows looking across London to St Paul's Cathedral and beyond to the hills of Surrey and Kent. There were two barn-like studios, 'A' and 'B', and a whole honeycomb of corridors, wardrobe and make-up departments and engineers' control rooms. The do-or-die pioneers chosen to lead this new adventure were headed by the indefatigable Cecil Madden and by that dynamic Scot D. H. Munro, fresh from his triumph on the sliding seat at the Christmas Day Empire Exchange Programme. What a debt the development of television entertainment owes to men like these. There was little material reward for them – just the challenge and excitement of pioneering in a new medium and they gave it all they'd got. D.H. was lucky in his announcing staff – the blonde Jasmine Bligh, and Elizabeth Cowell, dark and elegant. Leslie Mitchell was transferred from Broadcasting House to join them in the new art of talking and smiling straight into the camera lens. There was a television orchestra conducted by Hyam Greenbaum, and as second violin a round-faced young man called Eric Robinson. Marvellous feats of production were carried out in the two studios, measuring just 70ft by 30ft, and Cecil Madden soon launched one of the most successful television magazine programmes of all time, 'Picture Page'.

The make-up in the early days was quite alarming. Most artists looked as though they had been disinterred, with matt yellow faces and lips in a dark shade of blue. The cameras also disliked colour contrasts in dress. Black and white were the worst. So, for evening dress men had to wear yellow shirt-fronts and collars, which was a carry on from the early days of film production.

There was a long haul ahead for the new medium. For the Coronation Service in 1937 there were no cameras in the Abbey: the event was still in the main an affair for radio. And yet television scored a triumph by having three cameras and Freddie Grisewood at Hyde Park Corner to give the first ever, high definition, television Outside Broadcast in the world. It was an impressive start in its way even though not much more

74

than a few thousand viewers in a limited range round London had sets to see it.

Apart from the general junketing which surrounded the Coronation, the trumpet fanfares and magnificence of the Service from Westminster Abbey itself, there was one broadcast never to be forgotten. The Fleets of the World were gathered off Spithead on 20 May for the Great Coronation Naval Review. Top BBC Commentator Thomas Woodroofe, an ex-Naval Commander himself, returned to his old ship HMS *Nelson*, which became the broadcast headquarters. That afternoon he gave cne of his fluent, concise, descriptions of the scene. The quality wasn't as good as it might have been but millions were waiting eagerly for the evening broadcast of the illuminations.

Perhaps we were all suffering slightly from a plethora of portentous imagery after so many Coronation occasions. This was to be different, just a joyous, festive sight.

With a few colleagues I was waiting in the Announcers' Room at Broadcasting House. After the usual hand-over from London, we heard a pause, then a voice, it was Tommy Woodroofe, but not quite himself and he kept on saying, 'The Fleet's all lit up!'

The awful truth dawned: he was sloshed. With what must have cost him considerable effort, he tried again: 'It's like fairyland; the ships are lit up with little lamps – yes all covered with little lamps!' He let that sink in and tried yet again: 'Even the destroyers are all lit up.' Then he said something about an American ship being lit up too – after which there was confused mumbling, followed by, 'Shut up!' Then quite a pause, as he managed to say with an air of finality, 'The lights have been switched off – it's all gone – There's nothing between us and heaven – the Fleet's disappeared!' With which an engineer somewhere along the line mercifully faded him out and the Announcer closed the programme from the studio without comment.

That came the next morning with banner headlines in the popular Press. Back at Broadcasting House, Tommy wasn't exactly clapped in irons, but he was suspended from the microphone for a time and I don't think he ever fully recovered his nerve as a Commentator. But millions still remember him with affection and gratitude for giving them the most hilarious broadcast of all time.

The Coronation came in the fifth year of Empire Broadcasting, and in this same year of 1937, under a new Charter, the BBC was at last given official instructions to expand the Service. A sixth Transmission came into use and we were now installed in a studio on the fourth floor, 4D. Not only did the Announcer now have two gramophone turntables under his control, but he could also fade up Big Ben when required or by turning the main fader, coloured red, take the whole Service off the air. Also, our numbers had increased to seven.

On the Home air about this time, the BBC, not for the first time, was in trouble with a politician. Sir Kingsley Wood, the Minister of Health, felt he had been slighted when on turning up for a broadcast he had, owing to a misunderstanding, been kept waiting. So, on the next occasion he was due at Broadcasting House no chances were taken. Sir John Reith himself escorted the Minister to the studio for his talk on State pensions. Everything went beautifully, except that in another studio Lionel Marson was waiting to read the News summary. With a few moments to go, the News editor brought in a late item. It was about some tiresome nut of whom Lionel disapproved. In fact being a forthright chap he expressed his views quite strongly to the editor. What he didn't know was that Sir Kingsley's talk had already ended and the News studio was on the air. So, astonished listeners at home heard one Announcer say: 'That was a talk given by Sir Kingsley Wood, the Minister of Health.' Then, immediately, came Lionel's voice saying with feeling: 'That bloody man!' The newspapers had a fine old time next day.

It was also Lionel who was reading the six o'clock News on the day the Coronation stone was removed from Westminster Abbey by a dashing Scottish nationalist. This message was brought to him as a late item and he didn't have time to read it over before giving out the News at the microphone. He started beautifully but then continued: 'The stone has rested in the Abbey since the days of Edward Isst.'

He left the studio at the end of the bulletin looking rather puzzled. No so puzzled perhaps as some of the listeners. I don't know who he thought Edward Isst was – one of those obscure Saxon monarchs I suppose.

7 The Shadow of Hitler

In Europe, the big slide went on and obviously Spain was being used as a dress rehearsal for World War II. Hitler, Mussolini and Stalin were busy trying out their new toys, and anyone who thought at all could see it wouldn't be long before we were all caught up in their lunatic game. The BBC's motto was 'Nation shall speak peace unto Nation' and certainly to me the whole idea of nationalism or racism seemed absurd. I had read as much French and German literature as English and, although I'd formed no clearly defined politics, was a convinced pacifist. This was why I spent so much time and energy on foreign languages, feeling, naïvely I suppose, that if only people from different nations could learn to speak freely to each other, barriers could in time be broken down.

Early that summer of 1937 my old friend Dick and I decided to have a look at Hitler's Germany. We hadn't booked in anywhere, but just bought train tickets for a round-trip. From the frontier at Aachen to Cologne, what we saw of the countryside was neat and well-tended with the farmhouses newly whitewashed.

We weren't long in Cologne, but there was just time to visit a fairly English-looking pub. Two middle-aged Britishers came up and seemed keen to know how things were at home. They'd been there nearly twenty years, staying on after the Army of Occupation in 1919 ; they'd married German girls and settled down reasonably well with grown-up families of their own but, somehow, there was a trace of sadness about them. When the balloon was to go up for the second time, a year or two later, they can't have found it easy.

That evening we caught the train for Coblenz and, after a comfortable night in what had once been an old coaching inn, boarded one of the small Rhine steamers for the stretch of river down to Mainz. A few years earlier I remembered Prime Minister Baldwin saying: 'When you think about the defence of England, you no longer think of the chalk cliffs of Dover. You think of the Rhine.'

But for us it was a perfect day on that dramatic stretch of the 'castled Rhine'. On either side, the banks swept up sharply, terraced with vines; now and again an extraordinary fantasy castle soared above us on a pinnacle of rock. Then we passed another great towering rock in the middle of the river, the Lorelei, where Heine's maiden legend used to sit combing her golden tresses and luring sailors to destruction. It's a romantic, but slightly sinister skyline: all very Germanic and Wagnerian.

Aboard, everyone was getting slightly tipsy and we had a splendid lunch of fresh Rhine salmon washed down with well-chilled Hock. In fact, afterwards I fully agreed with the sentiments of that nineteenth-century wag Charles Stuart Calverley, who wrote on a similarly euphoric occasion:

> For king-like rolls the Rhine,
> And the scenery's divine,
> And the victuals and the wine
> Rather good.

At Mainz we took the train for Munich and we noticed that the hideous swastika flags were much more often to be seen here. In Munich it was hot, so, as soon as we had settled in, we set out to find a swimming pool. There was no difficulty about that and in no time we were stretched out on the grass sunning ourselves and idly smoking cigarettes. We were getting rather interested in two girls some twenty yards away, when a policeman suddenly loomed over us. Evidently we hadn't seen a notice which said smoking was *verboten*. Move two yards to our right and all would be well. He wasn't very nice about it and it all seemed rather pointless; after all the grass was exactly the same and we were in the open air anyway. But this was Germany and *verboten* was *verboten*. There was one good thing, the two girls had seen what was going on and were smiling, so that, of course, helped the introductions. Knowing the language gave me a horribly unfair advantage, and so I was able to team up with by far the prettier of the two. She was slim and straight with enormous dark brown eyes and sleek black hair and was just nineteen. I wasn't surprised to hear her say she was half Hungarian; her name was Lise. Dick's girl, unfortunately, didn't really rate at all, but that evening we all went to a café together and decided to meet the following afternoon.

In the morning, I had arranged to visit the Munich Broadcasting set up, the Rundfunkhaus. I wasn't prepared for the black uniformed sentries at the gates or the general barrack-like appearance of the place. Unlike the BBC, it was all too

78

evident here that broadcasting was a direct arm of the State. Once inside, the officials were courteous enough and allowed me to see everything I wished. It was all very efficient, but the military style and atmosphere were depressing.

One of the good things about Munich is that a short way out of the city there are beautiful woods. Lise knew the best route to take and it seemed the perfect way to spend an afternoon. As we walked through the streets of Munich to the bus stop, she suddenly dragged at my arm and said in a hoarse, tense sort of voice, 'Quick, we must turn off here, if we go straight on we'll have to give the Hitler salute as we pass the Nazi memorial.'

I remembered she was half Hungarian, and perhaps a little Jewish too, but neither of us felt like talking politics. We were young and the sun was hot. It was very beautiful when we reached the woods: the sun filtered down through the trees, and, after walking for a little, we stretched out by a stream. There was no one about and we were quite startled when a hare suddenly appeared and rushed straight by us. I swear his eyebrows were slightly raised.

Back in Munich the next morning there was an art exhibition I particularly wanted to see. It was an interesting sidelight on Nazi Germany. The paintings and sculpture were arranged in different halls of the same gallery. One contained the Approved Art, the other half consisted of what the Nazis decreed to be Decadent Art. The Approved section was dull beyond belief. Many totally uninspired portraits and groups with, of course, the Fuehrer well to the fore. One huge painting even showed him as a knight in shining armour on a fiery steed. It was as corny as that. In contrast, the Decadent Art was welcome relief, because it was at least trying to say something, however obscurely.

The next stop was Heidelberg and the first evening there Dick and I called in at the Rote Ochs, the famous old inn near the University, which is a traditional meeting place for students. We sat on benches at one of the long wooden tables and, like everybody else, were soon clutching large *steins* of beer. Two young Germans, spotting we were British, came over to join us. They seemed surprised and delighted that I could speak the language and, as more beer went down, we were soon linking arms and swaying to and fro to the choruses of German student songs.

Their names were Hans and Peter – and they were as different as could be. Hans, bullet headed, red faced, jovial in a hearty way, while Peter was slim and pale and more restrained. But they had in common the fact that both were Nazis and their constant theme throughout the evening was that Germany and Britain must never fight again. Through the haze of smoke and beer fumes, Hans, his red face shining, would keep insisting that we were *Blutbrüder*.

Blood-brothers or not they were wonderfully hospitable and said we must meet again in the next day, as Hans was going to drive over to see a friend, who owned a paper mill in a village in the Black Forest. So there we were next morning, careering along the country lanes at fearful speed, roaring through villages, with chickens and people alike scattering in all directions. Hans was singing and bellowing with laughter all the time he was driving. Wasn't it H. G. Wells who said our civilisation was like a high-powered racing car with a monkey at the wheel?

Kappelrodeck turned out to be a charming village and our host there could not have been kinder. He owned this small paper mill and lived with his aged mother in one of the pleasant, wooden Black Forest houses. It was all very relaxing after the hair-raising drive and he insisted that we sample the local liquers, which he produced from a huge, carved, pinewood cupboard. Under the influence of all this effusive friendliness, it was impossible to think our two countries could ever go to war again, and yet I remember feeling a certain uneasiness.

Why were they being so friendly? Could it be that Nazi Party members even at that level were under orders to be especially pleasant to Britishers? Perhaps it was all part of Hitler's plan to lull us into doing nothing to resist him. I can't understand otherwise why they should have made such a fuss of us. Or was it just that they were astonished to find a young *Engländer* who could speak their language?

On the return drive to Heidelberg, we passed several columns of young people, looking dusty and cheerful, but marching and singing in a purposeful, military way. Hans explained they were just students helping with road-works, but I wondered why they carried their spades at the slope like rifles? Hans said it was *Kraft durch Freude*, 'Strength through Joy'.

Dick's holiday time was running out, so when we returned to Munich, he had to leave for home. As I had a week or so left, I decided to have a look at Austria. I had been given an address where I could stay in Seefeld, which was then just a small village in the mountains above Innsbruck. I believe it has since become a fashionable winter sports centre.

In that summer of 1937 it was still largely undeveloped. Every evening and morning there was the haunting sound of cow bells, as the cattle went on their way to and from the lush, green meadows. Each little herd seemed to know exactly where to go, as they swayed heavily through the streets back to their byres, without supervision. In Austria I found no forced friendliness, but much gentle courtesy and charm. I stayed in a wooden chalet in the foothills of the Hohe Munde mountain.

There were only two cafés in Seefeld then. One was rather shabby, but typically Austrian, and called the Hohe Munde. The other, grander, more efficient in every way, was called the Sport Café. The German border was not far away at Mittenwald and this was the café the Germans in cars always visited.

I spent most of my time there with an Austrian girl who was on holiday from Vienna. Lene was ash-blonde with light blue eyes and her hair done in braids over her head. At first, I couldn't understand why she should be so subdued, but then she explained one of her parents was Jewish. She was very afraid.

Every evening we went to the Hohe Munde Café and drank a little and danced a little and talked a lot. On my last night there, as we left and walked up the village street, there ahead, drawn up outside the Sport Café, was a large black saloon and on the front of the bonnet – the swastika flag. It looked sinister. It was an affront. As we passed it, I grabbed the pennant and snapped it off cleanly. A pathetic gesture perhaps but what could one do. There was a heavy sadness hanging over Seefeld that night. It was only a few months before the German tanks were to come roaring over the frontier at Mittenwald and down that village street. When I returned to London I had a few letters from Lene, and in the last one she said she was 'down with her nerfs'. I didn't hear from her any more.

That autumn the BBC started preparations for foreign language broadcasts – to conteract German and Italian propaganda. Sir John Reith had insisted all along that the new service should be known to be a BBC and not a Government service, as he put it: 'The BBC would be trusted, where the Government might not be.' But, it was January 1938 before the first of the foreign language broadcasts took place: in Arabic.

To demonstrate the BBC's independence the News bulletin reported the execution that morning of a Palestinian Arab, on the orders of a British Military Court. There were some protests, but the Director pointed out in true BBC style: 'The omission of unwelcome facts of News and the consequent suppression of truth runs counter to the Corporation's policy.'

Part of the programme consisted of a reading from the Koran. The recording engineers weren't too well up in Arabic but, on the night, it seemed everything had gone off splendidly. It wasn't until the postcards started coming in that we heard they'd played the tape backwards.

A couple of months later saw the start of the Latin American Service. This was broadcast at the same time as our North American Transmission. Therefore, we shared several programmes, particularly those given by the BBC Empire Orchestra. This was a rather ludicrous business, as all announcements were made in three languages. George Camacho did the Spanish, Manuel Braune the Portuguese and me the English. With the three of us lined up at the microphone it was a set-up for giggles and we had to steel ourselves to keep straight faces. The announcements took such a long time that the orchestra hardly had time to play anything and finished by being faded out.

This expansion of the Overseas Service meant that we had to call on relief Announcers to help us out. They were usually radio actors and apt to be rather nervous, so, sometimes, a little fortifying went on with the help of a hip flask. This led to one Announcer getting carried away and closing down the North American Service with the National Anthem, a whole hour too soon. When this was pointed out to him by the astonished engineers in Control Room, he, with infinite resource and aplomb, announced the: 'Transmission for North America – Part two!' as though he were handing out a special bonus.

Another of our new boys had a horror of oversleeping, especially when down for duty on the early Transmission starting at 6 a.m. He would retire at about midnight to the Announcers' bedroom for a few hours of uneasy sleep, having asked the telephone exchange, his wife, the commissionaire on duty at Broadcasting House Reception and a few other people to call him. Not content with that, he also had two alarm clocks, just in case.

He had clocked in successfully one morning and was launched into the 7.a.m. News for Australia in Studio 4D, when one of his alarms suddenly went off. It was making an unholy racket but for some reason he did nothing about it, just carried on reading, looking rather tense. This set the News editor quite a problem. The clock was obviously concealed somewhere on his person, but where? All he could do was to creep up behind him and begin fumbling about in the poor chap's jacket pocket. Just as he was about to extract it, the clock gave a final admonitory gurgle and expired.

Australia must have thought we were at action stations or something. Anyway, our new recruit got a good mark for imperturbability.

This was a useful quality with the war looming ever nearer and when in March Hitler sent his tanks and planes into Austria, I remember hearing the dramatic broadcast from Vienna, as the Austrian service went off the air with a string orchestra playing their National Anthem. It was followed immediately by a military band crashing out German marching tunes. The music said everything. That night, thousands were arrested in Vienna and G. E. R. Gedye, the *Daily Telegraph* correspondent, wrote that women, whose husbands were taken away, soon received a small parcel with the injunction 'to pay, 150 marks for the cremation of your husband – ashes enclosed, from Dachau'.

Perhaps partly because of the gloom and foreboding we all turned with relief to the first regular comedy show on radio. 'Bandwagon' had started at the beginning of the year and brought almost overnight stardom to Arthur Askey, who had often compèred our Empire Variety shows, and his partner Richard 'Stinker' Murdoch from the Fol de Rols Concert Party at Hastings.

The programmes went out 'live' from St George's Hall and it was all good clean fun. Hitler was always 'Old Nasty', then there was 'Lewis the goat' and Mrs Bagwash, the char. The jokes mostly centred round Arthur's combinations. At least for a short time it took our minds off other more pressing things.

About this time, D. H. Munro, the Television Productions Manager at Alexandra Palace, invited me to have a look round the studios there. I was pleased to see Cecil Madden again in his office on the fifth floor. It was his job to sift all the new ideas and to fashion the lay-out of advance programmes. D.H. told me he had six or seven shows in rehearsal every day. All this in the two studios. There were seven television cameras, two telecine cameras and two mobile units. Leslie Mitchell was looking very smooth and unruffled and the make-up used was more natural. He just looked bronzed, if not exactly fit, and was wearing his usual red carnation. 'Picture Page' was in rehearsal, but I couldn't stay long, as I had to return to Broadcasting House.

The next morning I was summoned to see the Director, J. B. Clark. As I went into his office, he looked up coldly and pointed to a copy of the previous day's *Evening Standard*. There was a section ringed in blue pencil. It read: Bob Dougall, a young Announcer from the Empire Service, is being groomed to replace Television Adonis, Leslie Mitchell. Today he was seen visiting the studios with the Production Organiser.' I did my best to assure him that some reporter had merely put two and two together, and made five, but he obviously thought I had been up to something – a nasty, suspicious mind.

Soon it was September and Hitler began putting the screw on the Czechs. Off went Prime Minister Chamberlain with his umbrella on the first of his appeasement trips – Berchtesgaden, then a week later Godesberg and the final humiliation of Munich. This meant a strenuous time in the News studio with some bulletins running for up to as much as forty minutes. It meant not only long spells at the microphone, but, very often, reading straight off the tape and editing as best one could.

Meantime, there were great changes at the top in the BBC. Vice-Admiral Sir Charles Carpendale, Deputy Director-General, was 'piped ashore' at a ceremony in the concert hall in March, ships' bo'suns and two buglers being provided by the Admiralty. Then, at the end of June, Sir John Reith himself accepted an appointment as Chairman of Imperial Airways, leaving without ceremony of any kind. I supposed he wished to fly higher. The *New Statesman* carried a poem by Sagittarius, which asked:

> Breathes there a being fit to sway
> Reith's self-made Empire of the Air?

The Governors finally chose as his successor a man unknown to the public: Mr F. W. Ogilvie, Vice-Chancellor of Queen's University, Belfast.

Nobody seems to have given an entirely satisfactory answer as to why Reith left the BBC when he did.[1] I suppose he felt his job there was done – that he had set British broadcasting on the right course and cast it so indelibly in his mould that it could be left safely in other hands. He must also have thought that with the war so clearly looming up there would be for him a higher, even more important service to perform.

It was Reith's tragedy that he was never to be fully stretched again. Churchill was soon to become Prime Minister and there simply wasn't room for them both: it was a clash of Titans. There is a report that on one occasion, when Churchill had had a talk with Reith, he afterwards turned to the Secretary of the Cabinet and said, 'I never want to see that old Wuthering Heights again.'

Many years later, Reith was to protest movingly about those lost years in a letter to Churchill: 'You could have used me in a way and to an extent you never realised. Instead of that there has been the sterility, humiliation and distress of all those years – "eyeless in Gaza" – without even the consolation Samson had in knowing it was his own fault.'

I don't think he could ever reconcile himself to the way television developed. Lord Hill (when he was Chairman of the BBC) once told me that when Admiral Carpendale died it was arranged to hold a Memorial Service at St Martin-in-the-Fields. Knowing that 'Carps' had been the Director-General's deputy for many years, Lord Hill sent Reith an invitation which he promptly declined, saying he didn't want to meet all those television people. But the Chairman was, of course, a man of some determination, so he returned to the attack three times, pointing out to Reith that it would appear very strange if he were to stay away.

Finally, after much thought, Reith said all right he would come, but he would not read the Lesson.

At least, Lord Reith would have approved of his own Memorial Service at Westminster Abbey on 22 July 1971. The Westminster Abbey Choir, the BBC Chorus and the BBC Symphony Orchestra were conducted by Sir Adrian Boult. There was a congregation of 1,400, probably the largest gather-

[1] Andrew Boyle gets as near the truth as humanly possible in his probing biography of Reith. He says he was out-manoeuvred by Prime Minister Chamberlain and others. (*Only the Wind will Listen,* published by Hutchinson, 1972.)

ing of BBC staff ever seen outside the Corporation's premises and there were 300 retired members of the staff who had served under him. I must have been one of a handful of contemporary staff there who had joined in Reith's day.

At the end of the service, there was an inspired moment, as a lone piper of the King's Own Scottish Borderers materialised dramatically playing a Highland Lament, and moved slowly through the standing congregation, across the crowded Abbey from the Henry VII Chapel to the West Cloister Door.

Afterwards, outside, there was a great gathering of the clans and I saw a host of faces I hadn't seen for twenty years or more. There must have been many interesting comings together and much good talk and reminiscing, but for me there was work to be done, so I regretfully hailed a taxi to get me back to Television Centre. As I climbed in, I overheard someone make a remark – a sort of irreverent postscript to the service – the voice was saying: 'A difficult time ahead now for the Deity!'

In 1938 a difficult road certainly lay ahead for Reith's successor, although some plans for the wartime organisation of broadcasting had already been made. The danger that the BBC might come under the Ministry of Information had been taken care of before Reith left. The BBC was to keep its independence, subject to guidance and direction on policy. Ogilvie was liberally minded and charming. But what was needed in the BBC of 1938 was a strong man who could shape a mushrooming organisation. The expansion must have been very much more rapid than Reith could possibly have foreseen, otherwise, he would surely have decided to stay on.

The new Director-General found the BBC a very different proposition from a university. He's reported to have said to Jack Payne, the dance-band leader, 'If you want to talk business with another department it is not just a simple matter of telephoning; you have to write "memos" and have them passed from hand to hand.'

The most important development was the start of News bulletins to Europe in French, German and Italian, which were put on the Regional Transmitter normally serving listeners at home. Ogilvie agreed there would be informal contact with the Foreign Office about these broadcasts, but no direct FO control. Preparations were also made for the start of a BBC Monitoring Unit listening to foreign stations round the clock; and another measure with the war in mind was the acquiring of properties outside London to serve as emergency headquarters.

Early in 1939 the Director of the Overseas Service, J. B. Clark, called a meeting of Announcers to outline contingency war plans. All staff were placed in categories, as regards call-up. I was now the Senior Empire Announcer, Joe Shewin and Basil Gray having moved on to other things. I and three colleagues were 'indefinitely reserved', which meant we were unable to join any of the Services. There was so much going on we had no time for regrets.

To work on broadcasting at that time was to feel right at the centre of things. Days and nights seemed to pass in a blur as, in the newsroom, we tried to keep pace with the flood of reports coming in from all over the world. Hitler went on ranting and raving over the air. So much so, that I felt there was only one effective reply one could make to him. It was flattering him too much to try to answer in a rational way the wild charges he was making.

What I should have liked to do was simply play a laughing record without comment. There were some first class ones around at that time. You never know, ridicule, might have worked. Laughter is perhaps the best means of international communication.

At the time of the Munich crisis, great gas-proof doors had been fixed in Broadcasting House, which made it even more difficult to move around. We had also got used to the idea of gas masks. All staff were issued with brown cardboard boxes containing respirators. The trouble was people were always losing them and I just couldn't bring myself to try the beastly thing on.

Another new move was that the BBC for almost the first time in its seventeen years started sampling home listeners' likes and dislikes. Before this, there had been scarcely any means of knowing when people listened or what they liked. Producers and planners only had a guidance from Press critics or newspaper ballots and, of course, a certain amount of mail.

Another incidental source of information was provided by the Water Board. Thus, during the first half of, say, the Cup Final the demand would be minimal. Come half-time and the flushing of cisterns would send demand rocketing, only to cease dramatically with the resumption of play.

Dramatic Call from London

APPEAL OVER B.B.C. TO GERMANS	NEW APPEAL TO GERMAN NATION
	Dramatic Broadcast by "Englishman"

A BRITON TELLS GERMANY

DRAMATIC APPEAL

NEW B.B.C. BROADCAST TO GERMANY

"WE FIGHT IF YOU ATTACK POLAND"

B.B.C. Peace Plea

It was thought something rather more scientific than the pulling of a chain was desirable, so 3,000 listeners were asked to fill in forms, saying which type of programme they liked and why. The BBC was beginning to realise more and more the importance of giving people the programmes they really wanted to hear.

During this time, when I could slip away, I would see how my parents were getting on in Croydon. They were still in the same flat at Grove House. Mother was busying herself with the Red Cross and my father was doing a little clerical work at the Town Hall.

What I liked best was driving down in my little green Morris tourer to my favourite Kent village of Kingsdown near Deal. I had many friends there and no difficulty in finding somewhere to stay. There were marvellous cliff walks to Dover or across the windswept downs at the back. For me, there was a certain magic about the place.

It was just a fortnight before it all started. We'd had a superb, sun-soaked weekend. A ginger cat was curled up asleep right in the middle of the village street that meanders down to the sea.

The following Sunday night I was on duty at Broadcasting House. The news was getting desperate. The Russo-German Non-Aggression Pact had been signed and Hitler was poised to attack Poland. At about 7.30 that evening, Bill Newton, the Head of Overseas Talks, grabbed me in the corridor and said: 'Bob, this is a terrible thing to do to you, but we want you to put out a last-minute appeal to the Germans. It will be at eleven o'clock. You will be speaking as an anonymous Englishman.' I asked if I could see the script, but it still wasn't written. There had to be consultations with the Foreign Office.

Just before eleven, I was waiting in the studio and the script was still being translated into German. I got the first page with about three minutes to go. Then, the red light came on and it was up to me. It was an intensely dramatic script and most of the pages were fed to me at the microphone, so I had to get it right first time. God knows I put my heart into it.

We all felt this might just make the difference. At least it was leaving the Germans in no doubt that Britain had finally taken her stand and that, if Hitler went into Poland, it would be war. This was the one time when he wouldn't get away with it.

At the end of the broadcast, I felt completely drained, so we all went over to the Langham Hotel opposite and the night porter managed to find us a bottle of Scotch. I had seldom needed a drink more.

Next morning nearly all the papers carried a report of the broadcast. It had been put out on the Regional Transmitter, so had also been heard by listeners at home.

There was trouble with J. B. Clark, as he had not been consulted. Poor old Bill had a terrible time, and eventually driven to distraction told J.B. to f—— off! He then had a bit of a breakdown. The fact is we had all been under pressure for quite a time and nerves were getting strained.

Television was about to get the chop too. The only public television in the world at Alexandra Palace had to go off the air – for lots of reasons. The principal one was that the Transmitter would have given guidance to enemy aircraft. At Alexandra Palace there were also five acres of glass roofing, so at 12.10 p.m. on Friday, 1 September 1939, after showing a Mickey Mouse cartoon, ending with the catch phrase 'Ay tink ay go home', television closed down.

Saturday was a grim, gloomy day. The National and Regional Programmes had become the single Home Service, consisting of gramophone records, News and public announcements. Everything was prepared for carrying on the broadcasts, if necessary, from the emergency studios in the sub-basement. The BBC and the whole country braced itself to meet the Blitz.

Next morning J. B. Clark and a number of my colleagues were gathered round the large black loudspeaker cabinet in the Overseas Announcers' Room. There we heard Neville Chamberlain, as quietly and gently as though he were tucking us up in bed, telling us we were at war. I had to go straight to the studio on the fourth floor immediately afterwards to give the News to listeners overseas.

I had only just started, when I heard the distant wail of air-raid sirens. Then, I saw J. B. Clark, looking even whiter than usual, peering through a glass partition over the studio door. His arm was raised and with his forefinger he kept pointing in a downwards direction. I took the hint, put the Bow Bells record on the turntable and before dashing to the emergency studio announced as calmly as possible: 'There will now be an interval in the News from London.'

8 'Fortress' Britain

Somewhat to our surprise, we weren't immediately blown sky-high by Hitler's bombers. It was to be just on a year before he tried to rub us out and there wasn't even much of an interval in the Overseas News from London.

On the Home air, the BBC engineers' well thought out plans for keeping broadcasting going meant there was no interval at all and no mention even of that first, false alarm. The Home Service was put out on two medium wavelengths, each shared by a number of secret Transmitters. When enemy bombers approached a Transmitter, that particular one closed down, but listeners were still able to receive the programme from another, more distant, source. In this way, the broadcasts gave hostile aircraft only minimal, directional help.

This was fine, except that the bombers just didn't show up on cue. It wasn't long before blacked-out Britons set up a moan about the monotony of the programmes. The News was welcomed. That was on the hour, every hour, from 7 a.m. to midnight. But the weather forecast was a conspicuous war-time casualty and in fact every programme was scrutinised to ensure that no mention of weather cropped up that could possibly be of assistance to the enemy. This gave sports commentators a particularly difficult time. If the demand for News had greatly increased, it was what went on in between that caused the trouble.

This was mostly just gramophone records and request programmes by Sandy Macpherson, a tall, raw-boned Scot, who churned out a medley of nice mechanical noises on the BBC theatre organ, then situated in St George's Hall. His homely, slightly transatlantic tones were to become a national institution. But, even where Sandy was concerned, enough was enough.

Fortunately, it wasn't long before 'live' contributions began to come in from provincial centres, to which London producers and broadcasters had been dispersed.

Difficult, confusing months they were for everyone, those months of the 'phoney' war. There was little sense of purpose in the country. We were living in a kind of limbo. I was sharing a flat above Boots in Marylebone High Street with two of the News editors. It was only about fifteen minutes' walk from Broadcasting House.

About this time I got involved in an Announcer's nightmare. HRH the Duke of Kent had recently been appointed Governor-General of Australia and he was to broadcast in Transmission I, the Pacific Service. It would be my pleasant duty to introduce him on the air. This meant arriving at Broadcasting House just before 7 a.m. as the talk was scheduled for 7.30. As luck would have it, the telephone at the flat was out of order, so I relied on my alarm clock to wake me at six. Fearing to oversleep, I couldn't get to sleep at all. That is not until about 5 a.m. when through sheer exhaustion I went flat out. When I opened a bleary eye to look at the clock it said five past seven! Either the clock had gone off and I had slept through it or it had not gone off at all.

Never in my life have I moved so fast. By 7.15 I was in a taxi heading for Broadcasting House, my head in a whirl and with every traffic light at red. Out of the cab like a scalded cat, up in the lift, heart hammering and there pasing the third floor corridor was J. B. Clark with 'Where's Dougall?' written all over his face. It was 7.25 a.m.

When I entered the small talks studio, the Duke was already sitting calmly at the microphone, his script on the table. He was wearing RAF uniform and looking immaculately composed. He could not have been more charming or understanding. In the two minutes remaining we talked about working at odd hours and then I explained that I would have to lean over his shoulder to make the announcement. As I was anxious to redeem myself I gave the announcement all I had got. It was unfortunate that the Duke had an exceptionally light voice, so the effect was rather odd. I had got away with it by the skin of my teeth but I felt J.B. had yet another mark against me.

Social life seemed to be more or less confined to the BBC pubs. First among them was The George, otherwise known as 'the Gluepot', in Mortimer Street. Like so many pubs, it has now been given the modern treatment, but in 1940 it was a solid Victorian house with a stimulating clientèle of broadcasters. Among the regulars, poets Louis Macneice, Roy Campbell, Dylan Thomas and John Pudney. Then, right alongside Broadcasting House in Hallam Street was a smaller hostelry,

The Devonshire, with slightly less elevated company. This was my favourite. The landlord, 'Casey' Jones, was always telling me he had a quantity of very special sherry in his cellars, but he was determined to keep it for the peace celebrations. The other two principal places of refreshment and good talk were The Cock in Great Portland Street, favoured by the News and Sport-loving fraternity, and The Dover Castle in Weymouth Mews. Luckily, all but the sadly missed Devonshire have survived. Throughout the country, the talking and the speculating went on; but this was the war no one could understand.

There was even one old lady who was supposed to have said rather touchingly: 'Oh well, if the Germans win, at any rate I have my pension and they can't touch that.'

The initiative was all with Hitler and in May he took it again – this time the Low Countries paid the price – Brussels was bombed and Rotterdam set ablaze. But Churchill had, at last, taken over and the fight was on. In a few weeks came Dunkirk; and by the end of June with the fall of France, this country finally knew exactly where it stood – alone. At least, the situation was clearer; it was almost a relief.

King George VI expressed the views of millions of us when he wrote to one of his family: 'Personally, I feel happier now that we have no allies to be polite to and pamper.'

The change that came over the country was quite extraordinary. With Churchill at our head, we were beginning to behave more like Popeye after his can of spinach. Of course, old 'Jairmany Calling', William Joyce, the American-born Irishman and renegade we all called Lord Haw Haw, was in top gear on the radio from Berlin trying to chill our blood: 'England must now take the full fury of the German attack upon herself – England is now ripe for invasion.'

The raids began about this time in earnest. The mournful wail of the sirens became more and more frequent. 'Banshee howlings' as Churchill called them. There was one fixed to the wall just outside the flat in Marylebone High Street, so we got full benefit. It was always good to hear the steady note of the 'All Clear', but, as it was slowly dying down, the sound was even more bloodcurdling than the alarm – like some great wounded beast, subsiding with a sobbing moan.

I had my little green, open Morris with me in London and very glad I was of it. There was no parking problem then but, every time the car was left, it was necessary to open the bonnet and fumble away in an attempt to remove the rotor-arm from the distributor. This was to ensure that, if German Paratroopers came, at least they wouldn't be able to use our transport. I forgot to do this one night, when staying with a friend in Surrey, and on coming out at 7 a.m. found the car had vanished. The police had removed it to one of their stations some miles away.

Although there was very little traffic, the total black-out made night driving a dicey business. All signposts and railway station names had been removed, supposedly to confuse the enemy ; it certainly confused us. Traffic lights were still working, but all you could see was a glimmer from a tiny cross of red, amber or green, left in the centre of the lights. As car headlights were also heavily masked with black, visor-like fittings, allowing the merest chink of light, it meant driving with eyes on stalks, if you were going to keep out of trouble.

Another hazard to motorists came from trigger-happy Home Guards. The 'Dad's Army' Brigade had been called for in the early summer of 1940 by War Minister Anthony Eden. At first, they were known as Local Defence Volunteers and I remember a strange, unreal Press Conference at the War Office, soon after they were formed, when Colonel Walter Elliot announced that, owing to a shortage of rifles, it would be necessary to issue them with pikes.

Later that summer, they began to get their guns, but not always with the happiest of results. There were reports of motorists being fired on at night in an excess of enthusiasm, and some were even shot dead by over-zealous members, who stoutly maintained that the drivers had not stopped when challenged. And that autumn a warning was issued that any Home Guard who shot someone out of a personal grudge was liable to be suspended.

All the same, they did a tremendously important job, not least along the coast. Although there was petrol rationing, by saving up my coupons, I still managed now and again to get to Kingsdown, a few miles along the cliffs from Dover, for a long weekend. This was the invasion coast, 'Hell-fire' corner, as it came to be called. Long, hot, summer days, but no more sea-bathing to be had. The beaches were cluttered with all kinds of defences from coils of barbed wire to iron tank traps. There were pill-boxes and mysterious devices for spraying the sea with burning oil against the invasion barges, expected at any time. In the skies above the Channel, hourly dog-fights, as the RAF Hurricanes and Spitfires mixed it up with the German bombers. A strange, unreal sort of fight thousands of feet above, but we peered up there into the blue until our eyes hurt.

The weekend of 7 September one of the News editors offered to lend me a country cottage in Essex. With the girl I liked most in the world at that time, we set off from London in my car at about half past four. It was a glorious, sunny day and there was nothing to indicate that a holocaust of fire and terror was soon to fall out of the skies on East London and the Docks. But this was the evening Goering had chosen to switch his bombers from attacks on airfields and factories to deliver, as he put it, 'this stroke right into the enemy's heart'. Suddenly, the sky was full of noise, throbbing, droning, snarling. Then, the crump of Ack-Ack and bits started falling out of the sky all round us. We stopped the car in a suburban street and a man in a tin hat grabbed us by the arm and steered us to a shelter in somebody's garden. Up above, there were 300 German bombers with 600 fighters to escort them and they had it nearly all their own way.

We soon carried on again to Essex and found our cottage. It was one of the most run-down shacks I have ever seen, in a dank, weed-filled garden. The roof was holed in several places and the rain had obviously been getting in. We found a mattress which was reasonably dry and dragged it down the narrow stairs to the living-room below.

As it got dark, looking towards London the whole sky was a vivid, angry red, as though the entire city was ablaze.

I looked out of the cottage at the back to find a field full of red lights. Surely, it couldn't be a dummy airfield? It was, so next day we left the cottage to find a small pub, where we stayed for two heavenly days, surrounded by golden harvest fields.

During this time, Broadcasting House was beginning to look like a cross between a doss-house and a fort. The elegant concert hall had become a sleeping area with mattresses all over the place for staff who couldn't get back to their homes at night. Sexes were segregated by a curtain down the middle. Seldom in any dedicated place of music can there have been such a nightly symphony of snores.

The most remarkable thing that happened was that, as soon as things got rough, everyone was suddenly very friendly. Even the most aloof Controllers and Administrators became as jolly as Jimmy Young. Of course, it's not easy to look dignified clad only in a dressing-gown and a tin hat, and sometimes even less. A colleague of mine about this time charged into the News studio to read the News to North America only to find a large man in his underpants. It was one of the said Controllers about to crash it down for the night.

The canteen down in the basement sported a small bar for the duration. For those who preferred tea or coffee, there was just one metal spoon to stir it with and that was on a chain – by the cash desk. I suppose all the others had gone to be melted down, along with the railings from London squares, to make munitions, and plastic hadn't been thought of then.

On the night of 4 October 1940 I was on duty in the Overseas Service emergency studio, in the sub-basement. There was a raid on, and, when I looked outside at about eight o'clock, there seemed rather more going on than usual. The Ack-Ack guns were fairly thumping away and shrapnel was clattering down in the streets. I was quite glad to get back inside again. Soon after 8.30 the Civil Defence staff started rushing about in all directions. Someone said a delayed bomb had landed up in the building. There was a search on to find it.

Bruce Belfrage was the duty boy for the Home Service, just across the corridor. He was half-way through the nine o'clock News, when there was a hefty explosion and the whole building shuddered. A few bits of plaster floated down from our studio ceiling and a sprinkle of mortar-dust, but that was all.

Up above, it was a different story. The time bomb had finally been found in the Music Library on the fifth floor, to which it had penetrated, after crashing through the outer wall of the building on the Portland Place side. The upper part of the building was being evacuated, but in no great panic, as delayed action bombs were normally not expected to go off for twenty-four hours or more, but this one was different. It exploded only half an hour or so after landing, as monitoring staff in Studio 6A were moving their typewriters to a safer place. Six were killed, most of them girls.

Listeners to the nine o'clock News just heard a faint thud, a momentary pause, a voice whispering 'Are you all right?' and then Bruce's deep, reassuring tones continued. Next morning, the newspapers were full of it and Bruce became quite a hero.

My car had been parked outside Broadcasting House all

night, on the Hallam Street side. When I came out, bleary eyed in the early morning, I was quite relieved to see it still there. On the canvas roof there were some bits of rubble and dust and, bang in the centre, a larger object, which I took to be a brick. I picked it up and saw it was a fat, black book. The title, when I'd blown the dust off, was *The War behind the War*, by Professor Chambers. Somewhat ironical that this treatise on the First World War should have been blown out of the BBC Library, two floors above, by the second. I still have it on my shelves at home; and I expect the Library will now send me a chit asking for it back.

So, for the Overseas Service, it was now our turn to be off to Evesham and Abbey Manor. This was as improbable a place for a wartime broadcasting headquarters as you could possibly imagine. A draughty, rambling stately home, which once, it seemed, had housed the Duke of Orleans, Pretender to the throne of France. He'd certainly left his mark – the *fleur de lys* appeared in all the likely places and some unlikely ones as well. The royal emblem adorned the taps and plugs of the bathrooms and even graced the bumf holders in the ancient loo.

The approach was by a sweeping drive lined with soggy, overgrown shrubs and, at the back, terraced lawns sloped away to the River Avon. The first reaction was to laugh hysterically and, indeed, a hilarious company was gathered there. We regular broadcasters had been joined by a number of people from stage and films. Robert Beatty, the Canadian film star, Robert Harris, Reginald Beckwith, Beryl Measor, Terence de Marney, John Ellison and Alan Melville, to name but a few. George Inns, impish as ever, had to use all his showbiz knowledge in compiling and producing innumerable programmes of records.

For the first time, the war had brought the girls into the Announcing game and we were glad to welcome aboard Marjorie Anderson, Georgie Henschel, daughter of Sir George Henschel the distinguished musician, and Brenda Cleather. One way and another, it was quite a crew.

The first problem was to find a billet. Georgie fortunately was a great organiser, the girls are always best at this sort of thing, and she found us an old farmhouse about seven miles away along the Worcester road. Alan Melville, John Ellison, Bob Beatty and I settled for that. Transport was a problem. Alan had an ancient Ford that he claimed to have bought for

97

£7 10s, I had my little green car which was equal to every occasion, John had a large motor bike, he was constantly falling off, and Georgie and Bob found bicycles.

It was a very cold winter indeed – with hard frosts and lots of freezing fog. I enjoyed it least when I was on the Transmission for Australia and New Zealand. This meant turning out of one's cold farmhouse bed at about 5 a.m. and hitting the trail to the Manor.

My car always started like a bomb, but the difficulty was to see the way ahead in the total black-out and on an icy road. There were many mornings when the only way I could navigate was by putting the canvas roof down flat and lowering the windscreen altogether, which one could do on those old models. In this way, by peering into the surrounding murk, I could usually see about five yards ahead. The snag was that, on arrival, my jaw would be more or less frozen solid and it was minutes before I could even utter, let alone declaim the News.

Robert Harris, coming from the theatre, found things a bit confusing at times. On one occasion, he was standing in for me on the News and failed to see that the opening words, as written to be read by me, were: 'This is London Calling – here is the News, read by Robert Dougall."

He'd said this before he could stop himself, but then caused some merriment by saying: 'It isn't, you know – my name is Robert Harris.'

Perhaps owing to poorish reception on the short waves, Bobbie was also the subject of a letter from an overseas listener. She wrote to say that she realised the news was bad, but it didn't help when the Newsreader said it was 'rather harassing reading it'.

There was, of course, no central heating at the Manor. Any warmth came from gas fires or coal. The News studio had one of these open fires. I was launched on the News to Australia one morning, when, out of the corner of my eye, I saw the studio door open. Standing there was a man in a brown overall, holding a bucket of coal. No frenzied wavings of mine were going to deflect him from his purpose of making up the fire. He made a prodigious clatter. Down-under they must have thought the old country was really going through it.

The Manor was, of course, haunted – in fact, the whole area was pretty ghost-ridden – probably something to do with the fact that it was on the site of the Battle of Evesham. A headless man on a white horse was apt to appear in the grounds. On several occasions, a young secretary would arrive for night duty, shaking and ashen faced, having seen something in the drive. Whenever possible we provided escorts for them.

We had several transatlantic characters, apart from Bob Beatty, to help us with the North American Transmission. One of them was the actor and producer Stanley Maxted, who later became a Correspondent and dropped into Arnhem with the Paratroopers. Stanley, not surprisingly, had never seen anything like Abbey Manor before. A local historian he met in a pub tried to put him wise by telling him about Simon de Montfort and explaining there was a plaque dedicated to him in the grounds. When he got back, Stanley was even more puzzled. He was heard asking around: 'Say, who's this guy Simon D. Montfort? It sounds like the Americans have been through here.'

One way and another, after about three months, I'd had enough. I saw the boss-man Tony Rendall and told him, if he didn't give me something else to do, he'd find my body swinging from the banisters and adding to the ghosts of the Manor. Tony, a kindly and perceptive man, took the hint and agreed to give me a go as a reporter, or News Observer, as the term was then.

This meant a return to London, where an office on the third floor of Broadcasting House became our base. My principal colleagues covering stories on the home front were Robin Duff and Terence de Marney. A wonderful person called Mrs Vickers, who was supposed to be our secretary, looked after us like a mother. Vicky, who was perhaps nearing middle age, was very wise, intelligent, and much travelled. She gave us good counsel, had a marvellous sense of humour and was not surprised at anything. I don't know what we should have done without her.

We all felt it a tremendous time to be in broadcasting, when the country was under siege. Every time you went in front of a microphone, you felt you were reassuring someone, some-where, that Britain was still there. Once, after a description I had given of the London Blitz, I had a congratulatory cable from India. It was from my brother-in-law Pat, who a few years before had hustled me into St Thomas's when I got pneumonia. The eyes of the world were on London and we knew it.

Our job was to provide reports for 'Radio News Reel', then the most important programme in the Overseas Service schedule. Robin Duff and I had been involved with it from the start as narrators, now as observers. There was a dedicated team of writers and reporters, with my former announcing colleague Peter Pooley as editor. The programme had punch and impact and made use of as many actuality recordings as possible. We didn't just talk about the Blitz, we brought the sound of the bombs and the gunfire to listeners thousands of miles away. The programme was re-broadcast in all Empire countries and, significantly, in Canada by the Canadian Broadcasting corporation and by Mutual in the US. Great effort went into the North American edition, and to help us get the maximum impact for transatlantic listeners an American adviser was attached to the programme – Ted Wells Church.

Before long, Ted took an interest in one of my reports. Making recordings, which in those early war years meant cutting discs, was a cumbersome business, requiring the services of three men. On this occasion, my two assistants were Peter Thompson of Recorded Programmes and Eric Hough of Technical Recordings. The assignment was to tell the story of one of the east coast convoys from Chatham to Rosyth, one of Britain's life-lines, 'E-boat alley', in which the ships involved had to cope with attacks by dive bombers and E-boats, to say nothing of the ever-present menace of mines.

It was a gloomy December evening when we arrived at Chatham to join one of the 'V and W' class escort destroyers HMS *Versatile*. Dismantling the gear from the recording car was quite a business in the darkness and drizzling rain. Soon a launch collected us and we chugged out into the harbour until we drew alongside the long dark shape of a destroyer.

At about 5.30 p.m. on the second evening out I was playing darts with one of the officers in the wardroom ; Peter and Eric were resting in their hammocks. When 'action stations' sounded we rushed up on deck, just as our guns opened up on a group of enemy bombers. There was a hell of a noise going on and someone gave me a wad of cotton wool to put in my ears.

My luck was in and I was able to give the first commentary of an attack on a convoy at sea. All the ships were blazing off like mad and finally the Dorniers, after dropping several sticks of bombs, thought better of it and beat it for home.

There was great excitement when we eventually got back to

London with these first recordings of an attack at sea. Ted Church really went to town on the version broadcast to America. Robert Beatty made the announcement in stentorian, transatlantic tones and almost made me out to be the original boy standing on the burning deck. The version I prepared for other transmissions was more sedate and called simply 'In action with an Escort Destroyer'.

Another trip with the Navy was when I took recording gear in a minesweeper on the Channel run. We joined HMS *Deodar* at Portsmouth. She was the flotilla leader and we were to precede a convoy round to Sheerness. It was a blustery morning and at sea the wind was whipping up white horses. We soon cast off and nosed our way through shipping of various kinds, until we came alongside a dock, where barrage balloons were lined up like great silver codfish on a slab. After a few preliminaries, there was ours sailing serenely above us to keep the dive-bombers away. The balloons were smaller than the shore variety and more streamlined with metal fins. The other four minesweepers soon came up with us and the little flotilla steamed out to sea, and on for some distance to our rendezvous with the convoy.

Meantime I talked with the Captain – Lieutenant-Commander Moore, who was an Ulsterman from Bangor. He explained that, as leader, our ship was really the only one in danger. There was reason to suspect mines had been laid and the extreme danger point would be in twelve hours' time.

Soon, astern of us, we saw smudges of smoke and several dots in the sky – the barrage balloons of our convoy. As that strange, rather ragged collection of ships started its journey up Channel, everyone suddenly began to look business-like on board, as the order was given – 'Sweep out'. The gear was simple. It consisted of a grey float, looking rather like a torpedo, some ten feet long. This was swung out over the side and run out seventy feet or so astern. The sweep wire was kept at the required depth by two paravanes, or kites as they're called. One is the kite otter, which drags the wire out to the side of the ship, and the other is dropped astern.

There's one thing about life in a minesweeper – you can't help getting thoroughly dirty and greasy. The crew were bundled up in a variety of coats and sweaters and most were wearing brightly coloured woollen caps. As we headed into more dangerous waters, the gun crew were, almost lovingly, cleaning their proudest possession – a twelve-pounder, quick-firing gun.

The afternoon wore on without incident, except for the sight of an occasional squadron of Spitfires, streaking across to the French coast. I looked into the stokehold, as they were changing shifts. The heat was terrific down there and they were raking out the fires. Not much hope for them if we struck a mine.

Up on deck, there was a fresh wind and the sun was just going down. Something was going on aft, evidently the sweep had fouled something, possibly a mine. The kite and sweep were being taken in. The First Lieutenant told me they didn't enjoy bringing in mines, once it was dark. Suddenly, a grinding series of crashes as the cable snapped and the gear broke loose. Whatever it was the sweep had fouled, it must have been something pretty big. The convoy was warned to change course – it might have been a mine.

It was night now – with a glorious moon sailing through the clouds – the sea was black and shot with silver. There was no sound save the dull beat of the engines – the gunners were at their posts wearing their duffle hoods. I remember thinking how absurdly like monks they looked – those cowled figures silhouetted against the sky.

And then, where the French coast was, the blackness was stabbed with flashes of white, you could see the vivid orange streaks of tracer bullets and hear the rumble of guns. The RAF must have been raiding the invasion ports – it looked like a benefit night. It was getting cold up on deck. I turned away from the rail – below, the crew were singing – 'Yip-i-Addy-i-Ay'.

9 Reporting the Blitz

Civilians just went on taking it. In London, night after night, during the long winter of 1940–41, as soon as it got dark, the sirens set up their wailing and from then on the time seemed to be spent in smoke-filled rooms or dodging about in cavernous, deserted streets. One got used to sleeping anywhere.

Terry de Marney practically lived in a Turkish Baths in Jermyn Street. If you went in there at about 11.30 p.m., you could steam away happily, doss down on a sort of pallet bed for the night, and then the resident masseur, an old chap of Dutch extraction, known as 'Pro', would throw in an egg and bacon breakfast – for a total cost of thirty bob. I tried it once, but didn't like all that steam.

There wasn't much difficulty in finding somewhere to live as almost everyone who was able to stay away from the capital did so. The Marylebone High Street flat was a write off ; it had stopped a bomb one night, when fortunately no one was there. About this time, I spent a weekend with some well-heeled friends at their country house near Chalfont-St-Giles in Buckinghamshire. From there, you could see the glow in the sky over London and it was clear there were some tremendous fires. They asked me where I was living and, when they heard I'd been bombed out, promptly said why on earth didn't I use their London flat, as it seemed absurd to leave it standing empty. So, for a couple of months my base was in a suite on the fourth floor of Grosvenor House, Park Lane.

It was pretty fantastic, except that when the guns went off across the road in Hyde Park, they nearly blew you out of bed. Another drawback was that I could scarcely ever afford to eat there and would enter the plushy portals and cross the deep pile carpet, clutching a bag of buns. Sidney Lipton and his band used to play in the ballroom below ground. People dancing always knew when there was a bad raid on because the band just used to go on playing, sometimes till nearly 4 a.m.

Later, I shared a ground floor flat, which Robin Duff had acquired in Cleveland Row, opposite St James's Palace. There, you could lie in bed and watch the sentries marching up and down; and it was good to hear the striking of the Palace clock.

Whenever possible, I would visit my parents in Croydon, which was having as bad a time as London. There were heavy anti-aircraft defences and RAF Fighter stations quite near, so, when hard pressed, the German bombers would jettison their load over Croydon and beat it back to the Reich.

There were shortages of everything and even dustbin contents were salvaged for pig food. People were asked to put their bins on the pavement for emptying. A milkman's horse had become notorious locally through his practice of grasping with his teeth the handles on the lids, which then fell to the ground with an almighty clatter. This done, he was able to rummage about inside. So, his progress along the road could be gauged by the crash of dustbin lids coming nearer.

One afternoon when I was visiting mother, there was another kind of crash. We were just clearing away lunch, when there was the familiar sound of a stick of bombs. Three came down on a descending note – then there was a noise coming straight at us like an express train and getting louder all the time! The house shook, glass and bits of plaster were flying about. We picked ourselves up, dusted ourselves down, and looked around. There was a nasty crack in the ceiling and nearly all the glass had gone from the window. We looked out to see a fair-sized crater in the road, and the milkman's horse was in it – dead. As far as I know, he was the only casualty.

That evening, I called in at a club where I used to play squash. One of my friends had just got back from the City, where he told me he'd been firewatching the previous night. The raids had gone on until four in the morning, then there was a lull for some minutes. After that, yet another wave of bombers. The old watchman, who was with him on the roof, sucked at his pipe: 'Here comes Jerry to give us a goodnight kiss.' He'd hardly got the words out, when a dozen bombs screeched down. The old boy picked himself up, as he growled, ' 'Ee doesn't 'arf put some passion in it.'

I enquired about one of the girls I used to know there. They told me Audrey was driving ambulances. One night on a trip to the mortuary with the bodies of six children, who had been dug out of the ruins of a school, she had a macabre experience. In the back of the ambulance was a speaking tube. Usually, there was an attendant and, if he wanted to speak to the driver, he would blow down the tube, which whistled in the driver's ear. That night there was no attendant in the back, just those six bodies. Then as she was driving through the rubble strewn streets, Audrey heard a loud whistle down the tube.

A friend in the Home Guard joined in the talk round the bar. He told us he'd seen a bomber blow up in mid-air the night before and was particularly pleased because, a few hours earlier, that same night his own house had been burned down by incendiaries. I noticed his hand was bound up – 'Rubbed the skin off working a stirrup pump – it's hell, Bob,' he said, 'I can't play golf.'

As far as London was concerned, from September 1940 until Sunday, 11 May 1941, there were very few nights without the bombers. Around Broadcasting House, it began to look very different. Queen's Hall, the home of the Proms, and St George's Hall, headquarters of BBC Variety, were both totally destroyed. And so was The Devonshire. It was just a fluke I wasn't there – something had cropped up in Broadcasting House to prevent my going for my nightly tipple.

There was very little of it left when I saw it next morning. 'Casey' Jones and most of his family were dead – all that special sherry he had been keeping for Victory Night had gone too.

The last of the big raids, before Hitler turned against Russia, was the worst. That May night more than 500 bombers came over and 1,500 Londoners were killed. Westminster Hall, the Abbey and the Houses of Parliament were all hit. Every main line station, except one, was out of action and the Thames bridges blocked. When daylight came, hundreds of acres of the city were still burning. The capital had had about as much as it could take. I really felt a few more nights like that and London might have cracked.

At one time or another, all the big ports and provincial centres had copped it too, although the pasting was less prolonged. In the early spring of '41 it was Plymouth's turn. Mr R. G. Menzies, the Australian Prime Minister (he hadn't received his knighthood then), was visiting Britain. There were thousands of Australian servicemen here and Mr Menzies wanted to see as many of them as he possibly could. 'Radio News Reel' had arranged to cover his visit to an Australian Coastal Command Squadron based at Mountbatten near Plymouth.

We left London in the recording car late on the afternoon of Friday, 21 March. Arthur Phillips, one of the senior Recording Staff who is now Chief Producer (Outside Events Recordings), was with me, and the third member was 'Skip' Arnell from Technical Engineering. Plymouth had had its first heavy raid the night before. The inhabitants had previously been kidding themselves that there was some mysterious reason why the Germans were unable to get through to bomb them in strength – atmospheric conditions or something – but they found to their cost there was no reason at all. The Luftwaffe simply hadn't got round to it before.

As we sped across Dartmoor, we were discussing whether Plymouth would catch it for the second night running. Soon, an ominous flush across the sky provided the answer. We stopped the car for a moment to have a look. The flush was merging into an angry red glow, like some fantastic sunset – we could see each other quite plainly – and those bangs we were hearing were guns all right.

So, we had two stories for the price of one – Mr Menzies' visit plus the Plymouth Blitz. As the car came into the outer suburbs, it lurched a bit, crunching its way over broken glass and rubble. Near the centre I could read the *Evening Standard* I'd bought in London in the light from the fires. Then the road ahead was blocked, so we got out of the car and started recording.

We were standing just across the street from a large department store. It was well ablaze – the wax models in the windows looking like bizarre victims ; as they melted, they seemed to be writhing in the flames. The upper stories were soon alight too and, in no time, we could see the whole side of the building was going to crash down. It leaned outwards slowly, almost imperceptibly, and then down it came with a great rush. Dust, rubble, and broken glass were everywhere and a fierce heat, like opening the oven door, drove us back – but we'd managed to get a memorable recording of the whole scene with commentary.

It was useless trying to get any further in the car, as all the roads seemed to be blocked, so we set off on foot. The whole centre of Plymouth was burning down. There were a few firemen about, doing their pathetic best, but the conflagration was on altogether too vast a scale. Much of their fire-fighting equipment and even some of the water mains had been destroyed by the raid with high explosives the night before.

On top of the chaos and confusion, the Luftwaffe had rained down incendiaries and now, on every side, churches, halls and other historic buildings of Plymouth were ablaze. Sparks were cascading into the sky and floating down, thick as snowflakes. As I stumbled down one of the poorer streets, little knots of people were standing about dazed and bewildered. One old woman standing by a heap of smouldering rubble looked back as I passed. 'That was my home,' she said. 'It's all I have.'

In all the confusion, I'd lost touch with Arthur Phillips – 'Phil', as I always called him – so I made my way down another street, where soldiers and some Naval ratings were helping the firemen salvage what they could from burning homes. There seemed to be no water for their hoses. I noticed a pack of cards scattered in the gutter and wondered if a game had been suddenly interrupted. Some people were squatting down on the kerb outside their houses, while policemen and air-raid wardens were showing others to shelters. In the midst of it all, incongruously, I saw an old salt leaning over his front gate and sucking at his pipe. As if there wasn't enough smoke that night. Certainly it was billowing out of the upstairs window of a tobacconist's shop down the road. Next door was a grocer's with the counters piled high with food. I joined a group bringing out crates of eggs, tea, butter and jam, and stacking them in a cinema nearby to save them from burning.

Meantime, Phil, I discovered, had broken into that cigarette shop and was doing a bit of fire-fighting on his own. I joined him upstairs and, between us, we hurled down through the window a sofa and some tables, which were smouldering. There wasn't much we could do, but I suppose we may have stopped a few fires from taking hold and spreading.

One of the most vivid impressions I have, as we stumbled wearily to our hotel, was the memory of a young girl. She was in WRNS uniform but without a hat. Her hair was flying about and her face, lit by the flames, had an expression of ecstatic bliss. She said gaily their headquarters had been bombed. What an enduring, resilient species we are! It was about 5 a.m. before we found the Grand Hotel, where we were booked in for the night. Miraculously, it was more or less undamaged. Plymouth was still burning all round, but we had had enough. I've never enjoyed sleep more.

We were called at 8.30 with breakfast because we had to get to Mountbatten by 10 a.m. for the Australian Prime Minister's visit. It was a slow business getting there, as street after street was closed because of unsafe buildings or unexploded bombs. But we made it eventually and it wasn't long before Mr Menzies showed up at that Australian Coastal Command Squadron.

He had been up most of the night too. You would never have known: he was even wearing a sprig of mimosa, or wattle as the Australians call it, in his buttonhole. Big, burly 'Bob' Menzies was a reassuring sight on that 'morning after'. He said all the right things to those young countrymen of his, who were helping to keep the seas round Britain free of U-boats, as they flew mission after mission in their Sunderlands.

That afternoon, before leaving for London, I arranged to record a short interview with Lady Astor, the redoubtable 'Nancy', Plymouth's representative in Parliament. Remembering she was American born, some words from her would be a must for the North American Service. I decided to record her, for maximum effect, in the open, standing on the famous Hoe with Plymouth still smouldering behind her. I shall always remember her opening words, but then, after all, I expect she had been up most of the night too. She started off, 'I'm standin' here lookin' out over Plymouth Po.' 'Cut!' I said. And we had to begin all over again.

We rushed back to London, tired, but pleased with the material we'd got.

I was to return to Plymouth several times in the following months. In May, I travelled down by train to check up on its recovery. The countryside was at its loveliest – fields and woods gay with primroses, cowslips and bluebells and then, abruptly, a desert of rubble. In the studio there I talked to Viscount Astor, the Lord Mayor, who told me they had improvised a system of communal feeding and would soon be serving 10,000 meals a day. He had also organised an Air Raid Distress Fund and had received gifts from all over the world.

There were gifts too from nearer home. Lord Astor said his house in Plymouth had had its windows blown out and the gas cut off, so he was living outside the city. In the evenings, he used to give a lift to some of the thousands who trekked out every night. The previous night he had picked up an old character who didn't exactly look like a millionaire, as he had a two-day growth of stubble and appeared to have been living rough. When he dropped him off, the old man mumbled something about relief. Lord Astor was about to tell him how to apply, when the old chap dredged up something from his trouser pocket and thrust it at him, saying would he please put it in the Air Raid Distress Fund – it was a ten bob note.

There wasn't much wrong with the spirit of Devon. A couple of nights later they were even dancing to a band, in the open on the Hoe.

Earlier, at the end of March, I had been with the small party of Newsmen at Bristol Airport when 'Bob' Menzies weighed in, all 250 lbs of him, before taking off for Australia and home. I thought he was in a rather quiet, reflective mood, especially when I asked him about the elections he would soon have to face. I believe he knew he was returning to electoral defeat – Australians prefer their leaders to stay at home.

Soon it was Mr Peter Fraser, the Prime Minister of New Zealand, who visited Britain. A far less colourful character with none of the Menzies panache. For a fortnight we slogged round the country with the recording car, while he visited the thousands of New Zealanders with the Forces.

First stop, the Navy's shore establishment at Brighton – *King Alfred*. The German broadcasts had put up a black a month or so before by claiming to have sunk it!

From there, to a clearing in the New Forest and a maori war-cry greeting. Watching those tough, wiry men of the Forestry Unit going to work on our timber, I felt, if I were a tree, and saw a New Zealander coming – I'd hide. Mr Fraser's last port of call was Portsmouth Naval Barracks, where he lunched in HMS *Victory*. From Nelson's quarter-deck, I recorded messages from a number of young New Zealanders to their parents back home.

Then, there was the day the tape machine stuttered out – Bombs on New York. The one in Lincolnshire. Off we dashed in the recording car. On arrival, I found no panic – the citizens were shaken, but resolute – all one hundred of them. There was a bomb crater in a wheatfield opposite a small farm and I talked to the owner, who had lived in New York, in the heart of the fen country, for seventy years man and boy. 'Tanty' Trafford was also the local grave-digger. Luckily the bomb had not given him any extra work. He told me his total score of burials to date was 215 and he'd just put down one of the heaviest men for miles around – a big horseman, who weighed over twenty stone, and was a noted gentleman all over Lincoln-shire.

As it happened, it was my privilege to meet many noted gentlemen from overseas about that time. Charles de Gaulle made an unforgettable impression on me when I first met him at a luncheon at the Savoy. In France resistance was building up against *les boches*. A French friend who had escaped to this country via Lisbon told me: *'ça commence à chauffer',* things are warming up. As for de Gaulle – it was like shaking hands with a bean pole. Slim and straight he was then – austere, remote, dedicated.

There were many kaleidoscopic meetings. Among them I remember Joseph Kennedy's successor as American Ambassador in London, but, unlike him, having faith in Britain – John G. Winant. One of the most charming and diffident Americans I have ever met, who later was to die so tragically. As a broadcaster, he was the despair of recording engineers, because of his hesitancy. One of them suggested that, with a little doctoring of the disc, the pauses could be removed. 'Don't do that,' said Winant, 'if you make me sound too good – no one will think it's me.'

Then, a boyish looking Malcolm MacDonald was given a great send off at a luncheon in London on his appointment as High Commissioner to Canada. He told me his young godson thought he'd been appointed Lord High Executioner and wanted to go with him, so he could sit in the front row, when he first carried out his duties.

Canada was playing an immense part in the war effort, not least as a training ground for the Empire Air Training Scheme. I was soon reminded of this on a cold, grey day in the harbour at Liverpool, as our launch took us out to where a liner shaped itself black against the mist. Her decks were a mass of khaki and blue and the faces formed a pink necklace round the ship.

Soon it was Mackenzie King, the Prime Minister of Canada, we were welcoming. All charm and distinction with his shock of white hair and keen blue eyes. He told me he was here to emphasise the intention of Canada to give of her utmost.

That wasn't quite the way a party of United States isolationist congressmen impressed me near the end of '41 when I said goodbye to them, after they'd made a short tour of inspection over here. One of them said they didn't so much want a British victory, as an Axis defeat.

110

A month later, of course, Pearl Harbour changed all that, and, from then on, America was in it up to the hilt. All over the UK you could sense the great sigh of relief that went up. If in the short term the outlook was bleak, now, at least, we could see the light at the end of the tunnel.

By this time, the Overseas Service had left Abbey Manor and was back in new battle quarters in London at what had been Peter Robinson's – 200 Oxford Street. Not that I spent much time there, as I was always out on the road.

Inevitably, it was a rackety existence. There's nothing like a war for removing inhibitions and I would say morals have scarcely ever been as lax as they were then. In my experience, sleeping around is most often a short cut to misery, to say nothing of disease. I suppose it can only give pleasure if a person is totally insensitive to the feelings of others, because emotions are bound to become involved and usually it is the woman who gets hurt most. It horrifies me now when I think how thoughtless I must have been as a young man.

The trouble was I felt irresistibly drawn or impelled towards a beautiful girl, as though by unseen forces – dig my heels in as I might.

In fact, my opportunities for dalliance were few. 'Radio News Reel' kept me too busy for that. I came to specialise more and more in air stories. With the Blitz over, the emphasis was on the production of bombers to mount an all out offensive on Germany. It was, I suppose, the only way Churchill felt we could hit back effectively. I flew on training missions in most of the heavier types of aircraft – the Blenheims, Stirlings, Halifaxes, Beaufighters and Bostons. The most stimulating was a flight with a test pilot in a Halifax.

The previous day I'd been at the christening, when Lord and Lady Halifax did the honours for their namesake. The great, four-engined machine was rolled out of the hangar and looked absurdly frivolous, draped in a Union Jack with champagne bubbles dripping from its nose. When the test pilot took it up, I was in the bomb-aimer's position, lying face down, right up in the front. For its size the Halifax was astonishingly manoeuvrable and it felt like being on the Giant Racer, as he flung the plane about the sky. Then he made a simulated bombing run over a factory and I left my stomach behind as he dived down and the tall chimneys came zooming up to meet us. At the last second he levelled out and was up and away again with a mighty roar of engines. Soon that ninety-nine foot of wing-spread was casting its shadow over Berlin and far beyond.

Not all flights were official and not all were in bombers. On a routine visit to a Fleet Air Army Station at Lee-on-Solent in April '42, I ran into Lieut.-Commander Ralph Richardson.[1] I had met him only once before at Broadcasting House, but he hailed me as a long lost friend and, as things were quiet on this station, he suggested I might like to fly with him to another station in St Eovil in Cornwall.

We clambered into a light aircraft, I think it was a Vega Gull. There were two seats beside each other. One of the ground-crew pulled the chocks away from the wheels and, as he did so, grinned and gave a sort of knowing wink, which I thought rather odd at the time.

The take-off was satisfactory, but we had gone no distance before a black wall of thundercloud stretched across the sky ahead. Soon we were slap in the middle of the father and mother of a storm and the little aeroplane began bucking and bouncing about in the most irregular way.

I even found myself singing aloud to keep my pecker up. Ralph had one of his vague, lost looks and eventually decided to put the nose down to try and lose that cloud. For a few moments we glimpsed some built-up area below. He dropped a map on my knees, shouting over the engine noise, 'Can you navigate? Is that Bournemouth?' I hadn't the remotest idea.

We never did find out, because cloud closed in on us again. After half an hour of being buffeted about the sky, Ralph decided to make an emergency landing. A rough-looking field rushed up to meet us and we came to a bumpy, but blissful halt. He was quite pleased, because in the corner of the field was a Nissen hut and inside we found some RAF weathermen. They plied us with restorative liquor and a snack lunch, but said we had better forget about Cornwall, owing to more filthy weather ahead.

I would cheerfully have walked back to base, rather than go in that damned aeroplane again, but, mercifully, the return flight was slightly less turbulent. At the air station they seemed quite relieved to see us, but not half so relieved as I was to see them. I had the impression that Ralph had omitted to tell any-one where we were going. At least, I felt I knew now why that chap had winked.

[1] Now Sir Ralph Richardson.

This had been a dismal year and the news was consistently awful. The loss of Singapore with 60,000 British troops, the sinking of the battleships *Prince of Wales* and *Repulse*, and then the reverses in the Middle East with Tobruk falling to Rommel. In London, life with all its shortages seemed unutterably drab. At least, there had been excitement and tension during the Blitz.

I suffered from perpetual sore throats and only kept going by doses of the new sulphonamide drugs, which in those early days had a very depressing effect. By then I'd been fitted with a War Correspondent's uniform and spent a week on a landing exercise in the Isle of Wight with the Coldstream, but it only made me feel rather bogus.

The one bright spot in the war was the successes of the Red Army. Whereas, from America and at home there were constant reports of dissension and defeat, from Russia we heard only of a seemingly magnificent unity of purpose carrying them forward. It was sometimes difficult not to come to the conclusion that Russia was the only country of the Alliance fighting from a sound, social base.

Indeed, at this time in London, perhaps partly in gratitude, partly in guilt at the absence of a Second Front, many people began to idolise the Russians. I remember an instance of this at a cinema in Piccadilly when *A Day in Soviet Russia* was shown. Ivan Maisky the Soviet Ambassador was there with his wife. He was a popular figure in London then – with his smiling face and pointed beard. At the end of the film, that packed house of reasonably sophisticated Londoners leaped to their feet and clapped and cheered for all of three minutes.

There were many Britons, disillusioned with the social system and its inequalities, who wanted to believe in a dream society. I was one of them and the absence of negative news about Russia made us feel the Soviet Union might indeed be that society.

Meantime, Terry and I had become inextricably involved in a destructive triangular affair with an actress or rather enchantress. There is nothing in the world more lowering and awful than this, especially as in this case Terry was winning hands down.

My tonsils were now deep mauve with white spots all over. I took them along to C. P. Wilson, top Ear, Nose and Throat man at Middlesex Hospital. He seemed awed and said he couldn't remove them until they'd simmered down a bit. I booked a hospital bed for some four weeks ahead. The final pushover to my state of mind came when I heard that Dennis Johnston, the Irish playwright, had been appointed BBC Air Correspondent, Middle East. I had nothing whatever against him personally – I'd never even met him, but it made me feel that as an Overseas Reporter I would never stand a chance. The appointments were all made by Home News and they would be bound to pick their own men.

One morning, in this far from jolly state and with a fair amount of pique thrown in, I happened to meet J. B. Clark on the stairs at Broadcasting House. He was looking as self-contained as ever and, before I could stop myself, I'd blurted out that I would like my release from the BBC. I suppose he had never forgiven me for leaving the Newsreading team at Abbey Manor, so he just looked at me, as though I were mad, and said I'd better see Ryan.

A. P. Ryan was then Controller, News Co-ordination. A ghastly title, which implies correctly that the whole News scene was, at that time, being reorganised. He knew practically nothing about my work with Overseas and I had only met him once before in the corridor, so there was no problem – I got my release.

From a career point of view it was idiotic. If only some official had explained what BBC plans were and told me to go away, get my tonsils out and come back refreshed, all would have been well. As it was, eight years of training were thrown away.

I signed on with the Navy and said they could have my body, when the surgeon had finished with me, in October.

10 The Navy

I couldn't have left my tonsils in a nicer place than the Middlesex. Apart from the inevitable feeling that I'd had red hot tongs shoved down my throat, the effect of lying in bed with nothing much to worry about was highly therapeutic. As it was September, on most mornings my bed was pushed out on to a small sunny courtyard. It was the best holiday I'd had in years and I was quite sorry to leave.

My parents were still living at Grove House in Croydon, although the old place looked very much on the slide after the bombing. One of the outer walls was shored up with strong wooden supports, and inside it was pretty rough structurally too. Fortunately, my mother had a genius for making a place seem bright and cheerful, mainly by the force of her personality. She was also still working enthusiastically for the Red Cross, while my father and elder sister were carrying on with Civil Defence work at the Town Hall.

In the fortnight or so before delivering myself to the Navy, I thought I'd better try to get fit. I knew it would be a tough course, so I even tried a bit of skipping and also played a lot of squash. One of the very last things I did was to see my barber and ask him to give me the shortest possible haircut. He did his best and when he'd finished my ears were sticking out like bats' wings.

The day came when I was due to report to HMS *Ganges*, the Naval training establishment at Shotley near Harwich. At Liverpool Street Station there were a number of other characters with small suitcases and with their ears sticking out too. We eyed each other sheepishly. There was a pleasant young chap opposite me in the compartment, who had still got quite a lot of curly hair. He said his name was Geoff and he'd been reading Modern Languages at Cambridge. Geoff was wildly enthusiastic about Russia and even more convinced than I was that the Soviet system was the answer to all our troubles.

At Harwich we piled into Naval buses for the last stage of the journey. Next morning the Navy really set to work on us! That first week spent in the annexe at *Ganges* was quite an experience.

The object, I suppose, was to make us forget we had ever been individual human beings. To help us lose former identities, our hair was clipped even closer and it was extraordinary to see the difference as sideboards, moustaches and hairy fuzz of all kinds vanished to reveal pallid countenances beneath. Then came kitting out. One thing is certain, there can't be any uniform anywhere that feels stranger to put on for the first time than the British matelot's square rig. It was wildly funny to see the despairing efforts to get into it. We soon got used to eating off tin plates and drinking from tin mugs. I rather think that, in comparison, a present day Borstal would seem like the Ritz.

After being given the initial treatment, we were moved into the main establishment. Originally designed in peacetime for boys' training, it was now holding four times that number of men. The overcrowding was total. Queues formed perpetually. One seldom knew what was at the other end, sometimes it was a bar of soap or it might even be a jab for yellow fever. Some of the new intake were a bit slow and, having got their jab against something or other, would continue in the queue and then be given another one on the second time round. As I was a heavy smoker at the time, I became adept at palming a cigarette, because smoking wasn't allowed near the parade ground. It was a mistake to conceal a cigarette behind your back, because another jolly Jack would, as likely as not, filch it from between your fingers.

There was endless drilling from 7 a.m. and on the darkest days we had to muster by torchlight. England's east coast that winter was anything but sultry. I'm not sure which was more invigorating, the square-bashing with hands so clumsy with cold it was all we could do to hold our rifles, or the boat pulling in icy blasts on the River Orwell.

For the most part, in spite of, or even perhaps because of these unaccustomed rigours, I felt remarkably fit. This was as well, because attendance at the sick-bay was not to be recommended. There appeared to be only two treatments. If the complaint was visible it was painted with gentian blue; if invisible, there was the invariable dose of half a glass of castor oil. This, at least, had the effect of shortening the queue outside the sick-bay door, even if it correspondingly lengthened the queue for 'the heads', as lavatories are known Navy style.

There was another instance of Navy style at morning Divisions. Thousands of us, drawn up, blue and shivering, on the parade ground. Then, on the rostrum, a senior Captain would appear. He sported a monocle. There would be a hush, as with a marvellous coolness of nerve he tossed it in the air and, almost always, managed to trap it in his left eye, on the way down.

Although I could cope with the drilling, it was humiliating to realise that in almost all other important practical things and manual skills I was hopelessly deficient. At least, I succeeded in learning to do my own washing, or dhobi-ing. The most fiendish item to wash was the big square collar, as it was so difficult to prevent the blue dye from running into the white tapes, which ran round the edges. I found the trick was to rub the tapes with a bar of soap, before starting to wash the collar. The aim was to achieve as pale a blue on the collar as possible – this was considered 'tiddley', which in Naval parlance means smart or *comme il faut*. It was also tiddley to have smart horizontal creases in the bell-bottom trousers like a concertina and it meant a lot of pressing with the iron.

The one thing which totally defeated me, practise as I might, was the tying of knots, or rather bends and hitches. Anything to do with mathematics had me groping too and it seemed I would never make a Navigator. All the same, as the months went by, I managed to acquire many basic skills with paint-brush, squeegee, scrubbing brush and broom.

One morning during a make-and-mend session, Geoff, who was doing his best to sew a vital button on his trousers, suddenly grabbed my arm. He'd heard a 'pipe', or announcement, over the address system, which said volunteers were wanted for special duties at the Royal Navy base in North Russia. Further details could be had in the Ship's Office.

The Master-at-Arms strongly advised us to have a go, and, as it meant a twenty-four-hour leave in London, that in itself was an attractive idea. At the Admiralty, we had separate interviews and learnt that the proposition was to take a short, intensive, Russian language course, lasting a few months, and then, provided we passed an exam, we would join the Royal Navy party up in North Russia, concerned with the smooth running of the convoys from the U.K. These interpreter liaison duties would mean sailing in Russian destroyers to meet the RN convoys, so it sounded as if there would be a fair amount of sea time.

117

Some of the questions were puzzling: could I ride, skate or ski? Then, I remembered the Germans were at Petsamo, only about sixty miles from the base, and it might become necessary to leave by unconventional means, and in a hurry. It sounded an interesting challenge and my News antennae were already beginning to vibrate – I was as curious as hell to find out what the Russian system was like. A few days later word came from the Admiralty to say I'd been accepted, but that Geoff had not. At the time he can't have realised quite how lucky he was.

It turned out that there were six of us from the Navy and two from the RAF on that first crash course in Russian and the main centre was the School of Slavonic Studies in Bloomsbury's Gordon Square. One of them became a great friend – David Chance – now living on a Norfolk farm with his charming Australian born wife Margaret. David and three of the others had been at Eton and university, the fifth was a former schoolmaster. The RAF men were David Floyd, now Special Correspondent on Communist Affairs with the *Daily Telegraph*, and Kenneth Maconochie, a former Announcer colleague of mine at the BBC.

Russian is not the easiest of languages and to get anything like a grasp of it in a few months meant working harder than any of us had ever worked before or since. There were, of course, no sophisticated aids to learning like present-day language laboratories, in fact all we had was a few text books and two dedicated mentors. When the time came for the exam, there was only one failure – the schoolmaster.

After that, the trouble was we, unwittingly, became the victims of a visa war. While the Admiralty was insisting on having a proper Naval base up in North Russia, Stalin, incensed at the Allies' delay in opening a Second Front in Europe, put every possible difficulty in the way. The Russians desperately wanted the flow of war supplies to continue, but without giving the essential harbour facilities to make it possible. When the convoys had finally battled their way up to North Russia, as often as not, they arrived with many wounded survivors needing urgent hospital treatment. There were bitter complaints from British and American seamen of conditions in the Russian hospitals – overcrowding, lack of drugs and of proper medical care. Therefore, on the Churchill level, there was insistence that an auxiliary Royal Navy hospital must be allowed. Meantime, we waited for visas and the months dragged on.

In the summer and autumn, the course transferred to Oxford University and St Edmund Hall. Finally, in December, we transferred to Portsmouth Naval Barracks for a further course and to be commissioned – Sub-Lieutenants. I was having a drink at the bar one evening, when a young, fair-haired Surgeon-Lieutenant hailed me. Eric Norman had been one of the first six pupils with me at Miss Polley's, twenty-three years before, and I hadn't seen him since. I remembered how Eric had very nearly disrupted an end of term play. I was King Alfred and Eric had been cast as the village woman in whose cottage Alfred took refuge. There I had sat by the fire, duly burning the cakes, for what seemed an interminable time – and no Eric. Then, from the direction of the kitchen, being used as a dressing-room, came the sound of fearful bellowing. It appeared that five-year-old Eric, affronted at being dressed as a woman, was refusing to appear. In fact, he was hanging on like grim death to the leg of the kitchen table. It took several minutes and much cajoling with sweets to get him to come out from under and make his appearance – a rumpled tear-stained figure. The memory of it and other incidents gave us a convivial evening round the bar.

Then at long last, David Chance and I heard that something was going to happen to us. Stalin had relented and the visas had come through. We had a few days leave, before we were due to report at Scapa Flow on 11 January 1944. I nipped home to say goodbye to my parents in Croydon, only to find they were about to move yet again. 'Grove House' had finally been condemned as unsafe after the bombing, and, to my sorrow, was going to be pulled down, so they were moving to a hideous Victorian block of flats called 'The Chateau' on the other side of the road.

David's parents were staying in London at Brown's Hotel and invited us to spend the final night there as we had to be at Euston Station fairly early next morning. It was to be our last glimpse of civilised living for quite a time. I haven't stayed there since, but even in wartime London, Brown's was still somehow managing to enshrine all the best English qualities of good taste, understatement and unobtrusive service.

Soon after breakfast we left for Euston and the journey north. In Scotland we found they had had quite a lot of snow and as there was little heat in the compartment, David and I put on our sheepskin-lined boots. That night in Scapa we reported to the Depot ship *Dunluce Castle*.

Next morning, a launch took us out to HMS *Savage*, the destroyer in which we were to take passage on this first convoy of the New Year. On Boxing Day just over a fortnight earlier, on the previous run, *Savage* under her Captain, Commander M. D. C. Meyrick RN, had played a vital part with her torpedoes in the sinking of the most successful warship in the German Navy, the battle-cruiser *Scharnhorst* which had been sunk in that now famous action off the North Cape of Norway. So, *Savage* had helped to end the career of a ship which in her time had accounted for an aircraft carrier, an armed merchant cruiser, two destroyers and well over 100,000 tons of allied merchant shipping.

We had missed that action, but the convoy with which we were sailing, JW 56A, was to have its moments too. This time, there were twenty merchant ships gathered in Loch Ewe ready to make the thousand mile journey, by way of Iceland, Jan Mayen, Bear Island and so to Kola Inlet and Murmansk or, for some of them, Archangel and the White Sea. All the way they would be open to air attack from the German bases along the Norwegian coast; the U-boats would almost certainly be waiting too.

With *Scharnhorst* out of the way, there was no longer need to provide the cover of a battleship force but, of course, the other enemy – the weather – was still at full strength. We sailed from Scapa at 9 p.m. on 12 January. There was bright moonlight and from our leading position the merchantmen strung out astern of us were so many black silhouettes. It wasn't long before the weather struck. We were soon tossing about in a force ten gale; I didn't much mind being sick, as a lot of others were very sick as well.

By Friday 14th we were off the east coast of Iceland and it was calmer. I even ate breakfast. Soon afterwards, at about eleven, we entered Seydhisfiord, a gaunt, brown, mountainous coastline interspersed with patches of green cultivation. Part of the day was spent taking on oil. For a time, sun and moon both showed palely together and then – darkness and my first sight of the weird Northern Lights flickering across the sky. But the best sight of all after over four years of black-out at home was the bright necklace of lights ashore.

Saturday was another quiet day. David and I inspected, with some wonder, our special issue of Arctic clothing. There were fantastic long woollen pants, so thick that they would stand up obscenely by themselves in the corner of the cabin, and fur hats with great long ear pieces that made one look like Flopsy Bunny. We heard that the merchantmen had been scattered by the gale and at midnight we sailed in an attempt to round up the convoy.

By the following evening we had found six ships, but a tremendous gale had got up again. In his book *A Window in Moscow* Alaric Jacob, who was on board one of the other ships in the convoy, described it like this: 'At first it was just grey pavements of water that came slapping against us, but within the hour it was as though whole roadways were turning over upon themselves and falling upon us. The convoy dispersed. It was not ordered to do so ; it just blew apart.' On one of the Liberty ships a heavy locomotive forming part of the deck cargo had broken loose and hurtled about like a maddened beast, until it finally plunged over the side. At ten o'clock that night we returned to Seydhis.

Next morning we left again for a day's patrolling in search of stragglers and I spent some time on the bridge. The Commodore in charge of the merchant ships had been obliged to take them into the northern Icelandic port of Akureyri to repair gale damage and restow the deck cargo. Accordingly at 7 a.m. the next day we too left for the north to rendezvous with them. Late in the afternoon we entered Akureyri fiord, which was a study in grey and white, but it was far too rough for us to anchor there, so we spent the night patrolling outside.

By 10.30 next morning it had quietened down a little and we were able to enter and drop anchor. The mountains were higher and less jagged than in Seydhis: there was far more snow lying and it was much colder. Again here the twinkling lights ashore were a splendid sight. Next day we enjoyed a closer look, when at three in the afternoon we tied up alongside the cruiser *Bermuda* and had a couple of hours' shore leave. Akureyri seemed like a toy town: there was a touch of unreality about the brightly lit wooden shops and houses and many a girl back in the UK must have been gladdened by the numerous silk stockings and lipsticks bought for them – there. This was a pleasant interlude, followed that evening by a brisk party after dinner in *Bermuda*'s wardroom.

We slipped our moorings early next morning, 21 January. Everyone was rather subdued, partly as a result of the previous evening, but also because the most serious stretch of the voyage was just beginning. Five of the original twenty merchantmen remained behind, their damage could not be repaired in time, so we sailed with only fifteen ships. As they had a close escort of eleven warships, prospects for this convoy's safe passage seemed bright. *Savage* sliced cleanly through the calm, grey-green sea. It was snowing and, at last, we were on our way.

On the Saturday the weather was still fairly calm. In January up in these northern waters there is very little daylight: just a grey gloom. It was getting distinctly colder and ice began to form on the deck.

The following morning at about eleven one of the merchant ships came up alongside and a loudhailer conversation ensued. They had an acute appendicitis case on board and wanted medical help. But the *Savage* was due to take on oil and the Captain was reluctant to waste time transferring our doctor to the merchantman. He accordingly instructed him to give what advice he could over the loudhailer. This he did with talk of hot waterbottles and so on and the Liberty ship went on her way.

The doctor had strong words to say about not being allowed to visit a patient, but there was nothing he could do about it. He had no means of knowing it at the time but the Captain, in refusing him permission to go aboard, was incidentally saving his life.

The next day there was a tremendous sea. Everything movable in the ship was hurtling about; chairs were all over the place in the Wardroom, and so was the lunch.

For some days, the convoy had had its shadowing enemy aircraft and we wondered if an attack would develop. In fact, an enemy agent in Iceland had tipped off the Germans when the convoy sailed and so a line of U-boats was awaiting it off Bear Island.

On the morning of 25 January our asdic started pinging and, from then on, we knew that sooner or later there would be trouble. It came in the blackness at six that evening. For some time the escort destroyers had been weaving about putting down depth charges. A pattern had just gone down from *Savage*'s stern, when there was an even bigger explosion than usual. Immediately, wreckage of all kinds floated by and sud-

122

denly all over the sea there were lights ; it looked like Piccadilly Circus in peacetime.

On deck, we didn't know what had happened. A 'buzz' went
round that one of the depth charges had got a U-boat. We
craned out over the guard-rail and then heard men shouting –
all around us. There were some on rafts and the lights were
coming from them, others were in the water. We slowed right
down to pick up as many as we could, but there wasn't much
time – the U-boat pack was still around. Some of us shouted
at them in German to come nearer and we began hauling up
over the side the black, slippery, oil-covered figures. It was then
we discovered they were, in fact, Americans from a Liberty
ship that had been torpedoed.

Tossing about with engines stopped in the middle of the
Arctic was a naked, exposed feeling. The Captain daren't risk
his ship for more than a few minutes and then, with a great
surge, we were away at twenty knots, the deck piled high with
bodies.

But there were yet more lights on the water and more despairing shouts ringing in our ears. The only hope was they
might be saved by other ships, otherwise they wouldn't last
long. Twenty minutes to half an hour was about all a man
could stand in those icy waters. When a count was made we
found we'd picked up fifty-one. And what's more, among them
was the appendicitis case we had heard about just two days
before. He was from Texas and his face was pale as parch-
ment with a straggly, sandy-coloured beard. So the patient had
finally come to our doctor, instead of the other way round.
The irony of it all was that a Medical Officer had been put
aboard the Liberty ship from one of the other escort destroyers.
But, in the event, an operation had not been found necessary
and, what's more, that unfortunate doctor had gone down
with the ship.

They were a great bunch those Yanks and so touchingly
grateful for being picked up. It is strange how men react when
their temporary floating home is sunk beneath them. One of the
Americans said his only sorrow was that he had lost his
favourite pipe when the bang came. As he put it – 'it was drawing real sweet'. Another regretting a doughnut he'd just been
eating – apparently it was a speciality of the ship's cook. Then
I remember another seaman telling me he had just taken off his
trousers to iron them, when the torpedo struck. The next thing

123

he knew he was in the Arctic. Not surprisingly, he kept feeling himself all over to make sure everything was still there. We had also managed to pick up another important crew member, 'Blackie' the ship's cat.

All that night and the following day, the U-boats stalked the convoy but, in spite of many scares, there was no further serious incident. The Germans cannot have been displeased with their score of three merchant ships sunk out of fifteen, as well as damage by torpedo to *Obdurate*, one of the destroyers. In addition two of the 'V' class destroyers had unhappily collided leaving one with her bows sheered off.

Our first sight of Russia came next evening – as we approached Kola Inlet. A desolate coastline with low snow-covered hills. Here and there, stunted birch and fir trees showed like black stubble. We entered the narrow, deep inlet of the Soviet Northern Fleet at Polyarnoe, which in Czarist days had been called Alexandrovsk, and tied up with the other Royal Navy escort ships at the wooden jetties. The prospect ashore was uninviting – a few shabby, grey, barrack-like buildings scattered about in the snow. David and I were regaled with many a tale about the horrors of life ashore and certainly none of the ship's company, most of whom had been there before, had any intention of setting foot on Soviet soil again. 'There's nothing there boy, nothing,' one of them said to me.

I looked out at the daunting prospect. There was an indefinable air of menace about the place – an alien, oppressive atmosphere – but I was determined not to be put off by anything anyone said. I thought they must be biased. It turned out that David was to remain at the main base in Polyarnoe.

I was sorry to say goodbye to *Savage*, when at eleven o'clock on the morning of 28 January a launch came alongside to take me the few miles up the inlet to the port and railhead at Murmansk.

11 Stalin's Russia

After a stop for lunch on the minesweeper *Hussar*, which had been stranded up in North Russia for many months and was crawling with cockroaches, I was collected by a Russian-speaking RNVR officer, Lieutenant Cheshire, who took me in a jeep over rutted tracks deep in snow and slush, towards the British Naval Mission in Murmansk. First impressions were confused and chaotic. It was dark and snowing hard. We passed a jumble of masts and buildings and a group of marching men with automatic rifles. They had round fur hats and long great-coats and were singing. Their voices seemed to come from their boots.

The Mission was housed on the second floor of a decrepit looking block known as Bolshoi Dom (Big House). Commander Morten RN was in charge and there were about six other officers and two Ministry of War transport officials. The work was involved with the innumerable problems of unloading the merchant ships and, as an interpreter, I was kept fully stretched. There were difficulties of climate, constant air-raids and a lack of mechanical unloading equipment in the docks. We even had to provide our own crane ship for the heavy lifts. The great bulk of the work was carried out manually by wretched, scarecrow figures dressed in rags. None of us who were up there in Kola Inlet will ever forget the sight of them. They were gangs from the notorious Stalin slave camps in the Arctic, which served three purposes: dissenters or would-be dissenters to the régime were silenced, the rest of the populace lived in fear of being sent to one, and an endless supply of cheap labour was provided for the Soviet economy. I had expected conditions in Murmansk to be rough, perhaps on the lines of a Canadian lumber camp at the turn of the century, but – not like this.

It is not easy for a person from the West to fathom the mentality of a people conditioned by centuries of slavery. Joseph Berger, once a foremost figure in the Komintern, who managed incredibly to survive twenty-one years in Stalin's camps, gives this explanation:

You have to get to know this people. The Russians will take their place in the sun precisely because they can be satisfied with very little. In no other nation will you find such a capacity to rise above material needs, even the most essential. All you have to do is hold a whip over their heads and feed them as little as possible. If you do that you can reach the Pacific Ocean and conquer the world.[1]

Like his predecessors, Genghis Khan, Ivan the Terrible and Peter the Great, it was clear that Stalin understood this to the full. Indeed, this I suppose was the secret of his success. While paying ceaseless lip service to the Revolution, he was, in fact, continuing the kind of rule which the Russians had been used to through the ages.

Suspicion was endemic and our contacts with Russians were confined to official business. The Soviet authorities would not allow us to have our own Naval launches for moving about the inlet, so we were dependent on two antiquated *Katyers* (launches) manned by seamen of their Northern Fleet. This was the only means of transport to Polyarnoe, where the Senior British Naval Officer (North Russia) Admiral Archer had his headquarters with the main body of officers and men.

Packs of semi-wild dogs roamed about the hills on either side of the inlet and it was curious how quickly they learnt to distinguish between Russian and British uniforms. Invariably, when a party of our matelots were seen ashore there would be a trail of dogs tagging along behind. The Russians on the other hand had no time for dogs and there was very nearly an international incident when a Soviet sentry bayoneted and killed two dogs at our ratings quarters in Murmansk.

Owing to transport difficulties several of us from the British Naval Mission applied to the Soviets for driving licences. There was a great deal of prevarication on the part of the local bosses and it was clear that difficulties were going to be put in our way. One obstacle was a medical examination. Six of us were summoned to report at a clinic. To our astonishment we were told to strip and await the Russian doctor. It was cold and, if we hadn't been determined to get those licences, we wouldn't have gone through with it. To our greater astonishment, the doctor turned out to be a grim-faced woman

[1] *Shipwreck of a Generation,* The Memoirs of Joseph Berger, published by Harvill Press, 1971.

with two nurses at her side. She came up to each of us, felt our testicles and marched out with a smirk. And, after all that, we still didn't get our licences.

The Liaison Officer with whom we had to deal on official matters was a Lieutenant Pankratov. His English was somewhat fractured, but this did not stop him from airing it on every possible occasion. Over the telephone, through the crackles and statics, came his booming voice with the invariable opening, 'I am speaking, who is talking?' His sayings became quite famous amongst us. One morning when I met him after a party, he confided that he still felt 'tightly slight'. On another occasion, when I asked for some of the half-starved wretches to be provided to help unload a ship, he was trying to tell me that he had no spare hands, but his English wasn't equal to it and so what he said with unconscious irony was, 'But I have no empty men.'

One of the irritations of life in Murmansk was the broadcast din of martial and folk music, interspersed with war communiqués, read in a bullfrog voice from Moscow. The loudspeakers were fixed high up on buildings and therefore difficult to reach. The same programme was belted out in the ramshackle intourist hotel. In the entrance hall stood a huge, moth-eaten, brown bear with yellow fangs and arms outstretched. Once past him, there was a confrontation on each floor with a Soviet female known as a *dezhurni*. Her function was to keep tabs on the occupants of the rooms and report to the local officials on all comings and goings. Then, once inside, high up on the wall was a black, conical object producing the identical noise going on outside. By clambering up on to a rickety chair, it was usually possible either to wrench it from its moorings or somehow to silence it.

Our daily path was strewn with time-wasting frustrations. A typical instance was when I called at the Intourist to collect a suitcase from the cloakroom. On presenting my ticket, I was told that I would have to get special, written permission to collect my own case. Eventually, after much questioning, I discovered the reason was that one of the American shipping officials staying there had deposited some clothes, then got high on vodka and lost a ticket. A Russian had found it, presented it at the cloakroom and made off with the clothes. So everyone was then made to produce official, written permission to collect their own belongings.

For the local inhabitants there was an almost total restriction on movement; they even required a permit or *propusk* to visit a neighbouring village. In fact *propusks* were needed at every turn. There was the story of a Russian seen carrying a small bundle of wood under his arm, while on his back was a large bulging sack. A comrade asked him what he'd got in the sack and the answer, understandably enough, was '*Propusks*'.

Not altogether surprisingly, an air of hopelessness hung over all. One evening, walking through the main street, I saw a body lying in the snow in the middle of the road. Every now and again a lorry rumbled past. There were people shuffling along on either side, but no one seemed to care. I thought it rather odd, so I walked out into the middle of the road and gave the body a shake. In a few moments, there was a grunt and the man got to his feet and started to move away. I shouted after him asking what was the matter; his answer was '*Nichevo osobyenovo*' (nothing special). Perhaps he was just tired of it all.

This was not an unlikely state of affairs. When aviation spirit was being off-loaded from the tankers, sentries had to be posted by the pipeline snaking along the dockside. This was found to be necessary after several comrades had broached the pipes and drunk their fill. Some went blind, others died. There were also several instances when these poor wretches from the slave camps, driven beyond endurance, placed their heads on the rails in front of a train.

For British personnel it wasn't quite as bad as all that. At least we had a degree of comfort. Perhaps the greatest lack was of any ordinary social intercourse and the infrequency of mail from home. We were isolated from the local people by the Soviet authorities and there was, of course, no feminine companionship at all.

In a despairing attempt to improve relations with the local Party bosses, I persuaded the Commander to throw a party and follow it with a film show. It was my job to organise the film. All I had to go on was a title and the names of the stars taking part. I studied the indifferent list looking for something light and jolly. Cary Grant and Rosalind Russell in *His Girl Friday* sounded the most suitable. There was no chance of getting a showing of the film beforehand, so I just had to keep my fingers crossed and hope everything would be all right. Well – it wasn't. It turned out to be a rather trite Hollywood thriller about American newspaper men. Not only that, but at one point in the film Cary Grant referred to one of the other characters by saying: 'That guy is crooked enough to be in the pay of Stalin.' At this point, I quietly left the room and nearly burst into tears.

As the months went by, most of us, in varying degrees, went round the bend – some were almost out of sight. One of the RNR types after a session in the Wardroom would down his drink, eye the empty wine glass, take it delicately by the stem and proceed to eat it like a piece of asparagus. Sometimes he would consume six glasses at a sitting and appear none the worse for it at the end.

The record for the shortest stay up in North Russia was held by a certain elderly RNR officer, who had had a fairly lively time of it in the convoy up from Scapa. On arrival at our Mess, he was, I think, secretly rather pleased with himself. In fact, he felt he'd earned a drink and so proceeded to let his hair down in no uncertain manner. After an hour or two of convivial relaxation, he rose unsteadily to his feet and, with a twenty degree list to port, set course for the door leading to the 'heads'. Not more than two minutes went by before there was the most unholy crash. Was it a bomb? On looking outside the door, there seemed to be water everywhere. We had forgotten to warn the new arrival about the loo and, in his state of exhilaration, he had tugged over-enthusiastically on the chain. The cistern promptly fell on his head and knocked him out. He was removed on a stretcher and put on the next convoy home. Having survived the worst the enemy could do, it was in Murmansk he met his Waterloo.

To help keep us on an even keel, every six months or so, with a bit of luck, we were granted leave in Moscow. When my turn came David arrived from Polyarnoe to relieve me and my companion on the journey was to be the Pay-Lieutenant.

Murmansk had been a total disillusionment, but it could not, I felt, be representative of Russia. It was, after all, on the outermost edge of the Soviet empire and even the locals called it *Kry zemli*, the edge of the world – we had another name for it. Surely it would all be very different in Moscow.

So, one morning in May, with hopes high and the Mission jeep piled with crates of food and drink, we left for the station. The distance to Moscow was over twelve hundred miles and that meant three and a half days of camping out in the com-

129

partment, as there was no restaurant car. We found the train already besieged by a swarm of Russians pushing and shoving each other in a bid to get on. Steam and smoke seeped from the huge, five foot gauge engine and lay in heavy swathes among the crowd. It was quite a performance clumsily clambering up the four iron steps to the compartment with our wooden crates and other baggage. We were privileged to travel 'soft' or first-class, but ten out of the twelve coaches were 'hard'. We were also favoured by having a whole compartment with four bunks to ourselves.

Although it was May snow was still falling in a desultory way and we were glad of our sheepskin-lined coats. Soon, with much snorting and clanking, the train disengaged itself from the station and headed south, Moscow bound.

We would be getting the opportunity of a look at quite a large section of the interior of Russia. At one time the Germans had succeeded in cutting this line, but now it was restored. Perhaps partly owing to the condition of the track, our speed averaged little more than twenty-five miles an hour, with a maximum of forty. Knowing the language, I was hoping to have the chance of talking to some ordinary Russians, as, with any luck, the green capped NKVD[1] men might not be so omnipresent as they were in Murmansk.

Our first stop was Kola itself, one of the oldest inhabited places in the Arctic Circle and just five miles down the line. There were a lot of oldish-looking wooden houses with high pointed gables and steeply slanted roofs, a small church with onion-shaped domes, the door of which was boarded up, a few drab-looking peasants and mangy goats and that was it. On a hundred miles to Kirovsk, a small township with a school, then to Appetit, where the fertiliser comes from which is a big Russian export. Nothing much to see here except oxen pulling ancient wagons.

We stayed in the corridor for quite a time – gazing out as Russia rolled by. Soon the train skirted the frozen expanse of Lake Imandra on our right and halted briefly at Kandalaksha, where the railway was only a few miles from the Finnish front. Deep craters on either side of the line showed the attention the Germans had been paying it. So, the vastness of this land unrolled in unrelieved sameness of wastes of snow and stunted trees – with just a few wooden shacks and near-primitive in-

[1] Now known as the KGB.

130

habitants. It began to pall on us and so we turned away from the window; we knew Russia would still be there in a few hours' time.

The compartment was shabby, but spacious and reasonably clean and comfortable. This was more than one could say for the lavatory accommodation provided at the end of the corridor. Although steeled by some months of Russian sanitation, I quailed at this. There was a small cast-iron seat and ancient wash basin and, as I opened the door, a spatter of water came down on me from a tank above. With every jolt of the train, and there were many, a ducking had to be endured. This was tiresome when seated on the stool. I suppose an umbrella would have been the ideal answer, but a raincoat draped round the shoulders helped a bit. The worst of it was that the lavatory did not, and evidently had not flushed for days – if ever. We over-industrialised British are perhaps fussy. Russia is a peasant nation and their nerves are stronger. The characteristic smell I found throughout the land was compounded of unwashed bodies, excrement and cheap tobacco with a touch of garlic thrown in.

On emerging from the loo I found a group of Red Army lads standing by the door. They were the usual types with short-cropped hair, round rosy faces, small deep-set blue eyes and crinkled foreheads, but they looked smart and clean in their tightly-belted, fawn-coloured greatcoats. There was no doubt of their friendliness; they were grinning and passing from one to the other a pint bottle of eau-de-cologne. Oddly enough, it hadn't occurred to me before that it was drinkable but, as they explained, their vodka had given out. What they wanted from me was a packet of English cigarettes. I handed them some and, in exchange, one of them unfastened from his belt a short hunting knife in a leather sheath which he insisted on my taking. At that time, cigarettes were only for the privileged in Russia. The ordinary serving man used to get a monthly issue of *mahorka* – greenish-yellow, powerful smelling, powdery substance, which came from anywhere except the leaf of the tobacco plant. This was then rolled in newspaper and smoked with some kind of satisfaction. So, when travelling, all British personnel had learnt to carry a plentiful supply of English cigarettes as this helped greatly to improve the atmosphere and was essential if any small service was required.

My companion, Lieutenant Fry, or 'Sec' as I always called

131

him, had started to prepare a meal when I got back to the compartment. Simple enough fare. We lived on corned beef and bread followed by tinned plums. In our crates we also had small tins of solidified 'meths' on which we could heat baked beans or brew some tea. The staff looking after the coach consisted of two youngish girl attendants and the inevitable man-in-charge or *nachalnik*. They looked after us extremely well, casting interested eyes at our stacks of tinned food, chocolate and cigarettes.

Having been deprived of feminine company for months, we too looked with some interest at the girls. The first was rather unprepossessing. Her face was coarse and her hair hung dank and matted from under a blue beret. Her colleague had a fresh face, blue eyes and a kindly expression. A full figure like almost all Soviet girls, but with it a refinement of manner which distinguished her. She said her name was Klava and she made up our bunks for us, and left us with a smile.

Outside in the corridor two Red Army officers seemed keen to have a natter. One was a major, big and hearty with a black, stubbly chin – he was puffed up and pleased with himself – and wore the Order of Lenin and the Fatherland War. The other, a captain, was younger with a pale, thoughtful face. Rather daringly, they invited me back to their compartment and suggested a drink. They promptly brought out from under the seat a bottle of vodka and slices of fat pork. I collected a bottle of Scotch and we were in business. Drinking vessels were white china breakfast cups. The Major promptly filled one with vodka and passed it to me. I filled his and the Captain's with Scotch. In Russia a drink is always preceded with a toast, so after 'a speedy victory' and '*do dna*', meaning bottoms up, we gulped it down.

They then began to talk more freely. All Russians were so deprived by their Press and radio of news from outside that they were insatiably curious and question followed question. The Major was particularly keen to know why the Communist Party was unsuccessful in England. At this point, the Captain whispered to him that the question was dangerous. I quickly reassured him and did my best to explain, as tactfully as possible. I noticed the Major getting uneasy and then he quickly moved over to the door and slid it back. Standing right outside was one of the secret-police chaps apparently admiring the scenery. So, that party was over.

I stood in the corridor to smoke a last cigarette before turning in for the night. At the far end of the coach stood a woman with a white knitted scarf drawn over her long fair hair. She approached me at once and asked for bread. Her monthly ration card was lost and the authorities would not issue her with another. How was she supposed to live till the end of the month, another twenty-two days? There were all too many question marks like that in wartime Russia. I was wondering what I could do for her, when the *nachalnik* appeared and she vanished like a shadow.

Next morning, there was nothing to be seen from the carriage window but a flat brown expanse of plain and scrub. In an hour or two, this gave way to a forest zone. Mile upon mile of pine and fir – we looked for signs of animal life but there were none. At intervals, we passed isolated anti-aircraft emplacements and sympathised with the comrades who manned them. The White Sea stretched away endlessly on our left and soon the train ran into the wooden station at Kem, a small township standing almost on its shores. This was a notorious place of exile in Czarist days. So little had the prisoners thought of it then that they named it by the initial letters of the three coarsest Russian words they knew – KEM. Now many ragged peasants were thronging round the train. They hoped to do some bartering, but had little to trade with except a few red berries and some small bottles of goats' milk. There were pitiful children with bare feet and gaunt white faces staring up at us, as they begged in weak, but persistent voices for *hleb*. Millions must have been without bread in Russia at that time.

On waking the next morning we were passing through a great open plain. From time to time, we saw an ancient peasant woman carrying a bundle and walking away up a cart-track leading apparently to nowhere – just an endless and empty horizon in front of her. People in Russia sometimes seemed like pieces of driftwood on the expanse of a vast sea.

By afternoon, we had arrived at the principal stop – the provincial town and railway junction of Vologda. They said there was to be a wait for two hours and Sec and I were curious to see something of a town deep inside Russia, so off we went, although a little scared that the train might leave without us. One never quite knew what might happen.

We set off up a rough, cobbled road; on either side were pavements of rickety boards raised over a sea of black mud.

Soon we reached a square with a market. The goods were displayed on trestle tables, behind which sat peasant women with lines etched deep into their faces, and in ragged clothes. This was evidently a black market for food. It consisted mainly of corn, small buns, scraps of cheese and salted fish. There were also a few very small eggs priced at twenty roubles each. At that time, there were only officially forty-eight roubles to the pound, but, as we hadn't seen fresh eggs for months, we bought one each. Shop windows were nearly all empty, except for pictures of Lenin, Stalin and Molotov. The only buildings we saw of any note were churches which were in a surprisingly good state of preservation, except that they had boards nailed across all the doors. Our uniforms caused a little stir among the crowd, although most of them seemed too exhausted and preoccupied with their quest for food to react very much. Under their dumb gaze, we returned to the station and, mercifully, the train was still there.

Soon after leaving Vologda, I got into conversation with a middle-aged civilian who said he was an engineer and had once visited Glasgow. He was intelligent and extremely friendly. We talked about the war and, to my surprise, he freely admitted that Stalin had left Russian's defences totally unprepared and was therefore to blame for the early reverses, when – in a flash his whole manner changed and pointing out some buildings he said at the top of his voice: 'You see those factories – we have to thank Stalin for those!'

I realised this was for the benefit of the green-capped NKVD man who had sidled up as we were talking. To make it quite clear that he had better watch his step the NKVD man asked the civilian pointedly: 'Well comrade, how is your political and military morale?' And that was that.

In the early hours of the morning, while I was still sleeping, we crossed the Volga. All the time the country was getting greener and there were more signs of cultivation. Eighty miles out of Moscow, our steam locomotive was changed for an electric one. I looked out hopefully on to the station at Zagorsk for any signs of improvement, but it looked much the same. The same drabness and poverty ; barefooted children ; ragged people carrying bundles. Strung across the station building, the same red banners proclaiming the new Holy Trinity of Lenin, Stalin and Molotov.

On the platform the great *kipyatok* scramble was on. *Kipyatok* is the Russian word for boiling water and this was the one thing obtainable on the stations. It was greatly in demand by all the passengers for a variety of reasons – principally for making tea and shaving.

Then, on to Moscow through a green fertile plain with many low wooden houses, goats and cows. Every inch of available land seemed to be cultivated and everyone was digging.

12 Moscow, Leningrad, Kronstadt

Feeling battered after the journey, we were met at the station by a smooth-looking RNVR Lieutenant. A large black Humber whisked us through Moscow's wide, almost empty, streets; the pavements, on the other hand, were thronged with hordes of shabby folk hurrying along, heads buried in their coat collars. At the Admiral's flat on the Arbat, where we were to stay for the next six days, a long soak in a hot bath helped us to feel more human. Then, still dazed with all these city comforts, we were driven to the British Military Mission housed in the former Czechoslovak Embassy on the Maly Haritonefsky. This appeared so palatial I could scarcely believe it was real.

We were introduced to several British Army officers, among them a Captain Lunghi, who spoke perfect Russian and was to look after us that evening. Hugh Lunghi, who after the war joined the BBC, was a dark, slim, extremely good-looking young officer who seemed to have Moscow thoroughly taped. That evening he arranged for us to go to a Tchaikovsky concert in the Bolshoi Zal – a splendid concert hall. I sat there in a dream listening to the surging sound of the Sixth Symphony, in a brilliant performance conducted by Ivanov.

The visits to the Bolshoi Theatre were even more out-of-this-world. This great organisation with its many thousands of State employees had been preserved intact from pre-Revolutionary days. Here the Soviet citizen, if he was lucky enough to get a ticket, could be transported to a world of colour, spectacle and pageantry, so lacking in his ordinary life. It was all on such a vast scale: the classical façade, the foyer and the immense, plushy interior with six great circles and private boxes.

The productions were lavish and breathtaking. I saw two ballets – *The Sleeping Beauty* and *Swan Lake*. In both, the overall technical excellence of the dancing was the finest I had ever seen, but I did not like the realism in the stage effects. Ballet is a world of fantasy: overdo the realism and the poetry and magic are lost. The one opera I saw was Borodin's *Prince Igor*. A sombre, opulent production with superb spectacle and singing, but the high spot was the wildly sensual, barbaric excitement of the Polovtsian Dances. Covent Garden could never match the raw, primitive sex that came flooding across the footlights that night. The audience, composed for the most part of sex-starved servicemen from various fronts, made the atmosphere the more electric.

In the interval, they streamed into the huge foyer for a promenade. Forming in lines six abreast, they circled round sometimes linking arms. Everyone was orderly and restrained. The Red Army officers had gold and bronze medals jingling from their chests ; the shoulders of their uniforms were adorned with Czarist-style epaulettes bearing gold or silver stars. For the most part, they were shortish and looked tough with cropped, bullet heads. Their women paled in comparison and many had blotchy complexions, due perhaps to lack of vitamins. The sobriety of the crowd may have been partly explained by the price of drinks. At a near-deserted bar, I was astonished to find that a bottle of beer cost the equivalent of nearly one pound sterling.

But for me the most lasting memory of the Russian theatre was seeing a production of *The Cherry Orchard*. This was at the famous Arts Theatre and since then I have never been able quite to accept London productions of Chekhov. However well they may be performed, they seem to miss the essential flavour of Russia. They cannot capture the smell, the frowstiness, the humour or the despair. And the sets usually look to me far too clean and smart.

On the Sunday afternoon of our stay in Moscow, a number of us visited a *dacha* twenty miles out of the city. In midsummer it becomes unbearably hot in the capital, so the big Party officials and members of the Soviet Establishment have these weekend cottages to which they can escape. The Admiral had one put at his disposal.

As we drove out along a broad highway, on either side in the fields, peasant women with bare feet and head scarves were digging ; many of the children too were unshod – and this only fifteen minutes from the Kremlin.

Arriving at the *dacha* at about five o'clock, we found the Admiral's secretary in a state. He explained that Admiral Archer had changed into civvies and gone for a Sunday afternoon walk in the woods alone. He had been due back at four o'clock, so he was already one hour behind schedule.

137

Just as we were thinking of forming a search-party, there was a commotion at the door and the large, bulldog frame of the Admiral hove into view. He was wearing a tweed jacket, grey flannels and a purple expression. Behind him were two tiny Red Army sentries with their Tommy-guns stuck in the small of his back. It seemed he had been arrested in the woods, questioned at an Army post, and marched back, under close escort. The Admiral wasn't best pleased, but had really only himself to blame.

After tea, some of us also wandered about on the springy green turf in the surrounding woods. At one point, we saw a small, ragged boy with tousled hair stuck half-way up a fir tree. I think he was after a kestrel's nest. In my diary, I noted seeing thrushes, pied wagtails, magpies and a wren, but in those days my interest in birdlife had not been sparked off and it is tantalising to think now of the number of species I must have missed.

We passed herds of goats with white kids ; an old peasant woman leading a black sheep on a string and a little girl in a pinafore with her fair hair in braids over her head. She was clutching a small bunch of lily-of-the-valley.

That afternoon was one of my pleasantest memories of the Moscow trip – an ageless, pastoral scene. I remember too with pleasure a visit to the British Embassy for lunch the following day. A huge building, once the home of a sugar king. It stands back from the road and has a fine view of the Kremlin. In the small back garden, His Excellency the Ambassador, Sir Archibald Clark Kerr, wearing just a singlet and grey flannels, was digging away like mad.

I was told that before he had last gone on leave, he had asked Stalin at a Kremlin reception whether there was any personal gift he would like brought back for him from Britain. Without hesitation, Stalin replied that he would like a genuine, English briar pipe. In London, the Ambassador duly called at Dunhills in St James's. The urbane assistant regretted that owing to shortage of the right kind of wood, they were making no new pipes at the moment. Sir Archibald explained that he did not want to disappoint Stalin. There was a pause ; the assistant then gave a polite cough: 'Excuse my asking, sir – would that be Mr *Joseph* Stalin? Oh well, in that case, I think perhaps something could be arranged.' So, Stalin got his pipe.

Our visit to the capital had been a great experience, but we weren't too sorry to leave. After a long stay in the north, we felt out of place in the Moscow scene.

Back at Kola Inlet, the auxiliary Royal Naval Hospital was now in being at Vaenga Bay and that is where I was based for some months. Vaenga lay a few miles below Murmansk on the eastern shore of the inlet. At the head of the bay was a wooden pier, where two destroyers could berth. Ashore were a few barrack-like blocks in one of which the hospital was housed. It had twenty beds and the staff consisted of Surgeon-Lieutenant-Commander Jenner, Surgeon-Lieutenant Tom Simpson and the 'Toothy', who was Surgeon-Lieutenant John Matthews, a gentle giant, later 'capped' several times for England at Rugby Football. There was also a Chief Petty Officer and about a dozen ratings. I was the only Russian speaker, so all dealings with the local authorities fell to me.

Perhaps because we were a small, isolated British community, it was a wonderfully happy set-up – and although there was an almost total lack of amenities, I can remember no serious discord of any kind.

Lying at anchor in the bay was the battleship *Royal Sovereign*, which the Navy had presented to the Russians, in place of a share in the Italian fleet, which had recently surrendered, and to which the Soviet Navy had laid a claim. I remember talking to some of the Russian ratings, who had been in the skeleton crew sent to Scapa to sail her back. While there, they had visited some Scottish towns, and these had been a tremendous eye-opener to them. They could not get over the fact that consumer goods of all kinds were openly displayed on shop counters and that nobody stole anything. The Russians had insisted that the British battleship should be fully stocked with provisions before sailing and these had been an eye-opener to them too. One of our Petty Officers, who had been on board, saw some of the Soviet ratings even dipping spoons into jars of blood plasma – they thought it was jam.

Royal Sovereign came up from Scapa with a strong escort force under the command of Rear-Admiral McGrigor. He flew his flag in the cruiser *Diadem* and there were in addition two carriers and sixteen destroyers. The Soviet Northern Fleet was intensely proud of its latest acquisition and she was promptly renamed *Arkhangelsk*.

Her function was to serve as a training ship for the big fleet the Russians were even then determined to develop. Some weeks after her arrival, in the middle of the night we heard the sound of heavy gunfire. It was clear that *Arkhangelsk* was pooping off with everything she'd got and we presumed she was under attack by enemy planes.

That night she notched up her first kill under the Red Flag, when an aircraft was seen coming down in flames. The rejoicing on board was in no way shared by the six luckless Americans who had formed its crew. Flying from Scotland on a special mission, they had sustained damage over northern Norway and so decided to fly on to what they thought to be the friendly Russian airfield of Graznaya, near Kola Inlet. Five of them had managed to bale out successfully, but only to meet with a less than friendly reception on the ground. Russian sentries posted among the rocky hills rounded them up ; then roughed them up and took them in for questioning. The Americans, to their great relief, finally ended up with us and we did our best to entertain them.

In the summer months of perpetual daylight, the Admiralty decided it was too hazardous to run the convoys. With reduced activity and no mail from home, Naval Party 100, as we were designated, slid further and further round the bend. As a Russian speaker, I was luckier than most and managed to keep reasonably busy.

In June I visited the Archangel base, taking passage in a merchantman, *Fort Vérchères*, whose Captain, Dixie Dean, was a friend of ours at Vaenga. He was a great character in the true tradition of British sea captains, but he certainly had plenty of worries. His chief stoker was one of his problems. The trouble was he kept on spitting blood, but then when he came up on deck he leapt about all over the place like a two year old. As Dixie put it, 'He must have a kind of galloping consumption!'

He was instructive on the subject of the corruption of port officials all over the world. In some South American ports it seemed there were Rat Regulations. The official would come on board, pull a handkerchief from his pocket and promptly shake out some rat droppings on to the snowy white deck. With a roguish smile he would then announce a fine of fifty pesos. When the money was handed over, the official would shamelessly scoop up the droppings in his handkerchief and replace them in his pocket. As Dixie said, it was as well to know the conventions of the game, then everybody was kept happy.

There was a delay before sailing from Murmansk – as four seamen had gone adrift in the town somewhere, but they made it with minutes to spare. Archangel lies 400 miles to the south-east, but unlike Kola Inlet, the White Sea on which it stands freezes over in winter. Dixie wasn't too happy about this trip as there was no escort and, with continuous daylight, he knew his ship would be open to attack. U-boats had taken to lurking in the area of the harbour entrance off Polyarnoe and a lone merchantman would be just what they were hoping to see.

However, in the event all went well, and three days later we entered the Gourlo, which is like a throat of water leading from the Barents to the White Sea. Ashore, instead of the grey, barren rocks of Kola Inlet there was quite a lot of vegetation and many wooden houses. We moored at a boom surrounded by a sea of logs. There seemed to be timber everywhere and I soon found that Archangel itself was a town built almost entirely of wood.

Captain Walker was the Senior British Naval Officer and had his headquarters in a building known as Norway House. It all looked pretty good to me; there was an absence of bomb damage and an awareness that this place had developed over the centuries. But here too there were rats as big as Alsatian puppies scuttling along the raised wooden pavements in broad daylight.

It was a reminder of Russia's past when Dixie Dean and I were shown one of the few Orthodox churches still open at that time. We found it in a village on the outskirts of Archangel. As we entered, a christening party was gathered round the font. A priest suddenly appeared from a low door set in the wall. His face was pale green, his hair dank and falling round his shoulders, his beard long and matted. He looked as though he had just crept out from under a stone.

While the christening was proceeding, at the other end of the church an old lady was waiting to be buried. She lay in an open coffin, as is the practice in Russia. Her face was yellow and no bigger than a man's fist; on her head was a tiny white lace cap. That afternoon in this small Archangel church the ceremonies surrounding birth and death were still being celebrated in the age-old way.

Dixie's premonition of trouble came true, when he was called back to his ship. One of his seamen, trying to clamber over the floating logs to reach a launch, had slipped and fallen through a gap. It was hours before his body was found, and he lies buried now up in Archangel. In addition to this fatality, there was a case of attempted murder and arson for Dixie to sort out, when the cook ran amok with a carving knife and then tried to set the ship on fire. We afterwards berthed at Ekono-miya to load some cargo and returned to Murmansk, without further incident.

For some time one of the most serious dangers to the escort ships had been a torpedo the U-boats were using, which was known to us as 'Gnat'. This was fitted with a listening device at the head, so that it homed directly on to the noise made by a ship's propellers. Thus, ordinary evasive action was of no avail. As a counter to this a noise-maker was devised called 'Foxer', which the escorts towed astern, so that the torpedo would home on that, but it was not the whole answer and some losses were still sustained. It was therefore of the greatest interest to the Admiralty when they learnt that the Russians had fished up from the Gulf of Finland a U-boat complete with the latest Schnorkel equipment and a Gnat torpedo.

Representations were made forthwith at the highest level and, after much prevarication, the Soviets agreed that a British Naval team might be allowed to inspect it. As I had a know-ledge of German and Russian, it was my good fortune to be a member of the party. The man in charge was our Chief Engineer, Lieut.-Commander John Pearson RN and the Flag-Lieutenant and I were to travel with him to Moscow and on to Leningrad and Kronstadt. John Pearson was the ideal travelling companion – a man of wide interests and with an enormous sense of fun.

The three and a half day journey to Moscow was again fascinating with the opportunity it gave of meeting a cross-section of people. The train was three hours late arriving there so we had a scramble to catch the night train for Leningrad, the Red Arrow. This was quite luxurious compared with the one on the Murmansk run and the coaches had Victorian refinements such as antimacassars on the seat cushions. From the station at Leningrad we were driven straight to the Astoria Hotel.

Leningrad has a more European feel about it than Moscow, although in neither city did I see any bomb damage remotely to compare with that suffered by London. Perhaps the Germans had wanted to take them intact. At dinner in a special suite 'Flags' was taken ill with stomach pains and was unable to accompany us to the famous Mariinsky Theatre, renamed the Kirov, and a performance of *Sleeping Beauty*. Again at the theatre the atmosphere was much more European and the ballerina Kirillova was enchanting as Aurora.

Back at the hotel afterwards for supper we were joined by a Russian scientist, who had been working on the U-boat project. Although a member of the Soviet élite, he knew almost nothing of conditions in countries outside his own and less than nothing about British and American contributions to the war. This was not surprising as the only occasion when the war outside Russia was covered in their Press was on 'D' Day itself. Otherwise, a couple of inches space on the back page was all the Soviet citizen was told.

I turned in feeling rather weary and glanced through a copy of *Izvestiya*, or 'The News', one of the national dailies, the other being *Pravda* or 'Truth'. Russians, I found, held their papers in little regard. It was often said there was no news in *Pravda* and no truth in *Izvestiya*. As I was looking through it drowsily, the telephone rang beside my bed. A sexy female voice purred into my astonished ear. Speaking almost perfect English it was asking what I was doing and suggesting we should meet. When I said I was reading the paper, the voice chortled that Russian papers were so boring they weren't worth reading anyway. This was, of course, an indisputable fact, but it was pretty clear to me that I was just being tried out by one of the NKVD girls. She was altogether too obvious, so I was able to replace the receiver with only a tiny twinge of regret.

An early start next morning for Kronstadt – the holy of holies of the Soviet Baltic Fleet. The launch which took John Pearson and me there was carefully blacked out, in case we should see any of the Russian warships berthed nearby. We were probably the first British Naval officers to be allowed in Kronstadt since the Revolution. After lunch in the Officers' Club, we were driven to the submarine pen, where the salvaged U-boat was housed.

To our utter dismay, the two items of principal interest had been removed. There were no Gnat torpedoes nor Schnorkel fittings to be seen. The wires were soon buzzing to Moscow, as the Chief reported on the situation. It was clear that more would have to be said on the Churchill-Stalin level. Meantime, all we could do was to crawl all over that U-boat and note any other points of interest. Among other things we guessed the Germans must be using half-trained crews, as screwed to the back of the door in the ratings 'heads' was a chart of the morse code, so they could learn it, while they contemplated on the stool.

That night we spent in the Kronstadt Officers' Club. It was quite a surprise to the Chief and me when at seven in the morning there was a knock on the door and there stood a 'Wren' of the Soviet Baltic Fleet wanting to know whether she could do us now. It was the first time either of us had been shaved by a blonde with a cut-throat. She made a good enough job of it, but I couldn't imagine this happening at Portsmouth.

Feeling cheated by events we returned to Moscow to report and await developments. We waited a week, compiled our report, then all we could do was return to the north, until heavy pressure could be put on the Russians at the highest level.

It wasn't until February 1945, three months later, that Churchill was able to lean heavily enough on Stalin to make him relent. Again, Pearson and I travelled down from Murmansk to meet up in Moscow with three high-powered Admiralty scientists flown out from London. One was a tall, thin, sandy-haired young man, who walked with a slight stoop. He obviously had an immense sense of fun, which frequently burst out into a high-pitched laugh more like a bray. I liked him immediately and he seemed amused by me. I had by this time been up in North Russia for over a year and probably looked pretty wild with a curly black beard I had recently grown. The young physicist said his name was Francis Crick. Perhaps I should have treated him with a greater degree of awe, if I had realised that he was to become one of the greatest scientific brains of our age. In 1962, with James Watson and Maurice Wilkins, Francis was awarded the Nobel Prize for Medicine and Physiology for his work in cracking the genetic code known as DNA. Many scientists would say this was the most important discovery since Mendel's law of heredity.

This time in Leningrad the Russians at last delivered the goods. Their scientists, over the months, had assiduously been unravelling the secrets of the German homing device and the results of their work were now put at our disposal. In the grim Peter Paul Fortress, where the submarine laboratories were situated, Francis and I spent the next fortnight pouring over their conclusions and tracing the intricate electrical circuits involved.

We got a lighter moment from time to time. My knowledge of electrical engineering was almost nil, so when I came upon the Russian expression *gnezdo holastyakov* I said to Francis: 'This can't possibly be right. It says something about connecting up with a *gnezdo holastyakov*, which means "a nest of bachelors". That sounds to me more like the homing device of a frustrated female than a torpedo!'

Francis gave one of his high-pitched brays and explained that 'a nest of bachelors' is a term used for a certain type of electrical plug.

In between times, we looked at Leningrad in the snow. A cold, grey, elegant city of granite standing as though suspended in time, its present day citizens seeming irrelevant to it with their dull eyes and felt boots. Planned by Peter the Great as a 'window on the west', his St Petersburg rose over the bodies of tens of thousands of serfs, who died while building it in the northern swamps. He and, later, Catherine the Great commissioned some of Europe's finest architects, among them the Scot Cameron, to construct it. Charles Cameron, although famous in the Soviet Union, is still little known in Britain. He was a great enthusiast for the Palladian style of architecture and wrote a book about it. In 1779 the Empress Catherine, having presumably read his book, summoned him to St Petersburg and gave him *carte blanche*. His success there was outstanding, especially at Tsarskoe Selo, which became one of Catherine's favourite palaces. He had a great career in Russia for twenty years and yet remained unrecognised at home; in fact, the Architects' Club in London refused to have him as a member.

We also saw the great Winter Palace with over a thousand rooms and facing it the Guard's Memorial – a magnificent triumphal arch commemorating the Napoleonic Wars and now renamed the Red Army Arch. We saw the red brick Summer Palace and the Kazansky Cathedral, off the Nevsky Prospect, with the words 'Religion is the opium of the people' over its entrance. Then there was the solid pile of the Isakovsky Cathedral built by a French architect, who had seen St Paul's. When completed, the interior had such a lack of light that he is said to have committed suicide. Everywhere there were women muffled in scarves clearing the snow with long wooden shovels and tiny children cocooned against the cold, as they were drawn along on mini-toboggans.

When our work was completed in Leningrad, we spent a further fortnight in Moscow compiling a report for the Admiralty – and that was that. Pearson and I entrained for Murmansk with Francis coming to the station to see us off and then he and his colleagues returned to London.

Back at Kola Inlet the worst danger to the convoys in the last months of the war was off the harbour entrance. The Schnorkel-equipped U-boats were able to move closer inshore, and since Asdic conditions were poor in that area, it was necessary to send escorts ahead of the convoy to keep the U-boats down, while the merchant ships were lining up to enter. These counter measures were reasonably effective, although the corvette *Denbigh Castle* was torpedoed just as she was entering the harbour, and the following day two merchantmen on passage from Archangel were sunk in the same place.

Unlike today, the Soviet Navy was then very weak and of little use in keeping the U-boats away. What a transformation since then. Russia's Navy now rivals America's and far surpasses it in the numbers of submarines. This is an entirely new factor in world strategy. Some people in the West seem puzzled as to why the Soviets support the burden of such a huge fleet when in Russia itself there are so many shortages. The Russians are a far-seeing people. Not for nothing are they a nation of chess players.

Lenin once said, 'So long as we have not won over the whole world, so long as we remain weaker, both economically and militarily, than the capitalist world, we must hold on to the following law: to make the best use of the contradictions and antitheses among the imperialists . . . but as soon as we are strong enough to strike down capitalism as a whole, we shall immediately take it by the scruff of the neck.' There is now no doubt at least of that naval and military strength.

Lenin's heart would have rejoiced at the words of Admiral Gorshkov, C-in-C Soviet Navy when in February 1970 he was able to say: 'Our Navy, together with the strategic missile forces, has become the Supreme High Command's most important means of solving strategic tasks.'

The grimmest aspect of life for all British personnel up there during the war was the feeling of isolation. If a Russian citizen were seen talking to a foreigner, he or she was immediately battened on by the NKVD. There was a typical instance at Vaenga when a young Petty Officer had a birthday party. A Russian girl attended it, but soon after disappeared. It was learnt that she had been arrested by the NKVD, put on a lorry, driven forty kilometres out into the Arctic wastes and dumped there.

There were also incidents when Russians tried to stow away in merchantships in the docks. Even if a comrade did succeed in escaping, the secret police promptly arrested any family he had left behind and they were then heavily sentenced. In the old days in Russia, there was a saying: 'We all walk under God' – in wartime Russia it was certainly: 'We all walk under the NKVD.'

So it was with a feeling of unmitigated relief that in April, after nearly eighteen months up in North Russia, I learnt that I was to return to the UK in a convoy at the end of that month.

It had been an interesting, but unutterably depressing experience. I remember John Pearson saying, in one of our innumerable discussions in those endless Arctic nights, 'This country is like a flower-bed in process of preparation. At the moment we don't like the smell of manure, but in time it will produce fine flowers and fruit.'

For individuals used to a Western way of life it seemed to me the system had nothing to offer. I only knew that few Britishers, whether Naval officers, ratings or merchant seamen, who had spent any time up in North Russia, would ever again harbour delusions about Communism or the Soviet system.

To fox the U-boats, the day before the convoy sailed, escort vessels made an intensive search of the area off the harbour entrance. Eleven U-boats were on patrol there and two of them were caught and sunk, but unhappily the frigate *Goodall* was torpedoed and thus became the last victim of the northern run.

I returned in the escort carrier *Campania*, which had become an old friend of ours up in Kola. Even in those last days of the war in Europe, we expected attack by U-boats or torpedo bombers but, in the event, all ships reached home safely. It was 7 May 1945.

Perched at the top of the mast on the launch bringing me ashore at Scapa was a huge, black-backed gull yelling his head off. He looked a bit crazy but, above all, he looked free.

13 The Prostrate Reich

I looked around me feeling rather like Rip Van Winkle. Compared with Kola, Scapa seemed a land of plenty ; but somehow even the Roman lettering on advertisements and notices looked strange after eighteen months of exposure to the alphabet in Cyrillic. In the tiny Post Office I queued happily enough to send arrival telegrams on a day when all the wires were buzzing. Then, a number of us piled into the train and much gin was drunk, but with reasonable decorum, because most of us were thinking about how things would be at home.

It seemed almost corny to arrive right on cue at Euston Station on VE-night itself. People were whooping it up all over the place and it was some time before I could get a taxi. Then, at last, I found one prepared to trundle me with all my gear through the shabby London streets, thronged with great crowds and uniforms of all kinds, to Charing Cross. From there to Croydon, where my parents were still living in the same block of flats.

They were well and I brought out the few little gifts I had stowed away – lacquer cigarette boxes, Russian dolls in peasant costumes and a hand-carved wooden bear. And afterwards, how marvellous it was to sleep in a proper bed.

Next day I decided to remove my beard, which I had worn for about eight months, and to which I had become considerably attached. My face, thus suddenly revealed, looked a pale shade of green and my chin seemed to have given up trying – I swear it had receded a good two inches. No wonder a former girl-friend recoiled.

It was a strange time. Everyone was feeling battered after nearly six years of war and in our hearts we knew nothing would ever be the same again. I avoided getting drawn into discussions on Russia. Most people had such a rosy, preconceived idea of life there, which they had picked up largely from our Press, that it seemed a shame to disillusion them. In any case, only events could do that.

Over the radio Churchill was now appearing in the role of Conservative Party leader and it was rather embarrassing to

148

hear the old warrior in the opening speech of his election campaign, as he indulged in some domestic political mud-slinging and tried to cast the Labour leader, Clement Attlee, as the head of a British Gestapo. The best thing about that speech was Winnie's pronunciation of Gestapo, which, as was his wont with German words, he thoroughly anglicised and so it came out as JESTAPO with lingering emphasis on the last syllable. In this Party role it was difficult to take him seriously and of course the voters didn't. But, it was all rather sad.

So, I did not really mind too much when the few weeks' leave was over and the Admiralty told me to report to an address in Princes Gardens, Kensington. There, I joined a Naval party about to set out for the British headquarters at Minden in our zone of Germany.

From Tilbury we crossed to Ostend in a tank-landing craft and then formed part of a road convoy of jeeps and lorries to Brussels, by way of Ghent. The war in Europe had been over only about a month, but in that early summer of 1945 Belgium, in spite of all it had been through, seemed to me a land smiling in the sun. The crops and livestock looked good, there were few outward signs of malnutrition and the roads were in reasonable condition too.

Brussels was a city with swarms of pretty girls in bright summer frocks but we had to press on. Nearing the Dutch frontier, everyone seemed to be riding bicycles – but none of them had tyres. I suppose all available rubber had been taken for the German war machine. The rims of the wheels clattered gaily enough over the cobbles, but it must have been uncomfortable for the riders – at least there were no hills. That night we slept out in the open in a field on the German frontier. It was a warm night with a soft breeze and a sky full of stars.

Germany was all dust and devastation. In Wesel there was not a building still intact. People were standing about looking stunned and hopeless. I saw several emaciated old women barefoot and covered in dust, which hung like a grey pall over everything. In between the horrors of the flattened, rubble-strewn towns, we passed through belts of woodland, so fresh and green and peaceful looking that it rested our eyes to gaze at them. Coming towards us there were little parties of refugees, nearly all women and children, piled up on farm wagons and hand carts. It seemed a ridiculous unequal confrontation. Dust-covered, grim-faced, uniformed men entering the vanquished land, peopled apparently by nothing but pathetic looking women and children. Our road convoy with its motorcycle outriders slowed down as we passed a group of them.

I can still see one woman now. She must have been about thirty-five with dark hair blowing about a sunburnt face and smiling blue eyes. There she sat perched up high on a small wagon with bundles all round her, a battered dog by her side and four ragged children. It was difficult to regard her as a defeated enemy. She looked to me an attractive and brave woman coping gaily against all the odds so – I winked at her.

Then the motor bikes revved up and the conquerors roared on. There were at that time of course strict non-fraternisation regulations. Allied Forces were supposed to ignore all Germans except those on official business. When we passed a bunch of charming looking girls clearing rubble, a Naval friend riding with me in the jeep said, 'Pretty girls, but they're bastards!' Then he added, rather ruefully, 'I'm sure they're bastards,' as though he were trying to convince himself.

After a short stay at the Minden headquarters, another officer and I were told to report to Wilhelmshaven. The town itself was a mass of rubble and there was a foul smell of death and decay, but the docks were not too badly damaged. Over the whole area there was still a curfew after 10.15 at night. Half the German Navy seemed to be assembled there – the *Nuremberg, Prinz Eugen* and a whole host of destroyers and smaller craft.

For the next year in Germany I was to be involved in the carve-up of their former surface Navy between the allies. The Germans were docility itself and only too anxious to show us everything. I met a number of *Kriegsmarine* officers and they all seemed incredulous that British, American and Russian unity could last. Nothing I could say was going to convince them that we would be able to work for long in amity with the Russians. For a few days I lived aboard a German 'Z' class destroyer. I was the only Britisher with a skeleton German crew and a Russian Naval party to whom they were handing over. Knowing something of both their languages, I was the go-between sorting things out and trying to keep everybody happy. As if that were possible in those circumstances.

Most British personnel seemed uneasy in their role as victors – even the Union Jack, flying over the main entrance of Heine's Hotel in Wilhelmshaven, which was one of the few buildings intact, looked apologetic. It was a miserable little flag and looked ludicrous flapping at the end of a long staff. The most awful thing though was that the Germans were so very anxious to please. One always had the disquieting feeling that it was only necessary to bark an order at them loudly enough and every German in sight would jump to attention.

In fact this actually happened to me on one occasion, I was in a car at the time. I was driving along quietly, when suddenly the horn developed an electrical fault and started blaring away hideously ; nothing I could do would stop it. I was in an area where there were a lot of former German servicemen and they fairly leapt to it, as I swept past feeling rather embarrassed. Perhaps they thought the Commander-in-Chief was passing by.

Another extraordinary thing about the Germans was their eagerness to work. No question of their just hanging about sucking their teeth, as we might have done, had the roles been reversed. At every available moment they were beavering away at something or other. One Wilhelmshaven dockyard matey, who was a skilled carpenter, made me a really splendid wooden chest, which I lugged about with me all over the place for the year of my stay in the prostrate Reich.

Towards the end of July we returned to Minden and with two other officers I heard that we were being posted to Berlin, where the main paper work of the Tripartite Naval Conference would be conducted.

At Helmstedt our car halted at the frontier with the Russian Zone. In spite of its very real implications, the barrier itself was unimpressive – just a roughish pole with the bark still on it and, on either side, what looked like oil-drums filled with concrete and painted red and white. A smallish Union Jack and the notice YOU ARE NOW LEAVING THE BRITISH ZONE OF GERMANY looked final and the sight of the Russian sentries a few yards on gave one a bit of a shock. Here they were right in the heartlands of Western Europe. Stocky, Mongol troops in their rumpled, smock-like Red Army tunics which were none too clean, but one didn't doubt the efficiency of the automatic guns they were clutching to their chests. There was an enormous red flag and then stretching away into alien territory the broad, deserted autobahn.

This was to be the first of many trips I was to make along this road, sometimes in company, sometimes driving alone. It was one of those roads that just seemed to go on for ever –

with pine forests and cornfields alternating. At dusk, particularly, there was a vague feeling of menace and on this first drive we hoped the car wouldn't have a blow-out; it was advisable to keep going because there were roving bands of DPs (Displaced Persons) from Poland and elsewhere, who had been brought to the Reich to provide cheap labour, and were now living off the land. Add some Red Army deserters and other flotsam of the war and, all in all, it was better not to stop for long. We made it eventually in one piece and after much confusion found the Naval Mess. All around in the darkness were spread out the remains of the great city that had been so recently a battlefield. There was a heavy silence; then I heard some random shots – Russians on the spree? A dog barked in the night – he might have been the only living creature left.

Next day we looked around. Our Naval Mess was in a rather splendid villa in Grünewald, the St John's Wood of Berlin. Most houses here were reasonably intact and some of the gardens including ours were still well tended. Clearly, the British were lucky in having some of the best parts of the city in their sector, among them the Kurfürstendamm, where, pre-war, the best shops and restaurants had been. Not that they were there now Berlin was a chilling, numbing sight. Mile upon mile of shattered streets with the jagged outline of buildings reduced to a crazy pattern of battered façades with great piles of rubble behind them. It was too much to take in. Choking grey dust over everything, but worst of all was the smell. The weather was warm and God knows how many thousands of bodies still lay rotting under the ruins. A sweet, nauseous stench hung heavily on the air and nearly made me retch.

Everywhere, pitiful groups of near-starving refugees were moving westwards pushing hand-carts piled high with bundles, their only direction – anywhere away from the Russians. Evidently, the crack Red Army divisions had been speedily withdrawn from the captured city. Perhaps the Soviet Government feared their contamination by contact with the decadent West? Whatever the reason, most of the Russian troops seen in Berlin at this time bore little resemblance to a disciplined army. It seemed inconceivable that this shabby looking lot with their broken-down lorries and horse-carts could have shattered the German war machine, but then one remembered their advantage in numbers of roughly four to one. There were so many tales of rape and brutality that allowing for German

152

exaggeration a very large number of them must have been true. As a result, the Berliners were terrified.

Everywhere among the ruins German women and girls were clearing rubble – the *Trümmerfrauen*. Some were even wearing smart summer frocks. One in particular I remember, with a lissom figure, blonde hair blowing about and an air of elegance, which would have served her well as a fashion model. She was wearing long, grey gloves to pass the bricks on to her neighbour in the human chain. Many of them doubtless soon found protectors among the allied soldiery, but for the moment – no 'fratting'.

The weird thing was how the Berliners were managing to live at all. People emerged from great piles of ruins, where perhaps there was one room left intact. It was close to cave-dwelling and yet in some incredible way they kept clean and gradually brought some order from the chaos.

One of the many unforgettable sights was the famous Tiergarten in front of the gutted Reichstag. Once a deer park, its trees were now reduced to blackened stumps and the statues of Germany's famous men were now ludicrously exposed. Overlooking it all the white slab of the Soviet War Memorial topped by the figure of a huge Russian infantryman. Already, some Berliners were calling it the 'Memorial to the Unknown Looter'. Here and there a burned-out tank was a reminder of the recent battle, although most had been taken away to dumps. Some of the air-raid shelters not blown to bits still had the letters LSR displayed outside. This means *Luftschutzraum*, but in Berlin they said the letters stood for *Lern schnell Russich* (learn Russian quickly). Your true Berliner can be as sharp and chirpy as a cockney and in this he seems quite unlike his countrymen in other parts of Germany.

The evenings I liked least. The main recreation was in the Officers' Clubs, which were fairly luxurious and where there was as much liquor to be had as anyone could drink and at very little cost. Understandably, there was much carousing. For the most part, each of the four Powers stayed put in their own sectors, so not only was there no fratting with the Germans, but not much contact among the allies. For me, the junketing in these approved clubs, although in some ways understandable, seemed slightly obscene with a starving city all around. It was a classic case of man's inhumanity to man. I found it more interesting by far to explore the 'off-limits' night-spots, which sprouted among the rubble and twisted girders of the Kurfürstendamm, where the gaunt, ruined tower of the Gedächtniskirche pointed like a warning to the sky. Here, in these improvised clubs, there was a kind of magic in the flickering light from candles stuck in bottles and at least for a time it was possible to feel a human being again.

My work was in connection with the Tripartite Naval Conference whose function it was to draw up schedules of what was left of the German Navy and to share out the craft between the three allies. The British and Americans weren't very interested, but the Russians having only a small Navy wanted to grab everything they could in order to build up the big fleet they were determined to possess. The war had evidently opened Stalin's eyes to the immense role sea power could play: he well knew the value of the tanks and lorries and aeroplanes the Arctic convoys had brought him and then there was the great armada, which had put the British and Americans in strength across the Channel on D-Day. These lessons were not lost on him.

Sometimes I even wondered if the Russians knew the war was over – or were they getting ready for the next one? Driving through their sector with a Soviet Naval Commander one morning I saw that new slogans were going up for the benefit of their Army of Occupation: 'Be on your guard, the enemy is always listening.'

'What's going on?' I asked. 'Who is the enemy now?' .

The Russian looked a trifle uneasy; I suppose he didn't like to say that Stalin, at least, thought we were.

At the end of July came the news from home that Churchill had lost the election in a Socialist landslide. For once, the Russians were awed. How could a victorious leader of his people be rejected in his hour of glory? I gave up trying to explain to them. Then, two weeks later, came the even greater shock of the atom bombs falling on Japan. This gave the Russians and all of us even greater pause for thought.

Towards the end of that summer, with the paper work and the wrangling round the conference table finished, preparations were made to send inspection parties to all the ports where German craft might be. So it was I found myself sitting one morning in the restaurant at Berlin's Gatow airport having a drink with Admiral Alekseyev of the Soviet Northern Fleet. The Admiral had never been in an aeroplane before and was frankly nervous. He kept on saying to me wistfully, with a twisted sort of smile: *'Loochay moryem'*, which being translated means 'Better by sea'.

In the party I was looking after were also two Russian Naval Captains and a Lieutenant and we were to fly in an RAF Anson from Gatow to Kastrup Airport, Copenhagen. There, we were to board the cruiser *Diadem* and visit all the Danish and Norwegian ports – right up to North Cape.

We duly took our seats in the twin-engined plane, taxied across the airfield and made an excellent take-off. But no sooner were we airborne with undercarriage retracted than the starboard engine spluttered and conked out. For a few minutes, the aircraft circled, banking steeply, and it was clear that it would have to land. It was also clear that it would have to land without wheels ; the undercarriage refused to come down. We cast sidelong glances, tightened our seat-belts and hoped for the best. In a moment the airfield seemed to be rushing crazily towards us. Then with a jarring bump we were down and careering along the runway with the starboard wing buckling and churning up the ground and the propellers biting the dust. Mercifully the plane did not turn turtle or catch fire and finally came to rest. None of us dallied in getting to the exit and we leapt thankfully down, as fire-floats and ambulances came screaming to a halt.

The Russians were looking a trifle discomfited and, no doubt, Admiral Alekseyev was more convinced than ever that it was *loochay moryem* but, all in all, they took it very well. It had occurred to me fleetingly that they might think the British were trying to liquidate them but, if so, they showed no sign of it and I was grateful for their truly Slavonic stoicism.

By now, a senior RAF officer was asking me if I were agreeable to taking off again with the same pilot. As he looked very young and his face was ashen white, I said it might perhaps be better for him to have a rest. The Admiral certainly seemed reassured when an older pilot with some 'scrambled-egg' on his cap was produced and our party was shepherded into another plane. This time all went smoothly and in no time we were translated to the delights of Copenhagen. No city in Europe could have provided a more extreme contrast after the devastation and despair of Berlin.

One got the impression that the Danes by comparison had not had too bad a war, even though their resistance movement had been active As everywhere else in Europe, the BBC had been its inspiration and its guide. I was told that the Nazis in occupation had complained over Kalundborg Radio that the Danes were taking their politics from the BBC. One of their newspapers had also carried an article which affirmed that 'many people have more faith in bulletins from London than in the words of the Bible'. Then, in the last year of the war, when the Germans had seized two thousand of the Danish police and taken them off to concentration camps, the ten thousand or so remaining were warned by BBC broadcasts and promptly went underground. But in spite of the struggle the Danes had put up, they were still enjoying a high standard of living and there was very little poverty to be seen. Everything looked amazingly clean and there were gorgeous looking girls all over the place sailing about on bicycles, their summer frocks ballooning out gaily round them as they rode.

In that first summer of peace in Europe, Copenhagen certainly seemed to me the perfect city. It was not too big – a capital to human scale. The whole place was like a fairy-tale. No wonder Hans Christian Andersen had been inspired to write as he did here. Even the Palace guards looked straight out of a musical comedy with their shaggy-looking busbies and free and easy style of marching.

Diadem was lying regally right alongside the Promenade at Langelinie, no distance from the centre of the town. There can't be many other berths in the world with a park and gardens at the foot of the gangway and, just near, on her rock gazing eternally out to sea Hans Andersen's famous mermaid.

I had often been on board *Diadem* up in Kola Inlet, so it was like meeting an old friend. It was clear that for the next seven or eight weeks at least the Tripartite Naval Conference was going to be quite a party, as we visited all the harbours and ports from Copenhagen up to Norway's North Cape. And so it proved. The Russians were, of course, in deadly earnest most of the time and determined to get their hands on every unit of the former German Navy that floated and even some that didn't. All this was greatly to the dismay of the Americans who, in any case, had all the ships they wanted and no desire to waste good drinking time inspecting a lot of old hulks.

My memories of the next few weeks are only sketchy. There was a fairly considerable alcoholic haze over all but in the Norwegian fiords there were moments of rare beauty and, incidentally, masterly navigation, as *Diadem* edged her way like a duchess through the deep, narrow waters along that fantastic thousand miles of coastline. At some points, standing at the guard rail, we were so close to the banks on either side that we could almost touch them. My memory is of great mountains and forests, farms and villages huddled on barren hillsides with lush, vivid green grass on the lower slopes. An elemental land of earth, sky and water, with strong, independent people, as the Germans found to their cost. At one time during the war, it took no less than six hundred thousand of them to hold down this nation they had thought to win over so easily.

I remember too the sixty miles or so of the Oslo fiord and the island fortress of Oscarsborg, which had sunk the cruiser *Blücher* on the night the Nazis invaded Norway in April 1940. As we neared Oslo, the fiord broadened out and on either side were brightly painted houses with white flagpoles and each with its wooden jetty.

We spent one evening ashore there in a restaurant, night-club place called, I think, the Rainbow Room. At an adjoining table, through the blue haze of smoke, was a face I knew well. There was no mistaking that Viking beard and I was delighted to meet again a friend I had last seen in North Russia. Haakon Jorgesson, a Commander in the Norwegian Fleet Air Arm, who often landed in his Catalina flying boat in Vaenga Bay after carrying out one of his secret missions over Norway and stayed in our mess. It was great fun, unexpectedly meeting him in his native Oslo.

From Oslo on to Stavanger, then to Bergen and Trondheim which had been used as bases for the U-boats, harrying the convoys to Russia ; and further north to Narvik, so important to the Germans for shipments of Iron ore. In May 1940 the Allies had retaken Narvik after landing twenty-five thousand men there, but it wasn't for long and in the evacuation that followed, the aircraft carrier *Glorious* and two destroyers had been lost.

From Narvik up to Tromsö where the RAF had finally nailed the battleship *Tirpitz*. She had been attacked early one morning in November 1944 by twenty-eight Lancaster bombers carrying 'block-busters'. Their aim was deadly and before they had finished *Tirpitz* turned turtle. It was an awe-inspiring sight to see the great ship lying there ignominiously up-ended.

Admiral Alekseyev and the other Russians were mightily

impressed. As the weeks went by, they gradually shed some of their suspicion and reserve. I think they realised that the British and Americans were shipmates they could trust. But they didn't let up in the diligent way they went about their duties and most evenings from their cabins we heard the tapping of typewriters until far into the night as they compiled their voluminous reports. All the same, slowly, they were thawing out and our comparatively free and easy way of life was making an appeal to them. As time went on, they joined our Wardroom parties and the Admiral, in particular, became respected and well-liked. One of *Diadem*'s officers was a first rate cartoonist and at a party he dashed off sketches of the Russian guests, as a memento for them and for me.

By the time we returned to Copenhagen, I think they were genuinely sorry to leave. In fact, as the members of the party waited at Kastrup airport to return to Berlin it looked as though two of the Russians had decided to defect. Then with just a couple of minutes to take-off a taxi arrived weighed down with parcels and lashed to the roof-rack were two gleaming bicycles they had bought as presents.

Soon all was stowed away and our Dakota was airborne and heading for Germany. We had all been celebrating the end of the trip with some Danish schnapps and a highly convivial party it was. As I was sitting there in a pleasant sort of daze, a figure on a bicycle wobbled past me up the passageway between the seats – then another – two of the Americans in a state of some elation were trying out the machines. With sundry diversions of this kind to enliven the flight, our party was finally decanted on to the airfield in Berlin.

By now it was autumn and the Berliners were hungry and fearful of the first post-war winter to come. Mass graves and flimsy coffins were being prepared against the famine and epidemics which were confidently expected. Acorns were being collected in the streets of Grünewald and so was everything else which could serve as food or fuel. Those Germans who had no work just stayed in bed. In this way, they kept reasonably warm and, by conserving energy, lessened the gnawing pains of hunger. Mercifully, the winter turned out to be a mild one and though many thousands died the number was far smaller than even the most optimistic had forecast.

The meetings of the Tripartite Naval Conference continued and more flights were made: firstly to the former German

Baltic ports in the Russian Zone. It was a curious experience flying with a Russian air crew, although the aircraft was familiar enough, that old work-horse the Dakota. The disconcerting thing was that the Soviet pilot never flew above factory chimney height. Either he was navigating by landmarks or, even more likely, practising his hedge-hopping techniques for avoiding radar screens. In nearly all the ports we found that the Russians were pushing ahead as fast as they could with submarine construction. The U-boat pens were filling up again. Who said the war was over?

Before Christmas we finished the paper work in Berlin and a party of us left for the ports in the British Zone – Lübeck, Hamburg, Wilhelmshaven and Kiel. This was the last phase of our work and entailed the division of all spare parts of the former German Navy. It involved a fair amount of driving on secondary German roads which at that time were in very poor condition. They were usually cobbled and quite often the camber went the wrong way. All they needed was a drizzle of rain or a spot of freezing fog to become deadly.

I survived until the early spring of 1946 – and then had my crash at about six one morning, when I was driving from Lübeck to Hamburg. In the half light of dawn, in the murk and drizzle I suddenly saw a post in the middle of the road. I think it must have been a sort of level crossing ; anyway, in trying to avoid it, I got into an uncontrollable skid. I remember thinking fatalistically – Oh well, this is it.

I must have been knocked out for a time. When I came to I was huddled in the back of the car with a great gash in my chin and more blood coming from a wound at the back of my head. The car was right way up in a ditch about six feet below the level of the road. I clawed my way up and waved down the first car to appear.

It was a little old German car with two male occupants and they didn't really want to stop. But they saw my British Naval uniform and decided they had better halt. All the same, they clearly did not wish to put themselves out for me, as they were in a hurry to get to work in Lübeck. Fortunately, I knew some German swear words, so I opened up on them and they decided that perhaps they'd better help me after all.

They took me to a small German hospital, which fortunately for them wasn't far away, and also very fortunately for me had a first-class surgeon on hand even at that early hour. He had me on the operating table in no time, and did a superb job of work in knitting my chin together and stitching up the back of my head. A telephone call was then put through to the British Forces Hospital in Hamburg and an ambulance came to collect me. They kept me there under observation for ten days or so, until I was fit to return to the Naval Mess at Travemünde just outside Lübeck.

As soon as I could, I returned to the scene of the crash to find out more about it, and incidentally to thank the German doctor and present him with a bottle of gin. I also came across two workmen who had seen the crash. They said that after the Mercedes I was driving left the road, it turned a couple of somersaults before landing right way up in the ditch. Clearly, I had been very lucky to get away with it. The curious thing was that I had felt no fear; just a cold curiosity and then total black-out.

A few weeks later my demob number came up – so now for me, after three and a half years, it was back to the BBC.

At the age of 8

'Alone with the
Empire' in Studio
7A, 1935

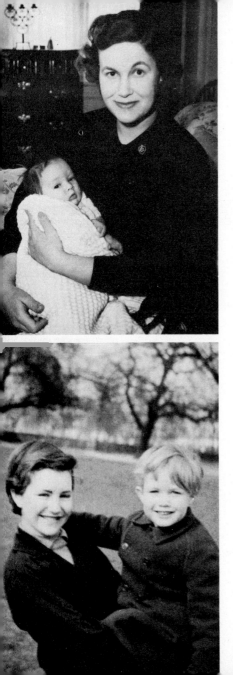

Alastair's first photograph

Miche and Alastair

With Nan, Miche
and Alastair after
the Investiture, 1965

With Quince and
Rollo

My turn to view

The first Royal visit to Sandy

At the Deaf Children's Society Autumn Fair, Luton, with Lord and
Lady Hill, 1969

Princess Anne meets Robert Dougall, Air Vice-Marshal
E. D. D. Dickson, C.B., C.B.E., President of the RNID, Marcel
Marceau and his assistant

Top hat chorus, 'Morecambe and Wise Show', Christmas 1971, *left to right*: Frank Bough, Cliff Michelmore, Eddie Waring, Patrick Moore, Robert Dougall, Michael Parkinson

The cover of *The Times* Special Report, 2 November 1972, to mark the BBC's 50th anniversary: Lord Reith with Vera Lynn, Peter Brough, 'Emperor Roscoe', Glenda Jackson, Richard Dimbleby, Warren Mitchell, Gilbert Harding, Robert Dougall

14 Return to BBC

'What grade were you on?' the BBC Administrator asked patiently. He looked a little askance when I said I hadn't the faintest idea. Up to the time I had obtained my release in 1942 salaries were a private matter. His question was a pointer to the way the Corporation had changed. I had only been away for three and a half years and yet was returning to a transformed organisation.

When I left, there were two Directors-General, Ogilvie having departed in January 1942. His successors, running in double harness, were Sir Robert Foot from the Gas Light and Coke Company, who looked after Administration, and Sir Cecil Graves running the Programme side. This joint reign prompted a wag on the staff to remark that the BBC 'now had one foot in the graves'. They lasted only two years and the Governors then appointed William Haley, who had recently come to the BBC as Editor-in-Chief after working in Reuters and becoming a Managing Director of the *Manchester Evening News* and the *Manchester Guardian*.

So Haley was the new D-G and presiding over a greatly expanded staff: it was over four times as big, the biggest change of all having taken place in the Overseas Service which was broadcasting in forty-five languages.

The BBC had been making up the difference between my service pay and my Corporation salary, which was very good of it, so I thought the least I could do was to settle into a job with as little fuss as possible. The first thing was an interview with the Resettlement Officer, General Sir Guy Williams. I remember him as a kindly, somewhat desiccated old gentleman and, I believe, he was even wearing a monocle. We had a polite, though inconclusive conversation and I then departed home to await events.

Meantime, my parents had moved yet again and this time to a pleasant house in Croham Road, South Croydon. London flats were almost impossible to find and it was a great stroke of luck when one day the telephone rang and my mother said there was someone called Francis Crick asking for me. His cheerful bray sounding over the blower so unexpectedly after our meeting over a year before in Moscow was the pleasantest of surprises. It became positively musical when he said he had a flat in Pimlico and wondered if by any chance I would care to share it with him. This was of course the answer to my problem and I didn't hesitate.

The flat was on the first floor at 56 St George's Square. There were two fair-sized bedrooms, and a large sitting-room with kitchen and bathroom at the end of the corridor. In the rather dark passageway Francis's bicycle leaned rustily against the wall. My room was empty so I managed to get a suite of rather horrible 'Utility' bedroom furniture, but with some scarlet curtains, a white sheepskin rug I had brought from Archangel and a wrought-iron candlestick made out of the twisted girders of Berlin it soon began to look quite jolly.

Francis had even organised a splendid little Welsh lady, a Mrs Thomas, to come in every morning to cook our breakfast and clean up for us. She was very pale and wore large steel-rimmed glasses and, for some reason, always burnt the toast. Each morning, one woke to the sound of conscientious scrapings in the kitchen, while agreeable smells wafted along the corridor. Mrs Thomas liked what she called 'a good fry'. She was admirable in every other way, not least in her impassive inscrutability at finding on occasions unexpected females in the flat. Francis's marriage had broken up and he was waiting for his divorce. I was entirely fancy-free.

We had some tremendous arguments about religion, politics, world affairs, Russia and so on and our viewpoint on almost everything was diametrically opposed. Unlike some scientists I have known, Francis seemed to enjoy the company of people with a totally different outlook from his own.

He came from a conventional home in Northampton and seemed determined to shake off any trace of stodginess in his make-up. After leaving Mill Hill School he read Physics at University College, London, until the war came when he joined the Admiralty Scientific establishment. He had done some important work there including the production of ingenious magnetic mines. It was through his Admiralty job of course that I had the good fortune to work with him in Moscow.

I think the war and the dropping of the atom bombs had a profound effect on him. Francis was a great humanist and determined not to work any longer for destructive ends. During the time I was staying with him he happened to read *What is life?* by Erwin Schrödinger and this helped to spark off his interest in biology. Schrödinger maintained that genes were the key components of living cells and that it was necessary to know how genes act in order to understand what life is. It became an obsession with Francis to find the key which would reveal how the genes decide, among other things, the colour of hair and eyes, govern the way in which we think and, in fact, determine our whole personalities.

When he and his two colleagues finally solved the structure of DNA, the fundamental genetic material, in 1953, Sir Lawrence Bragg described it as one of the major scientific events of this century. This was the work which nine years later was to win Francis his Nobel Prize. Of all this in 1946 I had no inkling. To me he was simply a pleasant person with whom to share a flat.

After a week or so of waiting I heard that the job the BBC had in mind for me was Staff Commentator, Outside Broadcasts, Television. The service had just started up again at Alexandra Palace after its wartime shut-down. Maurice Gorham had been moved from the Light Programme to take charge and my immediate boss would be Philip Dorté, who was Head of Films and Outside Broadcasts.

At my interview with Philip, if I was not very enthusiastic, it was because against the sombre background of world events, television seemed somewhat trivial and irrelevant. There were only twenty thousand sets in the country and reception was restricted to a radius of forty miles from London. Perhaps because I didn't particularly want the job, everyone seemed determined I should have it. There was an audition which was conducted from the roof of the pavilion at the Oval. Standing up there in a stiff breeze, I was required to describe the ground in a five minute piece to camera. This didn't worry me because as a schoolboy I had passed countless hours watching Surrey there and consuming countless bottles of ginger pop and sandwiches while doing it. I got the job all right. In charge of the OB Department and answerable to Philip was Ian Orr-Ewing.[1]

Under him and responsible for the production side was Peter Dimmock. Peter was entirely in his element and spent almost every spare moment working out camera positions in

[1] Now Lord Orr-Ewing, Chairman of the Metrication Board, 1972.

diagrams on the backs of envelopes. He had also been lucky enough to find an ancient but operable Ford Anglia in which he buzzed about purposefully. Peter's eyes were fixed firmly on the future with a single-mindedness I could but envy and no difficulties or frustrations ever worried him for long. Of course, there were plenty of laughs too.

One came during the England versus India Test Match at the Oval when Philip Dorté perpetrated a gaffe which made us roll in the aisles. During the interval, he launched himself into the pavilion to get the views for the camera of any prominent personages he could find. As it happened, Mr Attlee, who had recently taken over from Winston Churchill as Prime Minister, was taking a few hours off from his labours at Number Ten to watch some cricket at the Oval in the company of his wife. Philip plunged right in. In no time he was telling astonished viewers that he was going to have a word with the Prime Minister and *Mrs Churchill*. He then triumphantly confronted Mr and Mrs Attlee and, having elicited the PM's views on the state of the game, Philip turned to his wife sitting quietly beside him and did it again: 'And what does *Mrs Churchill* think about it?'

As far as I remember she was speechless; Mr Attlee just took it like the man he was. I believe afterwards someone led Philip away, quietly sobbing.

I had made it clear to everyone before starting the job that I had no expert knowledge of any sport, but was told that this did not matter. The theory was that the Commentator would simply represent a viewer with a ringside seat. The picture would tell the story; all I would have to do was provide a few vital facts and be, in general, a friendly guide.

Unfortunately, it didn't quite work out like that. In the first place even the business of getting to Alexandra Palace was difficult. Private cars were almost unobtainable and so most staff depended on the BBC buses, which made the seven mile journey from Broadcasting House through the north London suburbs at about two hourly intervals. Once arrived there, working conditions were far from pleasant. The Outside Broadcasts team were housed in draughty offices in the east wing of the cavernous, ramshackle old building. All television equipment had been stored away for nearly seven wartime years; it was now antiquated and suffering from lack of regular servicing. Our equipment was housed in enormous green vans which had to be left standing in the public parking space. It was only thanks to the dogged devotion of the engineers, who had to do all their maintenance work in the open air, sometimes in snow and freezing conditions, that any Service was possible. When the Outside Broadcasts unit did get on the move it looked like a travelling circus and, indeed, as Christmas approached, the circus at Olympia was our destination.

This was one of the occasions I enjoyed. Cyril and Bertram Mills who ran it were great charmers and there was a fascination in meeting all the varied circus folk and animals. Cyril was also complimentary about my commentaries and bothered to write and tell me so, which was very nice.

The ceremonial broadcasts I enjoyed too although there were innumerable hair-raising moments. At the Lord Mayor's Show, owing to traffic congestion, the procession halted for over ten minutes. Immediately opposite our camera position was a float with RAF men doing hand-stands, press-ups and the like. By the time they reached us they had already covered many miles and were understandably running out of steam. It took frantic efforts from me and many impassioned wavings and gestures to keep them up to strength and continuing their show for the viewers.

The Armistice Day ceremony at the Cenotaph in that winter of 1946, so soon after the end of the war, was tremendously impressive. The camera position was high up in a building on the east side of Whitehall and mercifully it was one of the broadcasts which passed off without any technical fault. My boss Ian Orr-Ewing was kind enough to say that, in his view, the commentary could not have been better.

This was not always the case, particularly when I was required to give commentaries on sporting events which were entirely new to me. I remember with embarrassment a visit to Herne Hill for cycle racing. I found this quite beyond me as for much of the time the contestants appeared to be vying with each other in going as slowly as possible without actually falling off. They would then quite suddenly start pedalling away like mad as if they were trying to get to the pub before closing time. At least I enjoyed the interval when I interviewed a splendid old man of eighty-two, who had brought his Penny-farthing along for the occasion. He was immensely tall with flowing white locks and wore plus-fours. In contrast, he had brought his great grand-daughter with him – an enchanting little girl of about seven with fair hair. They made a memorable picture standing there on either side of the gigantic front wheel of one of the very first bicycles.

Then there were visits to Speedway, which I had never even seen before. I didn't think it advisable to let viewers know this and I remember Peter Dimmock, who was in the commentary box with me, rolling about with mirth at my despairing efforts to show some expertise.

At Twickenham when commentating on a game of rugger in which the Harlequins were playing somebody or other, I was nearly thrown out of my stride seeing the huge frame of John Matthews, who had been our 'Toothy' in North Russia, lumbering about the field among the forwards. Seeing him there reminded me of the soccer matches we used to play against the comrades on the dirt-patch at Vaenga.

There were innumerable awkward moments when the equipment broke down. One of the worst was at Liverpool Street Station when the Royal Family were leaving for a holiday at Sandringham. A Television Commentator is dependent on his monitor screen which shows the picture being transmitted. Just before we were on the air, mine ceased to work. For the whole of that broadcast I had no idea what pictures the viewers were seeing in their homes, so that intelligent commentary from me was impossible.

On another occasion I spent forty-five minutes at the bottom of a test diving tank while wearing heavy diver's equipment. I was co-starring in this programme with Gillian Webb who was the current glamour girl Announcer. The cameras understandably were preoccupied with showing Gillian getting in and out of her suit and I was left roaming about with leaden feet down in the depths. The broadcast was planned to end with my majestic ascent. When the time came, I was so bored with being stuck down there that I pressed the little button on the side of my helmet over-vigorously. As a result, the suit inflated too quickly and I fairly hurtled up to the surface. On arrival, looking like Mr Michelin, I lay spread-eagled and helpless on my back. Not the ideal way in which to sign off a programme.

In between these outside assignments, I used occasionally to deputise for Leslie Mitchell, the immaculate, incomparable presenter of the Television Service's most popular magazine programme 'Picture Page'. This I much enjoyed doing: in the

166

studio there was at least a semblance of order in the chaos. But it was a disastrous programme of Old Tyme Dancing at a Palais de Dance which finally made me feel I had had enough. The particular producer handling it was suffering from fearful ulcers as a result of battling with all the broken down equipment. The poor fellow had really given up the struggle and in between nibbling at biscuits his main preoccupation had become the filling-in of football coupons. With no camera positions worked out and scarcely any plan of campaign, my job, as I stood there surrounded by a milling, cavorting throng, was impossible. That evening finally convinced me it was time I moved on to something else.

The world was in an unholy mess and I could not shut out my memories of Russia and post-war Germany. It was now January and we were having one hell of a winter to add to the gloom. All over the country, factories were closing for lack of fuel ; roads were blocked with snowdrifts ; villages cut off and ships bringing coal down from the north were held up by the weather. On top of this came a transport strike and the Army was called in to keep food supplies on the move. Water pipes were freezing in nearly every home and the power cuts were getting worse and worse. By the end of the month even the Thames began to freeze over and the whole country seemed to be slithering to a stop in an icy, grey stillness.

I had officially asked for a transfer to the European Service at Bush House and at last I heard this had been arranged. A few days after I left Alexandra Palace in February 1947 the fuel crisis became even more acute and the Television Service itself was forced to close down. It was over a month before it was able to get back on the air again.

Meantime, I had begun my attachment to the European Service of the BBC at Bush House. My principal interest was in the recently formed Russian Service and I broadcast several talks for them. Unfortunately, I found that I could not see eye to eye with the British staff running the programme. The trouble was that only one of them had ever been to Russia : he had spent a fortnight in Odessa before the war. It soon became clear to me that their idea of Russia bore little relation to the country I had recently left. The trouble was I suppose that the Foreign Office were reluctant to face facts and they were hoping against hope that the Soviets would co-operate with the West. Many years later, when I asked Anthony Nutting, then a Minister of State at the FO, about this period, he just said:

'The FO like the old grey mare was a long time turning round.'

Under Sir William Haley as Director-General, the BBC's Charter had just been renewed for five years. The post-war pattern of broadcasting was for three domestic networks – the Home Service, the Light Programme, and the newly launched Third. These and the Television Service were to be financed out of licence income. All external services were to be paid for by Grant-in-Aid, but the White Paper on Broadcasting Policy made it clear: 'The Government intend that the Corporation should remain independent in the preparation of programmes for overseas audiences.' This independence was of course the reason for the great trust the world had in them.

My problem in this newly reorganised BBC was to find some kind of niche. Not altogether surprisingly staff who had joined the BBC during the war were a little anxious about the return of fairly senior staff from the Forces and some of them were hanging on to their chairs like mad.

As already recounted, it was at this time when my morale was at its lowest that I first met Nan at Bush House. Two months' later we were married by special licence at Caxton Hall. It was the quietest of weddings as we had kept it very much to ourselves. On the way back from the Register Office we stopped the taxi at the White House in Bond Street and Nan popped in to get a super nightdress with some borrowed clothing coupons I had managed to get a case of assorted bottles and we returned to St George's Square for drinks with Francis and Odile. My old friend and colleague Basil Gray looked in with his wife Wendy and, by one of those corny coincidences life is always coming up with, it transpired that Nan and Wendy had once been at school together in Bedford. At the High School there, Wendy had apparently pinched Nan's first boy-friend at the age of sixteen. Nan claims to have been shattered at the time and says she sobbed her way all through the Schools Certificate Scripture exam. Anyway, all was now forgiven and we had a jolly little get together.

So, in a few months, I had acquired a wife and a two-year-old stepdaughter, but was no nearer getting settled in a job. Major-General Sir Ian Jacob was then the Controller of the European Service and he interviewed me for the post of Senior

Talks Assistant. Unfortunately, having been away for three and a half years, I had to admit that I was slightly out of touch with speakers.

It was at this time that I ran across a former Empire Service colleague Clifford Lawson-Reece. Clifford had become the head of the British Far Eastern Broadcasting Service operating in Singapore and he was on a visit to this country recruiting staff. The BFEBS was run by the Foreign Office and I pricked my ear up at once when Clifford told me it was proposed to start a booster station there for the Russian language broadcasts from London. The job of Programme Manager was vacant and he offered it to me. This was going to mean a secondment to the Foreign Office for a period of three years.

Life was looking brighter. The long dark freeze-up of the winter had given way to a scintillating spring and summer and I had even bought an old car. Nan and I drove all over London in it for most of one day but on arriving back at St George's Square I found I couldn't get out: my right knee had locked at an angle of about forty-five degrees. It was obviously cartilage trouble and probably sustained originally in that accident outside Hamburg just over a year before.

I promptly sought my brother-in-law Pat Sayers' advice and he told me to see Ronnie Furlong, who was one of the best orthopaedic men in the country and had been a Brigadier with Pat in the RAMC during the war. As I was shortly due to leave for the tropics, Furlong strongly advised me to have the operation first, and so it was agreed that I should enter Pyrford Hospital, near Woking, in Surrey.

By this time it was August. The ward was on the ground floor and in the days after the operation my bed was pushed out into the grounds and I was able to roast in the sunshine of that marvellous summer. Nan came down to see me fairly often and we discussed future plans. I was keen to go out by sea if possible, as the voyage would give me a chance to recuperate. Fortunately, the FO agreed and it was arranged that Nan should follow out also by sea a month later. The only snag was that Michèle, her two-year-old daughter, would have to be left behind in a nursery school, until we were able to set up a home for her there.

So it was that in September 1947, in high hopes, I boarded SS *Georgic* at Tilbury – Singapore bound.

15 Singapore

Georgic had had a distinguished record as a troopship during the war and on this trip too she was still packed with mainly service personnel. I found I was sharing an inside cabin with two other civilians, so it was not going to be a luxurious trip. This didn't worry me as almost anything seemed preferable to staying in post-war London and at least I had a job to go to. There was also the fascination of a sea voyage to what was for me an entirely new part of the world. I knew the frozen north, now I was to see what life was like on the equator.

My cabin companions were about as different from each other as possible. One was a huge jovial Scot from Aberdeen, Jimmy Murray, a planter returning to Medan in Sumatra across the Malacca Straits from Singapore. At that time, the inhabitants were far from friendly there ; he was going back to plenty of trouble and he knew it. All the same Jimmy was one of the most cheerful people on board and to ensure his spirits should not flag he kept a case of Scotch and rum ready at hand under his bunk. He was one of those massive, high cheek-boned Scots with legs like tree trunks, draped in khaki shorts. In fact, just the man to toss the caber, but like so many Caledonians he was under his rugged exterior a sentimental soul. After a dram or two Jimmy would fumble away at his bush-shirt pocket and out would come a much fingered photograph of 'Ginger', his young wife back in Aberdeen, whom he adored. He knew he was returning to an Indonesia in ferment and I think he was wondering whether he would ever see Ginger again.

My other travelling companion was a wraith-like man of about sixty. He had recently had an operation for the removal of one lung and, while he had any breath remaining in him, was determined to see as much of the world as possible. He was very brave and never once complained even in the most stifling weather. When he breathed he made a disconcerting rasping sound which sometimes kept me awake at night. For this reason I used to take my mattress up on deck for preference and sleep there in the open.

In general, there wasn't much comfort and the ship was still being run on the lines of a wartime trooper, but I enjoyed the three weeks' voyage thanks to some pleasant company. There were army officers and their wives and a charming fair-haired, vivacious woman, always known as 'Benny' Lister, who was going out to Singapore to be Second-in-Command of the WRVS. As usually happens on a voyage of this kind about eight of us formed a party and, as the days went by, we all became good friends. My knee was still rather painful from the operation but, at least, it was a marvellous excuse to duck out of all the hearty fun and games of shipboard life.

For me it was a time to take stock. I hadn't quite got used to the idea of being a married man with a ready-made daughter. It was a big responsibility, but I was determined to make a go of it. The war had caused so many broken marriages, so much chaos that it made me realise as never before the importance of a stable relationship. The war had taught me above all to take pride in Britain. I knew now there was no political panacea and, instead of seeking a solution for the problems of the world, I felt it was more to the point to try to create a small personal island of stability. As Voltaire said: *Il faut cultiver notre jardin.* I realised too how much I had neglected English literature and so instead of French, German or Russian I read for the first time George Eliot's *Mill on the Floss* and loved it.

As we steamed off the coast of North Africa, a golden eagle, exhausted and with a slightly damaged wing, alighted gratefully on *Georgic*. It was a young male and became quite a celebrity. Fortunately, one of the ship's officers was a keen bird man and knew how to handle him. The young eagle remained in his care, rapidly recovered, and I subsequently heard that he was released successfully on the return trip in roughly the same area.

Approaching Egypt, we were struck by the noticeable difference in the speed with which the setting sun dropped below the horizon. One moment it was there – like a great red behind on a dirty postcard – the next it was gone. Unfortunately, we were not allowed ashore at Port Said as relations with Egypt were rather strained, but in no time, we were surrounded with bum-boats and small craft of all kinds and brisk trading got under way. At the entrance to the Suez Canal the heat became almost unbearable, but the menu remained the same with steak-and-kidney pudding still featuring on it. As we edged slowly through the Canal, for the first time I saw camels, swaying lugubriously along its banks. We stood gazing out from the guard-rails and several of the *fellaheen* ashore reflected the state of diplomatic relations by raising their robes to their waists as we passed, not that they had much to show.

There was general relief as we left the Gulf of Aden behind us and headed for the Arabian Sea and the open waters of the Indian Ocean. Soon there were flying fish to divert us ; I never tired of watching them skimming over the surface like so many silver tracer bullets. For days on end we were escorted too by large playful schools of porpoises which seemed to appreciate our company as much as we enjoyed theirs.

I was grateful for the long voyage which was like being suspended in time ; for a few weeks at least there was nothing to worry about. All too soon we were past the Nicobar Islands into the Straits of Malacca and sailing down the west coast of Malaysia to the island of Singapore.

Georgic berthed alongside a quay and my first impression after days at sea was of the vivid green everywhere ashore. On a closer look there were many wooden warehouses and godowns and a sea of faces in every shade of black, brown and yellow. David Porter, the Programme Director, was waiting for me looking shiny and pink. He had very kindly come down in his car to collect me but his opening words were not exactly uplifting. He was saying ruefully: 'I'm delighted to see you, Bob, but I really don't know what you are going to do. We're hopelessly over-staffed. Perhaps you will be able to make a job for yourself.' Oh well, I thought, it's really too hot to worry.

For the first few days in fact the heat and, above all, the humidity overwhelmed me. It was necessary to change one's shirt at least three times a day and the air seemed so heavy that most of the time I felt I was walking on an eiderdown. At first I had to make do with temporary accommodation in the houses of other BFEBS staff. These were away from the centre of Singapore and gave me my first confrontation with mosquito nets, which I found stuffy and usually inefficient. Then there were the rather charming little house lizards or *chee-chaks* which chased each other upside down across the ceilings. The pursuer would sometimes grab his quarry by the tail, which would promptly be shed. Occasionally one of them lost its hold on the ceiling and fell to the floor with a tiny plopping sound ; another time I was at a friend's house for supper and a *chee-chak* even fell into a plate of soup, causing a splash and some

172

consternation. The cockroaches, on the other hand, were wholly unlovable, being about four inches long and a brownish orange colour with long waving whiskers.

After a week I moved into a house which I shared with a delightfully amusing man whom I had known at Broadcasting House before the war. Raymond Baker had at that time been one of the urbane receptionists in black jacket and striped trousers seated at the desk in the entrance hall, but during the war he had blossomed out as an administrator. He was now in charge of the business side of the BFEBS and the house was in a compound near the studios so there was no problem about transport. There wasn't much to do in the evenings and, as we sat drinking our whisky and water *stengahs* in the sitting-room, a sociable stick insect like a praying mantis used regularly to join us. He was nearly six inches long and pale green – we called him Wilbur.

The BFEBS was housed nearby in a handsome complex of white, single-storey buildings surrounded by beautifully tended gardens and situated off the Thomson Road about fifteen minutes' drive from the main part of the city. Its principal function was to serve as a relay station for the Far Eastern broadcasts from London. There were also News bulletins in English and in the vernacular languages of Malaysia and Indonesia as well as a small output of music programmes plus occasional features and plays. It didn't amount to very much and it was clear that David Porter had been absolutely right ; there were few enough programmes for him to direct, let alone for me to manage. I could only hope that an eventual expansion was planned but, certainly for the time being, there was scarcely anything for me to do. It looked very much as though this broadcasting station under direct Foreign Office control was an outwardly impressive, but no doubt costly, white elephant.

At the head of it as Controller was this somewhat Dickensian character Clifford Lawson-Reece, a portly, avuncular, kindly soul who at one time had been an actor. Then, Clifford had joined the BBC Empire Service as a Presentation Assistant and I remembered that in those days before the war he had been famous for his lengthy memoranda which he circulated widely throughout Broadcasting House. Few could understand what he was writing about but his memos were couched in such an erudite style and so full of classical allusions and Latin tags

173

that officials were soon asking who was this man Lawson-Reece, and in no time he had won for himself the reputation of having a mighty brain.

His secret I discovered was a photographic memory. At a dinner party I once heard him discourse at length on the mating habits of bees. Like everyone else I was impressed, except that a day or so later I found that he had been reproducing almost word for word an article on the subject in a Sunday newspaper. It was because of this gift of his plus his physical bulk, which must have amounted to at least fifteen stone, that in those early days, we had always called him affectionately 'elephant boy'.

Now, here he was again and at the BFEBS he had surely found some of his most satisfying roles: part broadcasting head, part colonial governor, part impresario, he played them all in turn and with the greatest gusto. By his side to sustain him was his charming wife Sybil, who had been his secretary, and was as pencil slim as he was rotund. To the FO, eight thousand miles away in London, the ways of broadcasters must in any case have been a closed book and perhaps they were in ignorance of the expansive way in which the station was being run.

I tried to find out all I could about the island, while I waited for Nan to arrive. A fascinating place in so many ways. An island about the size of the Isle of Wight lying at the southern end of Malaysia ninety miles above the equator and connected by a causeway to the mainland across the narrow Straits of Johore. But it is of course the mixture of races and cultures that gives Singapore its unforgettable attraction. In 1947 it wasn't long since the Japanese had left and yet it seemed they might never have been on the island. The Chinese were well in the majority; from their number came the big merchants, the seamen, and the coolies in the docks, the Malays were mostly policemen and fishermen, the turbaned Sikhs drove the taxis and the Indians sat behind counters as small traders or clerks. As for the British, they seemed already almost irrelevant except to keep order and, although superficially the Japanese had vanished without trace, in fact, the débâcle which first let them in had imprinted its mark for all time. The myth of white supremacy had now gone forever. There was no mistaking that this was now an Asian city and full independence, one felt, could not be long delayed.

Living conditions were not luxurious and most people could only afford one servant, a cook house-boy, but after post-war UK with its rationing, clothes coupons, queues and innumerable petty restrictions, life in Singapore had much to offer. One was always conscious of either the jungle or the sea. On the outskirts there was a great chorus of bullfrogs in the mangrove swamps after rain; here the primitive huts set among coarse, long grasses with the vivid green of banana and palm trees made the jungle seem an ever encroaching presence, waiting to move in again and take over. In the main part of the city on the southern shore it was the sea which dominated, all streets seeming to lead to it or to the Singapore River packed solid with sampans on which countless Chinese families lived and died. Over all hung the heady smell of the tropics: a mixture compounded of open drains, excrement, sweat, exotic spices, fish and food and heaven knows what else, but, once smelt, never forgotten.

The narrow Chinese streets appeared to be permanently *en fête*: long poles bedecked with gaily coloured washing stretched across from the upper windows and at ground level there were always family parties gathered round food stalls. The grace and speed with which even the children plied their chopsticks amazed me. More savoury smelling snacks were carried through the streets by emaciated-looking Chinese hawkers, who swayed along under the weight of containers at either end of the bamboo poles arching across their shoulders. They announced their coming, as they loped along, by knocking two pieces of hollow wood together to make a rhythmic, clapping noise. That was the haunting sound that even more than the inescapable Chinese and Indian music still evokes for me the magic of Singapore. If the Chinese teemed and bustled, the Indians and Malays appeared elegantly indolent. It was strange at first to see their young men often walking unselfconsciously hand-in-hand. The women for the most part moved with a slow sinuous grace which was a delight to see.

The business part of Singapore was a total contrast. Large, white soulless-looking blocks, but spaciously set out and overlooking the smooth green of the *padang*. Here rose the spire of St Andrew's Cathedral, which only a few years before had served as an emergency hospital for the British and Australian wounded in what must have been nightmarish days before the city finally fell. Here too the Cricket Club where, as yet, only

175

whites were allowed, the whole area having the atmosphere of a British cathedral city, except for the flame trees and the blue, shimmering sea.

After a month, I had a cable to say that Nan had sailed from Liverpool in the *Empress of Scotland*. I would now be entitled to married quarters. David Porter, who had a large flat in Singapore's only skyscraper, the Cathay Building, kindly asked me if we would like to share it. This was a wonderful stroke of luck as it was right in the centre of things and there would be no difficulty about transport. There was even a small cinema and two squash courts in the basement. During the war the Cathay had housed the Ministry of Information offices and the Malaya Broadcasting Corporation run by the Colonial Office. When the Japanese came they had used it for Head-quarter's staff and now it was partly offices, partly residential flats and the MBC were again operating in their studios on the third floor.

Nan's arrival date was 20 November. It also happened to be the wedding day of Princess Elizabeth and Prince Philip and Singapore was using the occasion as an excuse for celebrations and festivities of all kinds. The *Empress of Scotland* docked in the evening about six and I saw Nan at once, standing by the guard-rail, scanning rather anxiously the faces on the quayside. She spotted me immediately although there were hundreds waiting ; gave a cheerful wave and soon we were driving back to the Cathay flat.

Nan liked the flat at once and, after a quick look round, we switched on the radio to hear Richard Dimbleby's commentary on the Royal Wedding from Westminster Abbey. Richard was an old friend of hers and godfather to her daughter Michèle, so she felt quite at home. By now it was dusk and we walked out on to the balcony. The myriad lights of Singapore laid out below looked festive in themselves, but tonight they were being added to by fireworks going up on all sides. It was a marvellous night for her to arrive. Later, I opened a bottle of champagne I had managed to get from a little Chinese shop round the corner. Unfortunately, the champagne turned out to be rather flat, but that night, for once, it didn't seem to matter.

Next morning, we made a determined drive on the cock-roaches and I killed dozens by hurling a hair-brush at them. They expired with a crunching sound and left very little mess on the walls, which in any case still bore some bullet marks as a legacy from the war. We were also able to engage a diminutive Chinese *amah* to come in every day and help look after us. Ah Choo was only four feet six and her black pigtail reached right down to the floor; she looked charming in her white tunic with black trousers flapping round her ankles. As the months went by there remained only one thing about her which puzzled us. For some reason she used to sit in the kitchen in total darkness for hours on end. We could never make out whether she was meditating, communicating with the spirits of her ancestors or just having a kip.

We lived very quietly because we were rather broke. Not that it mattered too much, because it was an entertainment in itself just wandering about in the streets as there was always so much going on. Raffles Place was the centre of things for Europeans; there Robinson's, the general purpose store, was a meeting ground. Behind the square, Change Alley was where everything happened; a narrow, bustling street of small shops and booths in which the haggling went on. I wasn't good at this to begin with but soon learnt that one started by knocking a third off the asking price and negotiations then opened from there. To pay the price asked was almost bad form – nobody then had any fun.

'Benny' Lister, whom I had met on the boat, told me one day that an English girl from up-country, who had been missing, was now reported to be at a house near the docks. As a senior WRVS official she had been asked to investigate. Benny was very brave, but as it was a ropey district I couldn't let her go there alone. We set off in her car and eventually found the house in a rundown back street. The front door swung open, so we pushed inside. The ground floor was deserted and we started going upstairs. Half way up we ran into three villainous-looking Sikhs and for a moment I thought there might be trouble. We tried to look as fierce as possible and marched past them and through an open bedroom door.

There, in all this squalor, on a dishevelled bed was a deathly pale English girl aged about twenty. She was fair and must have once been rather elegant. She was wearing a sort of slip and clutching to herself a minute, mangy kitten. There were two Sikhs in the room but fortunately they left without any fuss. The girl had been adrift from Kuala Lumpur for nearly ten days and what with drugs and the attentions of the Sikhs was in a fearful state. Fortunately, she seemed prepared to come

177

with us but refused to leave the kitten. So eventually Benny and I more or less carried her down the stairs, still clutching the kitten, and drove her to the WRVS headquarters. She looked touchingly sad and frail. The hot, steamy weather had a dire effect on quite a number of European women.

Other, milder, effects of the climate were prickly heat, an irritating rash which affected almost everyone, and of course, Singapore tummy. Then, the humidity was such that mildew grew on clothes put away in cupboards and drawers; leather suitcases were also especially liable to go green and musty.

Soon after Nan's arrival Clifford gave a dinner party at his house, to which we were invited. I wore my white dinner jacket and Nan had a new, rather flowing, frock, which I suppose she thought would make an impact. When we got there, she popped into the cloakroom on the first floor for a moment and I joined the assembled company downstairs. Clifford was playing his colonial governor role that night and looked rather impressive with a black silk cummerbund draped over his ample stomach and smoking a cigarette in a long holder. After a moment, Nan appeared at the top of the stairs looking simply stunning; she took two steps, then caught her shoe in the long skirt and slithered the rest of the way down on her bottom. It obviously wasn't the impact she had intended. She always says she is sure that Clifford never forgave her, but I doubt if he minded all that much.

To help keep the rot out of my bank balance I used to read the News for Radio Malaya on two or three nights a week. This suited me perfectly because their studios were housed on the floor immediately below ours at the Cathay. Nan also managed to earn a few dollars by presenting a sort of Family Favourites record request programme. This made hilarious listening, for me at least, as most of the names and addresses were Chinese or Malay and Nan had a frantic time coping with the unfamiliar and often unpronounceable names and addresses.

So the weeks went by and we both revelled in the exotic fascination of this, for us, new world of sights and sounds and smells. But there was no sign of any expansion of the output and in fact as Christmas approached it became clear that the project was going to be cut down. In the corridors at BFEBS, huddles formed as staff exchanged rumours and tried to think out their next moves. Britain was in the middle of a financial crisis, the FO was forced to make economies, and the BFEBS was to be one of them. For me, what was to have been a three year secondment had lasted only a few months. I wrote to friends in Australia to sound out for possibilities of getting work there, but opportunities in broadcasting did not sound encouraging. In any case, Nan's daughter Michèle was still at the nursery school in Sussex, so we decided that we would have to return to England. I cabled the BBC requesting that I might go on a resettlement course until a job came along and this was finally agreed.

The next problem was to book a sea passage home. Ships were becoming few and far between. We had hoped to get berths in the Dutch liner *Oranje* but they were all taken. So we settled for the Messagerie Maritime's *André le Bon.*

There were many regrets at leaving and many goodbyes to be made. Oddly enough, the one we were sorriest about was our parting with the little *amah* who had looked after us so charmingly – Ah Choo. She must have become rather attached to us, in spite of the language difficulty, because, when we were packing, we found her curled up neatly at the bottom of one of the large cases.

We were waiting for the car to take us to the docks when Nan suddenly said she could hear a puppy squealing somewhere. From the balcony we could see part of a slummy-looking street and the sound seemed to be coming from there.

When the car came we asked the driver to take us there first and, sure enough, we found the puppy. He was a sad little scrap, and had been tied to a post by a twist of wire round his middle. Six Indian boys were busy throwing stones at him. They were enjoying their game, resented our intrusion and didn't want to part with the object of their fun. There was only one thing to be done, so with our last few dollars we persuaded them to sell us what was left of that pup and then took him round to the RSPCA. At least, there his troubles would be ended.

Mine were really just beginning, because I hadn't any money left to tip the porter at the docks. As it happened, he was a particularly vicious looking character and was sweating profusely by the time he had finished carrying our bags to the separate cabins allotted to us in *André le Bon.* I gave him all the cigarettes I had but he made it clear beyond doubt that that wouldn't do. By this time he was scowling horribly and looked quite capable of drawing a knife on us when, to our immense relief, we spotted a young FO official who had come down to see us off. After all, I thought, the FO had got us into this mess, now it was only fair they should get us out. This they did through the good offices of the charming and elegant St John Don Byrne I think his name was.

If only *André le Bon* had lived up to its name; but, for a start, she was a filthy ship with a pronounced list to port and packed with depressed French settlers getting out of Saigon. Also, we did not like having separate cabins. I shared mine with a Frenchman who never seemed to wash, but just smothered himself periodically with eau-de-cologne. Like idiots Nan and I had thought the food might be good in a French ship, but this was a crowded troopship and there was very little of anything. The butter was rancid and the coffee like mud. My chief recollections of that trip are of grime everywhere, the stench of stale eau-de-cologne, and Charles Trenet endlessly singing *La Mer* over the ship's public address system. In fact, for years afterwards every time I heard that song I had to suppress a tendency to twitch.

The first stop was Colombo which gave us a day ashore. Instead of dashing about the island trying to see as much of Ceylon as possible, we took a taxi to the Galle Face Hotel and booked a room. It was a rather splendid hotel, which remembered better days. After a superb curry lunch, with all the trimmings, we ordered tea to be sent up, but as soon as the silver tray was set down on the table there was a flutter of black through the window, a squawk, and there, as bold as brass, was a large crow demolishing one of our pieces of delicately cut bread and butter! Outside were more crows waiting their turn, so once I had persuaded it to leave, we had to finish our tea behind closed windows, with a lot of affronted birds looking in. Before leaving Ceylon, there was just time for a quick visit to the Forces broadcasting station, where a Wing-Commander showed us round and where a former BBC colleague Alex Moyes was making a first-class job of the presentation.

Back on board there was little to do except sunbathe on the upper deck, which also meant getting covered in smuts from the smoke belching from the funnels, as the old French trooper limped her way across the Indian Ocean to the next port of call – Djibouti.

Nan and I were both fairly volatile in those days and the

frustrations of the voyage were building up. Even the drink situation was very limited, which led to our having a session one night on Pernod. This unaccustomed tipple led to our having the mother and father of a row. We must have been overheard by an old China-hand, a hard-bitten doctor, returning from a Far Eastern station. As he passed me with a dead-pan expression, he said out of the corner of his mouth: 'Every man gets the wife he deserves.' Nothing particularly profound perhaps, although the remark has, of course, a solid basis of truth. Anyway, it has for some reason always stuck in my mind.

Afterwards, I dimly remember our wandering round the deserted decks. It must have been very late and the Indian Ocean was dead calm. There was an enormous moon and the wake from *André le Bon* stretched away like a broad silver ribbon. Suddenly, Nan wrenched off her rings and flung them over the side. Not to be outdone, I seized one of the hideous, ancient-looking rattan chairs and greatly relieved my feelings by hurtling it clean over the side; then, another and another. They looked a bit weird, floating away, in line astern – up-ended, on a flat sea, with the moon shining down.

At Djibouti we spent half a day ashore, which was more than enough. If this were a typical example of French colonial administration, we were not impressed. An arid, fly-blown place with many signs of real hardship. Some of the native inhabitants, especially the children, look half-starved with their matchstick legs and pot bellies.

Soon, we were on the last lap through the Mediterranean to Marseilles, which we reached after twenty-eight days afloat. The rail trip across France was the best part of the journey but perhaps the unkindest cut of all was at the Customs when we got back. For some reason, they really put us through it. Nan had managed to win a bottle of champagne in a tombola on board; we even had to pay duty on that. So, we were home again, flat broke and with no proper job; but on the credit side it had been an interesting trip and, at least, we felt we knew each other a great deal better.

16 Light Programme

The first official I had to see at Broadcasting House was the Establishment Officer D. H. Clarke, the very same who had given me a break as an Empire Announcer fourteen years before. This time he had my bulky personal file on his desk containing all the annual reports written about me by my bosses since I joined in 1933. By his attitude, he almost seemed to imply that it was my fault the Foreign Office had closed the Singapore Station, which was of course ridiculous. But the stark fact remained that, in the eyes of BBC Administration, I had fluffed three starts at resettlement and D.H. was making it clear that the Corporation had discharged its legal responsibilities towards me. This had an ominous ring about it and to emphasise the point he quoted a number of uncharitable observations made about me on the file over the years. Then, a trifle grudgingly, he said, 'Here's a piece of jam,' and proceeded to read remarks made by Bernard Moore, who had been Overseas News Editor, when I obtained my release in 1942. Bernard had written: 'he is a first-class microphone personality whom we are very sorry to lose. I should like to emphasise that his departure is entirely at his own request.'

I got the gist of the message however delicately it was wrapped up. If there was no job available for me at the end of the training course, then I would be out on my ear. There was a week to go before it started and, in that time, much to be done on the home front.

Nan and I were staying temporarily with my parents in Croham Road, South Croydon. We had hopes of a flat in West Hampstead, which an aunt of Nan's was about to vacate, but it would be a few weeks before we were able to move in. At the first opportunity, Nan and I went down to see Miche at her nursery school in Bexhill. She was unfortunately ill with measles and could not be moved, so we had sorrowfully to leave her there, until we could set up a proper home for her at the flat.

The course got under way at the training school off Marylebone Road. Archie Harding, one of the BBC's most senior drama producers, was the Chief Instructor with my old friend from Empire days Basil Gray as his assistant. I tried as conscientiously as possible to take in what all the theorising was about, but it has always seemed to me that, apart from the technical side, broadcasting is really a fairly straightforward business. The lecturers made it all seem very complicated. At the end of the course we had to produce and take part in a play and also write and deliver a ten minute talk. I chose as a subject my impressions of the Soviet Union. Later, I learnt that Harding had been a follower of Marx, so I suppose it would have been better if I had talked about something else.

Anyway, all they had to offer me was a job in the Announcers' pool, which meant a precarious existence shifting about between the various networks. I felt I deserved something better than that, so I invited a former colleague to lunch. Tom Chalmers had joined me as an Empire Announcer shortly before the war, then during it he switched to the Presentation and Programme Planning side of things and had risen to great heights. Tom knew my microphone work and, after a pleasant lunch in Soho, he said he would be delighted to have me on his announcing staff in the Light Programme of which he had recently been made Controller. The only snag was that the post had a lower salary grade than that to which I would normally have been entitled. But, in any case, in this much changed BBC I realised that there was for me, in the words of almost every Chancellor of the Exchequer on Budget Day, 'a long hard slog ahead.'

The Light Programme had taken over in July 1945 as the successor to the Forces Programme and during those years of the late forties and early fifties, before television began capturing the audience, it had by far the biggest share of the listening public. So at least I was to work on the mass audience network.

But this division of the broadcast output into Light, Home or Third, according to the height of the listener's brow, seemed to me a rather sad departure from the old idea of providing a balanced diet of programmes. Before the war, the two domestic networks, the National and the Regional, had both carried the whole range of entertainment and information. In this way, for instance, the BBC had built up an immense following for serious music by introducing listeners to it almost by accident. A symphony concert or a piano recital might be sandwiched between a variety show and the commentary on a football match. So, tens of thousands must have come to an appreciation of classical music, simply because their sets were left switched on after the lighter and more familiar fare they had first opted to hear.

Under the new arrangement, the BBC had fewer complaints and, superficially, more satisfied customers, but I felt, in the long run, the mass of the listening public might be the losers. The fact was that the majority tended to identify with one of the networks and always stayed tuned to that. To this extent, the new system was also socially divisive. I think Tom Chalmers, who was himself no mean musician, must have realised the somewhat deadening limitations and he, in fact, succeeded in building up a big following for chamber music in the Light Programme simply by calling it 'Music in Miniature'. In this way, the uninitiated came to accept and enjoy light classical music because it was played continuously, without announcements, and so they were not put off by all the opus numbers, or the foreign sounding words.

I had a lively bunch of colleagues, among them Franklin 'Jingle' Engelmann, Philip Slessor, John Webster, David Dunhill, and Jean Metcalfe. Although much of the programme content was strictly escapist, I took a pride in at least presenting it as slickly and professionally as possible. My chief interest was in the News. The main bulletin on the Light Programme went out at 10 p.m. and this was a job I always tackled with great interest and care.

Events in Eastern Europe were fulfilling all the worst fears about Russia. After leaning over backwards, Britain had given up hope of ever reaching agreement, and Foreign Secretary, Ernest Bevin, had delivered himself of the final word on Stalin: 'Now 'e's gone too bloody far.'

By the summer of 1948 all road and rail communication with Berlin from the West through the Soviet Zone was cut and the great British and American airlift got under way.

Apart from the compelling News, the Light Programme also gave me opportunities for planning and playing my own choice of records. Over the years, I presented long running series late on Sunday nights. Firstly there was 'Serenade to Sleep' and then, in similar style, 'Music for Midnight'. This meant spending many hours in the Gramophone Library listening to discs and leafing through catalogues. I aimed to play pleasing instrumental and vocal music, but avoided as far as possible the hackneyed pieces. Debussy, Ravel and the guitar music of Granados was the type of thing I chose and I always included an unusual folk-song or two.

On one of these Sunday nights, it was 14 November 1948, I was engrossed in the presentation of my programme, which in those days involved playing the records oneself in the Light Programme continuity suite in the basement of Broadcasting House, when the Controller, Tom Chalmers rushed into the studio. 'Bob,' he said, 'Princess Elizabeth has had a son – we'll have to put out an announcement.' As it happened my records that night were rather more skittish than usual, so I suggested the announcement of the birth of an heir to the throne should be followed by something more soothing and, after a frantic search, we came up with Brahms' 'Cradle Song'. It was just after half past ten when I interrupted my programme to give the nation the news of the happy event.

The 'Family Favourites' record programmes, which were peak hour evening listening, meant careful preparation too. Franklin Engelmann, Michael Brooke, Philip Slessor, Jean Metcalfe and I used to present them in turn. We each selected our own list of titles from the thousands of postcards sent in by listeners. It was during one of these programmes that I dropped one of my worst clangers. I referred to a medley of Scottish songs as being sung by the late Sir Harry Lauder. No sooner had the record begun spinning, than telephone lines to the Duty Officer in Broadcasting House were jammed with calls from all over the country to inform me that Sir Harry was at that time still very much alive.

At the end of the record I said: 'I am so sorry about that slip – of course Sir Harry is still very much with us and may he delight us with his songs for many years to come.' The newspapers picked it up gleefully the next day and it appeared that Sir Harry had been sitting in the stalls of a Glasgow theatre when I prematurely killed him off. Fortunately he took it all very well and was able to say, as had Mark Twain on an earlier occasion, 'the report of my death was an exaggeration'.

John Macmillan, one of the Light Programme bosses, later to be a big success in commercial television, liked the way I handled 'Family Favourites' and wrote me a note saying: 'I can't remember hearing the programme being so effectively presented.' This I appreciated because John was a highly professional operator.

Cliff Michelmore was then at the Hamburg Station of the British Forces Network and did a popular Sunday 'Family Favourites' with Jean Metcalfe in the London studio. Whenever he was on leave, he used to stick his head round the door of the Announcers' Room at Broadcasting House waiting for Jean to finish her duties. That was the start of one of the great radio romances.

By this time, Nan and I had settled in with Miche at a ground-floor flat in Fawley Road, West Hampstead. Fortunately, Nan had been able to get her job back as a studio manager in the BBC European Service at Bush House, so that with our joint salaries we were able to keep just solvent. We were both working irregular hours and Nan's duties also involved a night-shift every few weeks. None of this would have been possible without the services of a splendid Irish person, Nancy Burke from Tipperary, who kept house for us and looked after Miche. It was a battle, but we were determined to keep a stable home going for Miche, who had been messed about quite enough already in her young life.

Walking was the main recreation as we still had no car. My favourite walk was up to the top of the Heath, perhaps stopping on the way back for a drink at The Holly Bush. This was a Benskin's house and sold superb draught beer. Bill Brown, a splendid character, presided and lived on the brew. He seldom bothered with solid food – and indeed seldom moved from his seat behind the tiny bar. Hampstead and The Holly Bush had been Bill's whole life and his father had had the pub before him.

When I was feeling less energetic, I would sometimes walk Miche round West Hampstead cemetery. The place seemed to hold a morbid fascination for her. A diminutive figure, she stumped round holding my hand and asking innumerable questions.

On one occasion she gazed long and fixedly at two old people who were resting quite near on one of the stone benches among the gravestones. Suddenly Miche looked up and at the top of her piping voice put the question: 'Is that where people sit while they are waiting to die?' I bundled her away without daring a backward glance.

Nan and I toiled through the summer painting over the acres of dingy brown on doors and skirting boards. It took three coats before they began to look as if white were the colour we intended. Our furniture was distinctly basic, but there were several junk shops near and, as the months went by, we were able to add an item or two. I remember buying a huge sofa for ten pounds from a shop in Flask Walk, Hampstead. It was about as big as a bus and, if you pressed a large wooden knob, one end of it flopped down, so that you could sleep on it too. On another occasion, Nan and I bought a huge brass fender in Chelsea and carried it back in triumph through the streets. We called in at a pub for much needed refreshment and stood at the counter with the fender on the floor, forming a sort of stockade around us.

When not fighting the flat, I was battling with the garden. Stone steps descended to it from french windows and it was like lowering oneself into a knee-high sea of brambles, thistles, nettles and ground elder. Shakespeare, in Julius Caesar, refers to 'thou bleeding piece of earth'. This was nothing to what I called our patch. Some of the brambles were up to fifteen feet long and the sweat poured off me as I lashed about in all directions with a bill-hook. Eventually I uncovered a few paths and, if I didn't make a garden, at least one could move around. Nan thought there was just one thing lacking – a dog. I was finding life quite complicated enough as it was, and found it perfectly possible to live without a dog, especially in London. However, Nan is nothing if not determined and, as luck would have it, when she was out with Miche one day, they passed a pet shop at the top of Baker Street. My fate was sealed when they both instantly fell in love with a doggie in the window.

He was there in the sitting room when I came home that evening. He was small and black and soft and wriggly – a perfect example of a feminine *fait-accompli* and I realised I was beaten. He looked so absurdly like a black lamb I called him Larry. If I had been getting a dog, it would not have been a poodle, but, no matter. Unfortunately things didn't augur well with Larry from the start. When we'd got the ticks off him, we took him to the vet for his jabs against distemper.

A few weeks later, on a Saturday morning, he started coughing. By that evening, he was much worse and having fits. Then he tried to climb up the wall. Next morning, although it was Sunday, we took him to a Jewish vet, whose surgery mercifully was open. Larry had got hard-pad distemper, against which, at that time, there was no immunisation vaccine. All the Vet could do was pump him full of every antibiotic he could think of and then say he had only a fifty-fifty chance of survival. It depended on us ; and nursing.

For a start, he had to be kept in a darkened room. As soon as there was any light, he began to see things and would stagger about, chew his feet and start trying to go up the wall. So, Nan and I took it in turns to nurse him for about a fortnight, during which time the only food he could take was calves'-foot jelly, administered with a spoon. Eventually we got him through it, although he was looking like a concentration camp victim.

Thereafter, he slowly gained in strength, but the illness had left its mark. Larry, one had to face it, was now a nutter or, let's say, an eccentric – a pixillated poodle. I must have walked thousands of miles with that dog on Hampstead Heath or in Regent's Park. This meant a short journey in the car, during which he kept up a continual, high pitched yelping. He was also liable to attack furiously any person who appeared anywhere near the car – say on a pedestrian crossing. Once I'd arrived, somewhat shaken, at the exercise ground the problem was to keep him out of water, especially muddy water to which he was irresistibly drawn. The very word Poodle, I believe, comes from the low German *Pudl*, meaning a watery swamp, so apart from being circus and truffle dogs, they were also water retrievers.

Nan and I were once misguided enough to take Larry with us to Brighton for the day by train. The best of many good things about Brighton is the Undercliff walk along to Rottingdean. On this particular day, there was a lot of wind and a boisterous sea. Suddenly, Larry, espying a seagull, leapt, with vertical take-off, clean over the railing along the sea wall to land, apparently, in a raging sea. Automatically, I followed suit and grabbed him back from the waves. All of this, somewhat to Nan's consternation. Her main anxiety, as she cheerfully confessed, ever practical, was that she had no money and in my pocket were the return tickets to London !

By the autumn of 1948 we were in need of a holiday but, not having much spare cash, we hadn't any idea what to do. Then, one morning, in a wash-room at Broadcasting House, I ran into Charles Brewer, the Assistant Head of the Light Programme, and he said why didn't I take his cottage at Southwold in Suffolk. This was a part of England I had never visited so, after mentioning it to Nan, I gladly accepted. We packed

Miche off to stay with Nan's mother in Bedford, caught the train from Liverpool Street to Halesworth, and a hired car drove us the last ten miles of the journey to Southwold.

Neither of us thought then that this was a place we would come to know better than anywhere else in England, except Hampstead. Charles's cottage was called 'Pantiles' and it was at No. 13 Church Street – a narrow lane leading off the High Street. We both fell in love with Southwold from the start.

A small town with a population of about three thousand and situated on England's most easterly stretch of coast, there is just the one main street leading to a small market place, dominated by the elegant eighteenth-century Swan Hotel, a white-fronted coaching inn. From there, three lanes branch off to the sea. One of the chief delights of Southwold is that it consists of a series of nine greens with cottages clustered sociably round each of them. Inland, the broad agricultural acres of East Anglia stretch away to the market towns of Halesworth, Saxmundham, Bungay and Beccles. There is no coast road, so Southwold has something of the feel of an island – by-passed by time and it has changed less over the years than almost any other small coastal town I can recall.

It is rather odd that Nan and I should both have fallen under Southwold's spell on that first occasion we visited it, because we spent the ten days or so we were there feeling miserably ill. I think we were thoroughly exhausted – Nan had a wretched cold and I was stricken by a monumental sty, which affected not only my left eye, but the whole of one side of my face as well, so this meant a course of penicillin injections.

In the evenings we usually called in at the tiny bar, really more of a snug, in Southwold's second hotel, The Crown. The bar itself was rather dark with a small settle facing it. Behind the counter at the back, interestingly shaped bottles of liqueurs were ranged on shelves and lit in such a way that they glowed intriguingly in a variety of colours. We used to sit there for hours over a drink or two happily gazing at the bottles, and revelling in the peace of the place. Before we left Southwold we booked to stay at The Crown the following Easter.

These post-war years were a tough time for almost everyone in Britain. There was fairly widespread disillusionment with socialism, which had failed to produce the pie in the sky some had expected of it and in the General Election of 1950 Clement Attlee's Government had its majority slashed to a mere six seats over the combined opposition. But, at least, clothing and petrol rationing soon ended and, at long last, the streets and shopfronts became fully lit once more. Then, just as we seemed to be getting off our knees, that very same summer saw the start of the Korean War and rearmament began in earnest – it was all very depressing.

The Light Programme with its audience ratings based on the findings of the BBC's Listener Research Department was now in the ascendancy and doing its best to keep everybody as happy as possible. In the forefront were Jewel and Warris, Frankie Howerd, Terry Thomas, Jimmy Edwards and, of course, the nation's friend Wilfred Pickles in the earthy *bonhomie* of 'Have a Go'.

My personal efforts were concentrated primarily on the News bulletins and record request programmes. I also greatly enjoyed presenting the Saturday night Promenade Concerts from the Royal Albert Hall, where that husband and wife team of dedicated BBC musicians Anna Instone and Julian Herbage genially presided. The commentary position is in one of the boxes and a lip microphone is used so that one's voice will not be heard in the hall itself. It's necessary to be very much on the alert in order to time the announcements to coincide exactly with the conductor. In my day it was usually Sir Adrian Boult, Sir Malcolm Sargent or Basil Cameron.

Then there's the question of gauging whether a solo artiste will give an encore or not. After a time, a sixth sense is acquired and one can adapt the presentation accordingly. The last night must be one of the few occasions when trendy young students quite unashamedly and with immense enjoyment find they are able to sing xenophobic songs like 'Rule Britannia' and, of course, 'Land of Hope and Glory'.

That same year the BBC Repertory Company celebrated its 21st Anniversary and Queen Mary, who was a great listener to the plays, had consented to attend a special performance of Emlyn Williams' *Night Must Fall* in Studio 3A at Broadcasting House. The production was by Howard Rose and in the cast were Gladys Young, Hugh Manning and Laidman Browne. I was asked to announce it.

The evening arrived and a red carpet reception was arranged. Then, a message came that Her Majesty was suffering from a sore throat and to her great regret would be unable to come. The broadcast went ahead as arranged and so did the champagne supper afterwards, but it felt pointless without Queen Mary. It was, incidentally, one of the few occasions when I met the reigning Director-General Sir William Haley. I had always heard he was remote and lacking in small talk and, that night anyway, he was. Not for nothing had a wag called him 'the man with two glass eyes'. I didn't see him address a single word to anybody. Later the Queen sent a message requesting that the Producer and all involved should send their commemorative programmes to Buckingham Palace. This was done and she signed each one of them. That is how it comes about that the only autographs I have ever collected in a long life of meeting celebrities are those of Queen Mary and – yes – the Beatles. Strange bedfellows I know, but pressure was put upon me to get the Beatles to sign on another occasion by my fourteen-year-old son.

Meanwhile at Broadcasting House there were rumours of impending changes in the Newsreading set-up. Until this time, each of the three domestic networks had its own staff who presented all the programmes including the News. This was not a particularly happy arrangement as some Announcers, especially in the Light Programme, much preferred putting on Variety shows and had little interest and not always the professional skills to make satisfactory Newsreaders. I knew that this was a state of affairs which for some time had been worrying John Snagge, the Head of Home Presentation, who had been heard to refer to the Light Programme as 'that Augean stable'. So a committee of top brass was formed to listen critically to all Newsreaders over a period of weeks and then to choose a team of seven who would read all the bulletins in the three networks.

BBC reasoning behind this was that the pronunciation used in the reading of the News should be only the best standard British-educated speech, which had been arrived at after a great deal of research and experiment. It seemed to me that it was even more important that the Newsreader should convey interest and make it easy for the listener to understand.

Anyway I was quite pleased when the telephone rang one lunchtime in the winter of 1951 at the flat in West Hampstead and Franklin Engelmann, who was then Assistant Head of the Light Programme, told me that I was one of the selected seven. My six colleagues were to be Frank Phillips, Alvar Lidell, Lionel Marson, Colin Doran, Robin Holmes and Alan Skempton. It meant that I would automatically be transferred to John Snagge's Presentation Department in the Home Service and it also meant that I would get a little more pay.

The national Press gave it quite a splash – dubbing us 'The Big Seven' or 'Now we are seven' and so on, but the fuss soon died down, because we were still anonymous. It took major wars to make the BBC give Newsreaders' names. They had done so for security reasons in the last big one and then again in, for the BBC, equally desperate times, when ITA finally burst on to the air.

In the early summer of that year, at last, there was some cheerful news to give. King George VI standing on the steps of St Paul's declared open the Festival of Britain. He appeared to have made a complete recovery from the illness, which had affected the arteries in his legs a short time before, and the Festival itself seemed to mark a hopeful recovery for Britain. On the South Bank there was a complete break with the frowsty past, here everything was gleaming and new: it was essentially a Festival inspired by contemporary materials and contemporary art.

No sooner was the Festival over, than the Attlee Government seemed to run out of steam and the Conservatives took over with the seventy-seven-year-old Churchill at their head and a majority of seventeen. R. A. Butler, the new Chancellor, saying the country was 'in danger of being bankrupt, idle and hungry' slapped on even tougher taxes and slashed the foreign travel allowance down to £25. The News bulletins were again full of woe.

In spite of everything round about this time Nan and I bought a car, a second-hand one, of course, but it couldn't have belonged to a nicer person. Benny Lister, with whom we had kept in touch since Singapore days, sold us her Morris saloon. This meant, among other jaunts, that we were able to see my parents more frequently and also Nan's mother in Bedford. Other visits were paid to Nan's Aunt Lil who lived in Shamley Green, near Guildford. She was over eighty, but tall, erect and splendidly aristocratic looking. In her day she must have been a great beauty.

Then, over the loudspeakers one bleak February morning in 1952, came the announcement of King George VI's death. It was totally unexpected as he appeared to have made a good recovery from his illness of the previous year. At the beginning

of the month Princess Elizabeth and Prince Philip had even set
off on a Commonwealth tour and the news was broken to them
at the Tree Tops Lodge in one of the game parks of Kenya.
One picture remains in the mind: the twenty-five-year-old
Queen Elizabeth, wearing black, pausing for a moment on the
steps of the airliner which had brought her home.

These were great events to chronicle in the bulletins. Britain
might now be a half bankrupt little island, but the whole world
paid tribute to the continuity of our traditions, even the
Chicago Tribune carried the banner headline THE KING IS DEAD.
At Westminster Hall, queues four miles long stood quietly in
February snow waiting to file past the catafalque.

For most of that year there was much to preoccupy Nan and
me at home. Our visits to Aunt Lil in Shamley Green became
sadder, as she was now desperately ill with cancer. She had a
horror of hospitals and nursing homes and asked if we would
agree to share a house with her and look after her. She was
quite happy that the house should be in Hampstead, so Nan
and I started the great hunt. We must have traipsed round at
least fifty before we found one that was reasonably suitable in
Netherhall Gardens, just off Fitzjohn's Avenue, which runs
from Swiss Cottage up to the Heath.

It was a tall, gaunt, red-brick Victorian house, semi-detached
and on four floors – with, in all, eleven rooms. Not the kind of
house to fall in love with, but the price was about right and at
least we would have plenty of space. This was good because
not only would Aunt Lil be with us, but we also knew that Nan
had started a baby.

We moved in the early spring on a cold, wet day. The house
seemed vast, empty and rather hideous. The previous owners
had been French. We had never met them, but they must have
had some strange ideas of décor. For a start, the heavy wrought-
iron gate was painted red and the spikes at the top of it were
gold. Indeed, almost everywhere was grey and salmon pink.
Horrible. Every fireplace had been boarded up, which made the
rooms look soulless. It was clear that this was a house we were
going to have to fight.

Our bits of furniture looked self-consciously lost in the
cavernous rooms and the carpets were much too small. We
would obviously have to do some more rounds of the second-
hand shops. I don't think Nancy Burke our housekeeper liked
the change much. The Fawley Road flat had been small and

G

snug – and the buses passed at the top of the road. Here, the kitchen was huge and gloomy with condensation perpetually forming on the high ceiling and it seemed about twenty yards from the kitchen, along a corridor, to the front door.

Ten days after we moved in, I stood at that door just after breakfast, as the removal men advanced towards me from the front gate. Their enormous van loomed outside and it was clear that Aunt Lil's furniture had arrived. As luck would have it, Nan had had early morning sickness ever since she was sure about the baby, and she had become strangely self-contained and mysterious. I knew I was going to have to cope, but I didn't know the furniture very well and was faced with having to make split second decisions as to where to tell them to dispose of the sideboards, wardrobes, beds and tables which lurched and lumbered in procession up the path. Which floor to say taxed me. let alone which room, but hesitation was useless, so I just said something and kept my fingers crossed. I felt like Mickey Mouse, as the Sorcerer's Apprentice in *Fantasia*, when the brooms kept on bringing in the buckets of water and there was nothing he could do to stop them.

It was a perfectly horrible business and when it was all over the house looked like a nightmarish junk store. Some of the oak pieces were little more than 'Hiltons' for a host of wood-worm and dust hung heavily on the air.

Later that day, Aunt Lil herself arrived by ambulance. She looked desperately thin and pale, but managed to walk, still erect, up to the big bedroom in the front on the first floor. The main preoccupation was to get her settled in as comfortably as possible. She seemed fairly happy, but rather disappointed that Hampstead was so quiet. I think she had been expecting to see more people and traffic in the streets, whereas at that time Netherhall Gardens was a back-water.

I suppose it was the strain of the move but just three weeks later I began feeling ghastly and the doctor diagnosed a virus pneumonia. He stuffed me full of antibiotics and the weeks went by, but I still felt filleted and awful. The odd thing was that my temperature was sub-normal all the time.

It was grim for Nan too, having to cope not only with me but also with Aunt Lil, the aftermath of the move and getting Miche settled in a new school, to say nothing of growing a baby. I tried once unsuccessfully to get back to work and then came to the conclusion there was only one thing for it. I had to get away somewhere on my own. The various antibiotic drugs may have damped down the pneumonia, but they had also practically sunk me without trace. While Nan was out doing the shopping, I telephoned The Ship Hotel at Brighton, ordered a taxi, and by the time she returned, I had gone. I left a note on the mantelpiece explaining everything and fortunately she took it like a lamb. She was probably quite relieved to get me out of her hair.

After a week or so, I was able to totter unsteadily along the front and then began to make good progress. Soon Nan came to collect me and all was well. By June I was able to return to work.

At least twice a week it was necessary to sleep in Broadcasting House. The last News summary was just before midnight and the first News of the morning was at 7 a.m. The divan beds were in offices on the fourth floor. On these occasions I found sleep was only fitful. The typewriters and telephones even in repose seemed to leave a disquiet in the fusty air and the rooms smelt of files, waste paper and fag-ends.

Soon it was time to rise again and wish everyone 'Good Morning' as brightly as possible; and in mid-winter, when there was freezing fog, to feel sympathy for the poor blighters for whom my voice was probably a sort of alarm-clock. At least I was at my place of work, but many listeners would soon be groping through the still dark streets for their buses or trains. Over the years while reading the News, I had acquired the habit of unwinding paperclips and by the time the quarter of an hour was over the studio desk top would always be littered with twisted bits of wire.

The morning reading of 'Yesterday in Parliament' could at times be heavy going. One day I very nearly came to grief. A new sub-editor had recently joined the BBC Parliamentary Unit and an unlikely sort of chap he appeared, with a distinctly bucolic look about him. To convince all and sundry of his genuine academic attainments he had thought it judicious to pin up behind the office door a photograph of himself in mortar-board and gown.

He was exceedingly conscientious about his duties and, being very new, thought it was part of his job to sit in the studio while I was broadcasting. Perhaps he thought I might not read the stuff as written. Wading through it, I felt his presence as he kept moving nervously in his chair in the corner of the small studio. As I neared the end of what had been an unusually turgid report, he must momentarily have lost control and there burst from him a report of another kind – in fact, a rip-roaring raspberry. A huge belly laugh surged up in me and my hand shot out for the 'cough' key, which cuts out the microphone. Somehow I was able to compose myself and in half a minute came back on the air, saying sedately, 'I am sorry about the break in transmission.' Little did listeners know the cause of it.

In the summer of that year, 1952, there was another change at the top. Sir William Haley left to become Editor of *The Times* – and Lord Reith wrote to the staff magazine *Ariel* paying him handsome tribute: 'He has held the second most responsible office in this country with dignity, devotion, distinction ; to the general high acclaim.'

Then, with the threat of commercial broadcasting in mind, Reith added, 'His friends in the BBC and in the ex-BBC are sad at his departing ; and they are worried too – for there is menace ahead.'

From my lowly viewpoint, I felt he was the first Director-General since Reith to leave his imprint on the place. He had been masterfully efficient, but left behind him a somewhat de-humanised organisation. I still feel that the effect of parcelling out radio programmes by the height of a brow was culturally and socially divisive.

Haley was succeeded by B. E. Nicolls, a stalwart character from Reith's day who became Acting-Director-General until his knighthood and retirement a few months later. The appointment of Major-General Sir Ian Jacob came in the winter of that year. He had formerly been in charge of the Overseas Service, but came to the top job after a secondment to the Ministry of Defence.

Sir Ian was not particularly impressive to meet in stature or in personality, but he obviously had great administrative gifts and during the war had been Assistant Military Secretary to Churchill's War Cabinet. Perhaps it was felt that he was the man to hold the BBC monopoly secure against the assaults of its enemies. The commercial and show-biz boys were gathering in the wings.

These changes made little difference to me at the time. Far more significant were the events at the new house in Hampstead. That summer Aunt Lil, after a tremendous struggle and considerable pain, had finally died. A nurse had been practically living in the house and the doctor calling daily, so things had been difficult. Luckily, we were able to get away afterwards for a fortnight to Southwold – as always, it worked its magic on us and we came back better able to cope.

Nan was all the time getting bigger: I suddenly found I was married to a barrage balloon. An appalling moment came one October morning when I was helping her with the shopping. We had been in different shops and when I came out of mine I saw Nan crossing the road and coming towards me.

. There were roadworks going on and somehow she tripped over part of a wooden barrier. She tilted forward, off-balance, running as she did so, but with the weight she was carrying there was no hope of her saving herself. She saw me a few yards away and that may have kept her going. I did not know I could move so fast. I hurled myself across the road and caught her in my arms just as she was collapsing. It was a nightmarish moment for us both.

In mid-November Nan moved into Queen Mary's Maternity Home right on top of the Heath. There, just before midnight on Saturday, 22 November 1952 our son was born. The next afternoon I set eyes on him. He looked great, with hair and everything and I suppose it was the most marvellous moment of my life.

17 Alexandra Palace and Minsmere

In the meantime, up on London's northern heights the Corporation's youngest, if not favourite, offspring little Telly was flexing his muscles in no uncertain way, on emerging from the trials of adolescence. The staff at Ally Pally or in the two newer studios opened in 1950 at Lime Grove near Shepherd's Bush were apt to feel overworked, underpaid and above all misunderstood. At Broadcasting House the elders of the temple still looked with greater favour on that more manageable and less demanding radio trinity of Home, Light and Third. But one event, on 2 June 1953, was to bring television to the full flowering of maturity – the Coronation.

For the first time on a great national occasion, television had by far the larger audience: over twenty million compared with the twelve million or so who listened to it on radio. It was the greatest of all the BBC's technical triumphs, masterminded in Westminster Abbey itself by Peter Dimmock, with Richard Dimbleby of course providing the perfect commentary.

At that time in some respects, the BBC's monopoly can never have seemed more secure and yet the problems besetting television were immense. For one thing, it was a very much more expensive medium than radio in every way and, as it was a new form of entertainment, there were many restrictions put upon it by the Unions. The ban on pre-recording by the Musicians' Unions was especially crippling. This greatly reduced the amount of talent available because, if the musicians were not allowed to pre-record, other performers, who depended on them for their act, could not do so either. In addition some theatrical managements would not allow their contract artists to appear on television at all. The feeling was general among the staff that, if television were to move ahead, somehow a great deal more money would have to be found.

In July 1952 the Corporation's Royal Charter had been renewed by the Conservative Government for ten more years, but there was one important new clause: the Licence of the BBC was described as 'non-exclusive'. This followed the recommendation in a Government White Paper earlier that year which read, significantly and ominously, 'in the expanding field of television provision should be made to permit some element of competition, when the calls on capital resources at present needed for purposes of greater national importance makes this feasible.'

The great battle of monopoly versus commercial competition was soon to be fully joined. For determined seekers after enlightenment in this murky field the whole tortuous tangle of intrigue and lobbying by pressure groups has been admirably traced by Peter Black, the distinguished television columnist of the *Daily Mail*, in his book, *The Mirror in the Corner*.[1]

And yet, the sorry truth is that the BBC only lost its monopoly more or less by accident. It was a classic case of a resolute minority getting its way. The Beveridge Committee had been set up by the Labour Government to enquire into all aspects of broadcasting in this country and in January 1949 it began collecting evidence.

When the report was finally published in January 1951 it came down heavily in favour of continuing the BBC monopoly. The only member of the committee against was that staunch Conservative Selwyn Lloyd and he put in a minority report. It looked as though the BBC were home and dry.

And so it should have been, if the Labour Government had not allowed itself to get bogged down in detail. Six months passed by in discussion about trivial arrangements affecting broadcasting in the regions. And then, before the Charter had in fact been renewed, Attlee decided to go to the polls – it can't have been easy for him running the Government with his tiny majority of six. Presumably, he not only underestimated Selwyn Lloyd, but also overestimated his chances of winning the election. In the event, of course, he lost and when the Conservatives got back to power with a majority of seventeen the fight was on again in earnest. There were no holds barred and as the general public showed apathy the anti-monopolists, the business and advertising interests, in the end, narrowly won the day. The repercussions which followed the launching of the commercial channel in September 1955 have since permeated

[1] *The Mirror in the Corner*: *People's Television* by Peter Black, published by Hutchinson and Co. Ltd, 1972.

every aspect of broadcasting in radio as well as television. One of the fields in which its influence has been strongly felt is, of course, the News.

In the early fifties there was as yet no straight television News, but at the end of each evening's transmission, a repeat reading was given from Egton House of that night's main radio bulletin. There were no moving pictures, just a BBC symbol to fill the screen. The visual side of things was taken care of by the television newsreel run by Philip Dorté. This fifteen-minute film coverage, on the lines of the cinema newsreels, went out in five editions each week and had deservedly won a big following: it was highly professional, informative and entertaining, but it did not pretend to deal with the hard news of the day.

So, eventually, the BBC decided to take the plunge and in July 1954 launched a television News, under the control of News Division itself. The Television Service had left Alexandra Palace for new pastures at Shepherd's Bush and so the ancient new venture. In the job of presenting a News in vision the BBC pile, where it had all started in 1936, was bequeathed to the had big problems. One of the biggest was the man then in charge of News – an immensely tall New Zealander with an exceptional rigidity of mind. I had first met him back in 1941, at six o'clock down in the sub-basement studio of the BBC Overseas Service, which was then run from 200 Oxford Street. He was broadcasting a weekly talk in the Pacific Service and I had to put him on the air. At that time in the morning, one's mind is not at its clearest and I remember thinking his name must have been wrongly spelt. It was Tahu Hole. I found him to be a man of considerable personal charm, but even seated at the microphone in the small talks studio, he towered up like a graven image.

When he was appointed to the top editorial job after the war, he was taking over a BBC News Service respected and almost revered throughout the world. Determined that this reputation should remain inviolate, he followed a line of hyper-caution. The bulletins under his direction became colourless, long-winded and dull. Editors seethed with frustration. One of them, the novelist John Appleby who was a good friend of mine and lived in Hampstead, courageously burst into satirical verse in the BBC staff magazine *Ariel*. The opening stanza ran:

According to the Press Association,
'Britain is definitely on the map'
But we don't guarantee the information:
Somewhere, the item may conceal a trap.

Another senior editor of great physical strength relieved his journalistic feelings when on duty at Broadcasting House one night, by wrenching a lavatory cistern clean off the wall.

It was not surprising that a man like Tahu Hole, whose caution could drive his editors to such extreme measures, regarded the use of pictures with disfavour and suspicion. Likewise, he feared that whoever was chosen to read the News in vision might colour it or distort it in some way by imposing personal views. So, for a start, only top editors and correspondents were seen, but excellent journalists though they were, their skills did not run to the art of reading scripts to camera. They frequently appeared furtive and ill at ease. Soon Fleet Street was referring to them, rather unkindly, as those guilty-looking men, so, for the most part, only captions or a still photograph filled the screen. The bulk of the News was read out of vision by the team of Newsreaders who took it in turns to make the trek up to Alexandra Palace from Broadcasting House.

We found it all a nightmarish business, because most staff involved were required to learn these new skills on the air, and Television News looked inept and amateurish compared with the professionalism of the rest of the programmes. The subeditors for instance had to learn to write their scripts to fit a section of film – and this meant acquiring the discipline of writing with a stop-watch at the rate of three words per second. The Newsreaders for their part had to become more flexible and to catch the mood of a story. They had to learn among other things to vary their pace and pitch like commentators. Some of the sound Newsreaders found these new tricks difficult to acquire.

One of them in particular was so set in his ways that his deliberate, modulated tones would time and again be heard meandering on long after the appropriate section of film had ceased. Sometimes he would still be reading the script of, say, a funeral, when film of a motoring Grand Prix was on the screen. One evening a senior editor, driven to distraction, stood behind the said Newsreader's chair in the studio and, whenever his voice overran the film, the editor clamped his hand firmly over the reader's mouth.

On these occasions feelings ran high and sometimes in the canyon-like corridors at Alexandra Palace it nearly came to fisticuffs as skirmishes broke out among the staff at the apparent imbecility of their colleagues. Successful television can only come from perfect teamwork among engineers, production staff, writers and performers and in this respect the News was in the kindergarten stage.

In the control gallery, once the News was on the air, the production assistant was in charge of the operation under the anxious eye of the editor. Sometimes, in those early days, there was total confusion, especially when the order of News items was changed at the last moment. Once a distraught producer, not knowing which piece of film was supposed to come next, was heard giving the despairing instruction 'Run it! Whatever it is!' On another occasion, when the News was in a hopeless tangle, with everyone in the control gallery shouting at once, the editor, a man of caution, delivered himself of the stirring instruction: 'Whatever you do – do nothing!' But, on consideration, perhaps it would be kinder to draw a veil over those first growing pains of television News.

Around this time I had other worries at home. Our son, whom we had named Alastair Robert, fell ill with whooping cough and a mysterious virus and lay in bed pale and listless for many weeks. Nan decided to leave her job at Bush House and devote all her time to looking after him. It was undoubtedly the right thing to do because with her nursing and the expert medical care of a Hampstead children's specialist, a charming old man by the name of Dr Batten, Alastair suddenly began to recover. By the summer, he was well enough to come with us for the annual holiday to Southwold, where we rented a house near the church on St Bartholomew Green. I began to take an interest in the varied birdlife which abounds on that easterly stretch of coast, just 100 miles from Holland. In long walks on the deserted foreshore my attention was first caught by the small gull-like birds which flew over the sea with a graceful buoyant flight, their bills held downwards as they scanned the waves. They were more elegant than gulls and I saw their tails were deeply forked. Every so often one would hover for a few moments before plummeting down almost vertically into the water, to emerge as often as not with a small

202

fish glistening in its bill. At one point along the beach twenty or more circled round above my head, making high-pitched, strident cries. They were so agitated that I realised this must be a breeding colony. From time to time one of them swooped low over my head trying to scare me away. It was just then that I very nearly trod on some eggs. There were three of them in a slight hollow; they blended so perfectly with the sand and shingle all around that it was only at the last second I spotted them and stepped aside. By now, the parent birds were getting so worried that I hadn't the heart to stay long.

They were, of course, little terns, but the strange thing was that my attention had never been caught by them before, although I must have seen them countless times in various parts of the country. With binoculars (8 × 30) and a book of identification I was soon well and truly hooked by this new interest and in no time was delighting in the fluting of the redshanks over the marsh, the piping of the oyster-catchers and the distant boom of a bittern. How odd that I had lived for over thirty years without being really aware of the wonders of bird life. It was something I had taken for granted and now I was finding that a new dimension of interest had been added to my life. It so happened that just a few miles down the coast was a large bird reserve at Minsmere run by the Royal Society for the Protection of Birds. As soon as possible, I became a member of the Society and after writing for a permit made regular visits there.

I found it was a 1,500 acre stretch of mixed heathland, woodland and reed-beds on the edge of the sea, south of Dunwich. There were several hides placed at good viewing points: these looked like dark, wooden huts, some on stilts. I shall always remember the first time I entered one. It was black inside until the warden slowly and gently, so as not to disturb any birds that might be near, raised the wooden shutters over the narrow rectangular opening. It must have been beginner's luck because there – a few feet in front of our eyes – was the unforgettable sight of a kingfisher hovering. He stayed for a good fifteen seconds, as though suspended by an invisible wire. He was quite small with a large head and bill; the tail was very short. His back, wings and tail were shimmering bluish-green in the pale sunlight; the throat was whitish and the underparts a deep copper and gold. I have never seen anything look so vibrantly alive.

Do you know whom we have to thank, indirectly, for the creation of Minsmere? – Adolf Hitler. If it hadn't been for his war this sanctuary, now famous all over the world, would never have come into being. Before the war it had been just rough farmland, mainly used for grazing. Then, in June 1940 with the country facing the threat of invasion the area was flooded as a coastal defence measure and by the end of the war, when the sluices began operating again, a large expanse of reed-beds and marshland had developed and with it a whole new habitat.

It wasn't long before the birds got wind of it and in 1947 ornithologists became intensely interested when, after an absence of a hundred years, that elegant black and white wader, the avocet was found to be nesting there. In fact there were four pairs. The RSPB, which then had only a few thousand members and a headquarters in part of a building in London's Victoria Street, moved fast and in 1948 the local landowner Captain Stuart Ogilvie kindly agreed to lease the 1,500 acres to the Society as a sanctuary.

A few miles down the coast on Havergate Island in Orfordness another four pairs nested and this too was acquired as an RSPB reserve – Reg Partridge being appointed warden. The avocet has perhaps been the biggest of all the RSPC's success stories and the 1972 figures were up to 110 breeding pairs at Havergate and 35 at Minsmere, so it was not without reason that this graceful bird was selected as the Society's emblem.

Over the years, I have watched great improvements taking place at Minsmere, because obviously it is not enough just to have the land ; a careful conservation policy is needed and much work has to be carried out in order to create the right conditions for the particular birds it is desired to attract. The outstanding success has been the construction of what has come to be known as 'the Scrape', where there is food in abundance for the migrant waders and the right breeding conditions now exist for many species, especially the terns and ringed plovers, which have been forced off their former nesting places on the foreshore through disturbance by holidaymakers.

Dick Wolfendale was the first warden and what a fine bird man he was ; once when I was with him he even called a whimbrel down from the sky. He retired in 1959; his successor as Head Warden was Herbert E. Axell. Herbert came to Minsmere from the RSPB reserve at Dungeness in Kent. He had done great work there, but a nuclear power station was being built nearby and it was thought at first that this might interfere with the reserve. So Herbert and his wife Joan sold their house and came to take over at Minsmere. It was ironical that, shortly after arriving, the Central Electricity Generating Board decided to build a nuclear power station at Sizewell immediately adjoining this reserve. Since then, we are wiser and have found that power stations and nature reserves can live side by side in perfect harmony; it has in fact been a story of perfect co-operation.

Not unnaturally, Herbert was a little sad at leaving Dungeness, which was his home ground, to come up to East Anglia, but he very soon settled down and realised the full potential of Minsmere. Now, just on 100 species breed here and over 200 are recorded each year. Herbert is in every sense a big man and Nan and I are lucky to be able to number him and his wife Joan among our friends. I liked him at once. He has the direct open look that belongs to men who live their lives close to nature. The only things he cannot stand are bad manners and interference of any kind with his breeding birds – Minsmere is after all his kingdom. Soon after arriving, he realised there was a large area of dry, reedy meadowland which was almost useless for birds – it supported a few pairs of reed-buntings but that was all. Bert decided to change all that and play at being God.

Over the years with bulldozers and strong arms, an area of fifty acres has now been cleared and flooded with shallow, brackish water. Then a whole series of small islands, there are over forty of them, were constructed out of shingle and hobbin to provide a great variety of nesting conditions. What's more by a system of sluices it is possible to control not only the depth of the water but also the degree of salinity. To see the result all you have to do is dip a glass jar into the water and hold it up to the light and you will see a living soup for birds – there are worms, insects, snails and shrimps – vital food for many different species. As a result, fifteen hundred pairs of breeding birds have been added to the reserve and, at the time of writing in 1972, there are in addition to 35 pairs of breeding avocets, 500 pairs of sandwich terns, 240 pairs of common terns and 5 pairs of little terns to say nothing of a pair of common gulls breeding for the first time in Suffolk. These are like miniature herring gulls and although resident in Scotland and parts of Ireland are very rare in England.

In addition to the breeding birds a whole host of waders use the Minsmere lagoons as a stopping place on migration ; it is the perfect place for them to feed and rest before resuming their great journeyings across the world. Many of them winter in Africa and then return in the spring to their breeding grounds far above the Arctic Circle at the top of the world – a distance of over 6,000 miles.

Apart from 'the Scrape' with its lagoons and islands there is the great area of reed-marsh where in particular three rare species are found. One of them, the marsh harrier, is now among Britain's rarest breeding birds. There are usually two or, some years, three nesting pairs at Minsmere ; it is a magnificent sight to watch these large hawks quartering the reed-beds in their search for food, as they glide low over the reeds, their broad wings spanning fully four feet. Every now and then they swoop down to take a frog, a toad or snake, sometimes eggs or young birds, or it may be a small rabbit or a rat. Their plumage varies considerably but generally the adult male is brownish with grey on wings and tail. His small head is cream with dark stripes. As with all harriers the female is larger, usually without grey on wings. Her plumage is brown with a pale, lightly streaked head and a creamy margin to the shoulders.

The nest is large, rather untidy and low down in the reeds. There are four or five off-white, tinged with pale blue, eggs ; the female does nearly all the sitting. As the time taken before they hatch it is up to thirty-eight days she gets pretty hungry. The male will often bring her food, which she sometimes snatches in a spectacular aerial food-pass. I have seen these aerobatics several times and the sight never fails to thrill me. As the male approaches the nest with food, the female flies up beneath him, flips over on her back at the last moment and catches the prey which he drops to her from his talons.

Another of the Minsmere star birds is the marsh harrier's natural enemy – the bittern. This formidable heron-like bird requires almost exactly the same conditions and so there is inevitable rivalry between them for territory and prey. As the bittern spends most of his time skulking in the reeds, he is not the easiest bird to see. I shall always remember the first time I had a good look at one from the tree-hide at Minsmere. An expanse of reeds stretched away, but just below in front of the hide was a clearing. After waiting in dead silence for about ten minutes, I noticed an almost imperceptible movement at the edge of the reeds – and, suddenly, realised he was there. He was quite big, over two feet long and his colouring blended perfectly with the reeds, as he stood motionless and straight as a post, his dagger-like yellow bill pointing to the sky. After a few moments, he unfroze and walked on his long green legs with a curious gliding movement, head lowered and shoulders hunched. His colouring was buff and brown, streaked with black and although the sexes are alike, I somehow felt certain this was a male. Then he melted back into the reeds again, as mysteriously as he had come.

It is, of course, the male which produces the extraordinary boom, a sort of 'hoomp' sound like a fog-horn, which can be heard up to three miles away over the marshes. Sir Walter Scott immortalised him in *The Lady of the Lake*:

> And the bittern sound his drum
> Booming from the sedgy shallow.

You can hear the sound from February to June and, contrary to what people think, when preparing to boom, he is in a more or less horizontal position. First, he gives some short grunts, then, after a big intake of breath, slightly lowers his head and booms up to six or more times in succession.

Once there were all sorts of fanciful ideas as to how he produced this weird sound. In the nineteenth century, in some parts, country folk thought he made it by thrusting his bill into a reed and using it like an organ pipe to swell the note above its natural pitch. Others thought he put his head under water and blew violently.

Unlike the heron he does not breed in colonies; the nest is quite small, usually among dead reeds and close to the water. The bittern lives mainly on fish and can take a pike or an eel over a foot long. He also eats water voles, mice, shrews, frogs and newts. I must add that there was a time when he was considered good eating himself, especially the young.

The bittern was also used to some extent in falconry. As the hawk stooped on him from above he would set his bill perpendicularly upwards and legend has it that sometimes he even succeeded in spearing it. He has certainly won a reputation for bravery and some say he will defend himself against a dog by throwing himself on his back using his long green claws and bill as weapons. A strange, fascinating bird whose mysterious boom echoes down the ages.

The third of the three stars which regularly breed at Minsmere, but in very few other parts of the country now, is the bearded reedling or, as he is usually known, the bearded tit. Like the others, he depends for his existence on a large expanse of reeds. The confusion over his name comes from the fact that he is not in any way related to our woodland tits, but is unique in Europe.

His life is spent among or flying in groups just above the tops of the reeds. For this reason, he is not easy to see and you are much more likely to hear him first – a metallic 'ching' repeated several times ; then perhaps a reed top will sway and you may catch your first glimpse of the beardie. He is a most elegant and colourful character with a blue-grey head and black stripes like moustaches, though of course, he hasn't got a beard. The rest of him is mainly a handsome tawny colour and his tail is long and rounded at the end. Look more closely through your binoculars and you will see his underparts are pinkish grey with black under-tail coverts. The hen is paler and without the 'moustaches'.

There is a gaiety and spirit about a small flock of beardies as they skim low over the reeds in direct flight that is uplifting and somehow, I always feel better for seeing them.

I have said nothing about the long-eared owls which bred successfully for the first time at Minsmere in 1972 ; and nothing about the birds of the heath and the woodland, where rare warblers breed and nightingales set the night air throbbing.

And, of course, it is not only birds, but most summers there are butterflies, dragonflies and damselflies in abundance. Great fat red admirals, peacocks and tortoise-shells tumbling about in the air, as they used to do everywhere in the countryside before chemical spraying started.

Then there are the animals too. In winter or early spring you may catch a glimpse of a small group of shy red deer perhaps feeding in autumn-sown barley. There are a few foxes, rabbits which are becoming much more numerous in spite of periodic outbreaks of myxomatosis, hares, stoats and weasels. The red squirrel happily still survives here in fair numbers, although one or two of the familiar grey variety have been sighted recently and infiltration is feared.

The only others which are not welcome on the reserve are

the coypu, the mink and the brown rat. The coypu is a large rodent from South America, which like the North American mink was brought here to be farmed for its fur. He is a beaver-like creature with a large flat head, two long orange-coloured teeth and a spindly rat-like tail. The fur – nutria – comes from his underside. At the end of the fifties a number of them escaped in East Anglia and in no time became a serious problem – undermining the dykes and eating the root crops. It took a major campaign by the Ministry of Agriculture and one or two very hard winters to get them under control.

Now once again with milder weather they are increasing and up to as many as thirty wire cage traps are still set daily at Minsmere in runs and ditches. In this way nineteen were caught and killed in 1971. This kind of vigilance is essential because they multiply exceedingly fast, owing to their tropical breeding cycle, which enables them to produce three litters a year. Fortunately, that vicious little killer the mink is, so far, less numerous.

On one occasion an old male otter who had a holt near a sluice was caught in one of these coypu traps. I am told he appeared most indignant, and after being weighed and measured, 11 lbs of him and 35 inches in length, he was respectfully released.

For botanists there are two very rare plants which grow here – California borage, which looks something like a common bugloss but has tiny yellow flowers. It is in fact a pernicious weed and was probably first brought to this country in chicken food. The other is only to be found in this part of East Anglia and in North Kent – the marsh sowthistle. It too has yellow flowers and grows in clumps in the reeds up to seven feet tall. At the last count there were 1,700 stems of it at Minsmere.

Understandably, Nan and I were increasingly finding that we wanted to spend as much time as possible in this part of East Anglia and so when she was left a small legacy by her godfather she had only one thought: a tiny cottage near the lighthouse, which in Southwold is fully automated and on dry land, was coming up for auction and Nan was determined to make a bid. In a solid downpour of rain she left Hampstead to drive the hundred miles or so to the saleroom. It was such appalling weather that very few people ventured out and so with hardly any bids being made we became the owners of 'Corner Cottage' for £875. There was even a little money left over to put it in order – not that much needed to be done – just a few floorboards to renew and we gave the outside a coat of whitewash. The small door and window frame we painted pale yellow. It was in a sheltered position, tucked up in the corner of St James' Green and right alongside it, in perfect harmony, was a disused barn.

An enchanting cottage and we couldn't have been more delighted with it. On opening the low door, two wooden steps led straight down into the sitting-room. A small staircase wound round from the far corner up to the main bedroom, which was just large enough to hold a small double bed ; off this room was a tiny cabin-like space which would at least take two bunks for Miche and Alastair. Apart from that, downstairs there was a small kitchen and a bathroom and that was all. Behind was a tiny walled garden and at the bottom of it a narrow, two-storey brick shed with a steeply sloping roof which the fisherman who originally lived here must have used as a smoke house. This was rather a rickety structure but, as a traditional feature, we had it carefully restored and it provided us with much needed stowage space. Seldom have we felt more snug and secure than in 'Corner Cottage', especially at night when the pale beam from the lighthouse flashed intermittently on the bedroom ceiling.

18 Television News

At Broadcasting House during those years of the early fifties Newsreading duties continued for me as before and nightly, on the Home Service, Big Ben boomed out, chimes and all, heralding the nine o'clock News as he had done in the darkest days of war. But the country was not stilled for him now: many listeners had become viewers as the emphasis shifted to television. All the same, there was big news to give and, having seen something of Stalin's rule, I had no tears to shed when making the announcement of his death on 6 March 1953. He had certainly raised Russia up but by such awful means that it was as if an evil shadow had now been lifted from the world. The paralysis of fear in the Soviet Union would at least be partially relieved.

There followed the struggle for power among his successors in the Kremlin, but here at home we all had brighter things to think about with New Zealand sheep farmer Edmund Hilary and Sherpa Tenzing from Sir John Hunt's expedition conquering Everest as a Coronation gift for the Queen; some sanguine spirits even took this to be a portent of a new Elizabethan age. But soon it was foreign news which took the headlines again as the people of East Berlin fought with bare hands against Russian tanks. Stalin might be dead, but for the East European satellite countries there was to be no let-up in the iron-fisted rule.

In the Far East, at last, an armistice was signed in Korea, while in Indo-China France toiled hopelessly in the eighth year of her struggle against the Chinese-backed communists from the north.

The world was living dangerously – Russia too now had the hydrogen bomb – and not surprisingly there was increased interest in programmes dealing with news and current affairs. One of the most important was 'At Home and Abroad' which followed the nine o'clock News on the Home Service on two evenings a week. I was pleased to be chosen as one of the presenters of this series which was edited by Stephen Bonarjee. Over the years on Tuesdays and Fridays all the principal

211

people in the news came to Studio 4A in Broadcasting House to be interviewed at the BBC microphones.

Before each programme a running buffet was provided on the second floor where speakers were received and duly refreshed. This was presided over with Jeeves-like suavity by a stately character known to all as Mr Goss. Formerly Lord Derby's butler, he now served Sir Ian Jacob in that capacity and also consented graciously to lend tone to our proceedings. There was always someone of interest to meet, but it was advisable not to get too carried away in conviviality otherwise it would mean trouble ahead. George Brown was always stimulating, as was Ernest Marples, who usually brought with him a bottle of burgundy from his own vineyard. The ultimate terror of talks producers was Randolph Churchill, especially when he had dined over well.

Mr Goss was equal to every occasion and once when a Trade Union official from South Wales, after an arduous journey, arrived in a somewhat flushed condition he resolved the situation in no time. 'If I may presume to make a suggestion, Sir, I believe I have the very thing for you.' With which he handed the fuddled official a wine glass containing angostura bitters plus a dash of soda. A potent emetic. In two minutes flat the official was heading for the door. On return he was swaying a little but at least able to utter. Considering everything we thought the microphone interview went reasonably well but, of course, there was no fooling his wife. She was on the blower in a trice from Wales wanting to know why her husband didn't sound quite himself.

In addition to radio duties my journeyings up to Alexandra Palace also became more frequent as television News continued with its painful early struggles. It was considered a daring new departure when in September 1955, for the first time the BBC showed Newsreaders in vision, though still of course unnamed. This was only a fortnight before ITV's ceremonial launching at London's Guildhall on the twenty-second of that month. The BBC was no longer to have the sole responsibility for broadcasting in this country. It was with this very much in mind that the Director-General Sir Ian Jacob addressed himself to senior staff. In the light of what was to happen in the years ahead, it is perhaps worth recalling his words. He said he thought the maintenance of standard was of supreme importance to the Corporation's future. And he continued: 'There were two ways in which the BBC might fail: One was by allowing standards to slide downhill so that it could be said with truth that there was nothing to choose between the BBC and any other popular form of broadcasting. The other way would be for the Corporation to be beaten at its own game. That the latter could happen was not to be believed for a moment but it was conceivable that standards might be lowered in an understandable effort to maintain big audiences. This must be avoided at all costs.'[1]

Sir Ian anticipated a loss of audience owing to ITV's emphasis on cash quiz shows and the like but he believed the ratio could be held in the proportion of 40 to 60. In the event, only two years later, the percentage figure for the BBC was as low at 27 with the ITV rating 73. There were questions in the House of Commons as to why all viewers had to pay for a licence to watch BBC when over two thirds showed preference for ITV. It was then that the Corporation finally knew it would have to change its tune, enter the market place and fight back.

One of the new channel's successes was its News Service. Editor Aidan Crawley's great advantage was that he was starting from scratch. His staff could be hand-picked for television and, unlike the BBC, ITN had no prestigious reputation to maintain and no inhibitions about Newsreaders projecting their personalities. Robin Day, Ludovic Kennedy and Christopher Chataway were called Newscasters and great play was made that they were journalists and wrote their own scripts. In fact the writing they did was not extensive but at least they were members of a close-knit team.

In a sense the BBC when faced with tackling television News was the victim of its own resources. These had nearly all been geared and the staff recruited for radio; unfortunately the requirements for television were very different. The medium itself is more intimate and direct. The impersonal, objective style of writing used for BBC radio bulletins at that time and the anonymity of the sound Newsreaders simply would not do. In television one must talk *to* people not *at* them.

This meant the writers had to learn to use simple, everyday language, and the Newsreaders learn to relax in front of the

[1] Extract from the Director-General's Speech, *Ariel* (Staff Magazine) Winter 1955.

cameras as though 'telling' the News in a friendly, informative manner.

Believe me, it wasn't easy. There were so many off-putting things going on and unlike the sound studio where you could loosen your collar and sling your jacket over the back of the chair, at Alexandra Palace it was always necessary to look reasonably correctly dressed with tie straight, hair tidy and so on. That is to say nothing of the glare and heat of the arc lamps, the baleful eyes of the cameras, the flashing of cue lights, the sometimes incomprehensible hand signals from floor managers and, worst of all, coping with a script received for the most part just before the 'off'.

Apart from these difficulties, there was the handicap in those days of having no prompter machine or autocue. This meant being totally dependent on the script on the desk, yet the camera could not be completely ignored. Eyes flicked nervously up and down and there was the constant terror of losing one's place. And they said relax!

The television News editor of those days, S. W. 'Pat' Smithers, described my early performances like this: 'the top half of you on the screen looks all right, Bob, but I keep wondering what's happening to your legs under the table.' I knew just what he meant. In fact my legs were tying themselves in knots.

Not surprisingly the senior Home Service Newsreaders accustomed to the calm correctitude of Broadcasting House found these new tricks a distinct trial. Frank Phillips said coping with television News was like driving a Rolls-Royce after a Mini. Alvar Lidell liked it even less. Wallace 'Bill' Greenslade, the regular announcer of the Goon Show, felt rather more at home, though he had an uncomfortable moment one night when a still picture of the Queen Mother was shown in the News upside down. The producer promptly rang through to a very nervous Bill and asked him to apologise. This he did with due solemnity. In fact he was a bit too fulsome: 'We must apologise,' he said, 'for inadvertently, in error, putting the Queen Mother on the wrong way up.'

Perhaps I found it a little easier to adapt than some of the others because of the experience I had had as a reporter during the early war years, and then of course I was not entirely new to television, having had a spell with Outside Broadcasts. But the great thing, I suppose, was that I had a genuine interest in

214

world affairs and was determined that, unlike many other opportunities I had had in the Corporation, this one I was not going to fluff.

Certainly there were testing and exacting times ahead in the new service. Anthony Eden was now Prime Minister, Churchill having resigned in April 1955. Following a turbulent spring, when the country was hit by a succession of unofficial strikes and London had no newspapers for a month, came a general election in May. Most of the campaigning was on radio and television and for reports in the News it meant being thoroughly po-faced. The Conservatives increased their majority and Hugh Gaitskell said the strikes had contributed to Labour's defeat.

In Europe the cold war was at its most frigid with Western Germany being admitted to NATO and Russia and her satellites lining up in the Warsaw Pact. The Cyprus situation was going from bad to worse. Sir John Harding was now Governor and Colonel Grivas was organising the Greek-Cypriot forces in all-out guerilla war.

Then followed the most fantastic year for news since the war. For a start, in February 1956 at the Twentieth Congress in Moscow came Khrushchev's devastating attack on the dead Stalin. For many, even for communists in all lands, the myth was now shattered and Eastern Europe in particular was on the boil with mass demonstrations and riots in Poland and Hungary, leading to the tragic events of late October and the Hungarian revolution. A heartbreaking business it was to record the heroism of a small nation battling against all odds. Soviet troops poured across the frontier and, short of starting a third world war, there was nothing the West could do to help.

In any case, at the same time as the Russian tanks were battering Budapest, British paratroops were landing at Port Said. Suez was a crisis not only for the nation but also for the BBC. Prime Minister Eden was insistent that the BBC should treat the campaign as a national war like 1914 or 1939. But, as the country was split right down the middle on the issue, the Corporation stuck to its guns and insisted that the Opposition viewpoint should also be put to the people.

Never have I been more conscious of the need to show total impartiality in front of the cameras. It was certainly the most exacting News work I had been required to do since the Munich crisis and, as then, it entailed the reading of lengthy

reports received, as often as not, a few moments before the red
light came on or while actually on the air. The Suez fiasco provided one of the big 'ifs' of history; it also did deadly damage
to Britain's prestige and ended Sir Anthony Eden's political
career. It had also demonstrated to the world the BBC's
independence and incidentally gave television News a thorough-
going baptism of fire.

It was perhaps in the 'home' stories that ITN's fresh visual
approach made the biggest impact. In the late summer of 1956
there was a strike at the British Motor Corporation works in
Birmingham and the coverage on the two News services was
contrasted in a popular weekly journal of the time, *TV Mirror*:

> the BBC treated the subject with scrupulous fairness. A few
> brief newsreel shots were supplemented by long carefully
> modified verbal reports of what the people involved had
> said, and what the management and unions were going to
> do. Factual, but to the great majority of people dull. The
> ITN version consisted largely of lively, gripping film shots
> of the picket lines outside the factories (the part which, let's
> face it, had the greatest appeal for the mass of the public)
> backed by a simple lucid commentary giving the main facts.
> [The article then made another point:] BBC readers are nor-
> mally made as anonymous and self-effacing as possible. ITN
> readers are not only named, but are encouraged to express
> their individual personalities, in the belief that they will
> gradually bring to the viewer the same kind of 'friendly
> feeling' he gets from his favourite newspaper.[1]

Sometimes I wonder what main difference there would be in
our society today if BBC News had not been jolted by competition and had continued with its former, factual, if dull,
coverage? But to the viewer, of course, it was heady stuff to
see the punch-ups and the clashes in the streets. Once ITN had
shown the way there was no turning back – and since then it
is a long, violent road the two services have trod together.

Certainly the BBC was quick to get the message and not only
did we give the public plenty of 'lively, gripping newsfilm',
but the top-brass also realised that newsreading in television
was a highly specialised affair. For me and two of my colleagues the shuttling to and fro between the radio News at

[1] *TV Mirror*, 8 September 1956 (I.P.C. Publications).

Broadcasting House and the new goings-on at Alexandra Palace came to an end. On 3 September the *Daily Mail* was able to report: 'to keep up with the speed and punch of ITV programme presentation the BBC has chosen a team of young Newscasters to provide News bulletins – Richard Baker, Kenneth Kendall and Robert Dougall.' Young? I was forty-three and incidentally the only one of the old guard to have made the change to television.

About this time Stephen Bonarjee joined television News as an assistant editor and used his influence to ensure that the three Newsreaders would be not only seen but also named. This, as it happened, prompted a mother to write to me saying her five-year-old son was most indignant. Having become accustomed to hearing 'now for the News over to Alexandra Palace,' he had convinced himself that my name was in fact 'Alexander Paris' – and Robert Dougall wouldn't do at all.

So from 1957 onwards for me it was the regular grind of television News. One of the greatest difficulties was that the sub-editors had been trained for radio and were learning the awkward disciplines of writing to film as they went along. At the sketchy run-through before we went on the air it would often be found that their scripts did not exactly fit the action of the film. This would mean a queue forming round the News-reader's desk in the studio making alterations up to the last second. With the red light flickering it was a desperate business to shake them off and try, at least, to get the twenty or so pages in the right order. Then, somehow, to compose oneself and look reasonably calm for the terrors of transmission. It was difficult of course for all the members of the team but, when things went wrong, it was the Newsreader, the man at the end of the line, who got left with the egg on his face.

One of my many awkward moments came with a sequence of film showing a round-up of natural disasters in various parts of the world – a forest fire in Canada, avalanches of snow in Austria and flood scenes from somewhere else. The trouble was that my script was in a different order. When I was describing the fire, up on the screen came the floods, as soon as I switched to floods, up came the snow – it seemed impossible to coincide words and pictures until eventually I had to give up the attempt and laugh it off saying: 'I am so sorry but as you can see we have got our elements mixed.'

This brought me a double compliment when a woman wrote

217

saying she had seen all the great comics in her time, but none of them had made her laugh as much as I had that night.

On another occasion I was solemnly reading an item of Parliamentary news when smoke began belching out of the side of the camera. I tried not to look too astonished and then spotted the floor manager waving at me frantically to turn to the reserve camera and I had to finish the News on that.

I should perhaps explain that the floor manager is in charge of the studio. He carries out instructions from the Director who sits in the control gallery with his attendant experts (the superintendent engineer, the vision mixer, sound mixer, etc.) all under the watchful eye of the editor for the day. Wearing headphones, the floor manager passes on all the cues and directions to the Newsreaders.

Once when especially engrossed in a bulletin on the air, out of the corner of my eye, I espied a floor manager crawling on all fours towards me – ferociously drawing his finger across his throat. It was quite alarming until I realised that I was over-running my time and was being given the cut-throat sign.

In those days the worst feature of the job was that the Newsreader in front of the cameras was usually the only person in the team who did not know exactly what was happening. The newsroom itself was about fifty yards away along a gloomy corridor. Relays of messengers who were for the most part ex-service pensioners distributed the scripts. Some of them were not built for speed and to hear the heavy pounding of feet approaching invariably quickened my pulse rate because it meant a big news story was on its way.

On one occasion I very nearly had no news to give. Making a desperate last minute dash into the studio, I tripped in the doorway; the twenty or so pages of foolscap went flying in all directions. I just managed to grab the first page off the floor and so was able to get started after a fashion. But the appalling thought lurked in my mind – what to say to the millions out there when I came to the end of it? 'Sorry – that's your lot tonight!' Mercifully, the floor manager came to my rescue at the last moment with another script and saved a nightmarish situation.

Once on the air, the great thing was to try to look calm and sensible – come hell or high water. One night it very nearly did. During the main News there was an exceptionally heavy rain storm. The roof at Ally Pally was in a fairly decrepit state and suddenly I heard the unmistakable sound of water spattering down into the studio. Large drops even sploshed on to the desk. I began to wonder whether I ought perhaps to get an umbrella except that it would have been difficult to hold one up and turn over the pages at the same time.

So many odd things used to happen in the News studio, that I came to understand something of how a police horse must feel under training. Mind you I was spared having fire-crackers put under my seat. All the same, one Guy Fawkes night the rockets and things were making such a racket outside that they could be clearly heard in the studio. I thought it as well to explain to viewers in case they thought the natives on the northern heights were revolting.

When film broke down during the News or there was an emergency of some kind the producer rang the telephone on the Newsreaders' desk. My heart used to skip a beat as with studied calm I said 'excuse me' and lifted the receiver. But on one occasion there was no one there – not a blind sausage. One feels a charlie with all those people watching, so I just nodded wisely saying 'I see – thank you very much' and put the receiver down. By that time, whatever trouble there had been had evidently gone away – so all was well.

Michael Aspel joined us for a time and one night when the telephone rang for him in the middle of the News he said 'excuse me' and then turned to find the telephone wasn't there! A cleaner had left it in a drawer of the desk. That must have been one of his best ever television performances.

In 1960 Stuart Hood took over from Pat Smithers as Editor, Television News. Pat had done a Herculean job in getting the new project off the ground. The main problem now was to get more punch and impact into its editing, production and presentation. Hugh Carleton Green had been appointed to the new post of Director, News and Current Affairs. Tahu Hole vanished without trace in a matter of days and Stuart Hood made tracks for Ally Pally. He was one of the new wave of BBC men who came to the fore with Greene. After an adventurous war service operating with the partisans in Italy he had joined the Overseas Service at Bush House.

I remember my first meeting with him one morning in the Newsroom in the central tower at Alexandra Palace. He was sitting surrounded by editorial staff and there was obviously a general discussion going on. He looked lean, hawk-like and rather restive. As I came in, he glanced up and to my astonishment fired the question at me: 'What do you think is wrong with television News?' This was awkward because as a front man getting all the limelight I found it necessary most of the time to tread like a cat. So, I just said I'd need a large drink before I could answer that one – with which he jumped up and said all right, let's go and have one.

We went straight up to his office, Stuart opened the drink cabinet and over gins we talked like mad. He admitted he knew nothing about television and had a completely open mind. My main point was that I felt the style of writing should be simpler, crisper and more direct. He impressed me as a man who meant to get things done and certainly within a year or so the improvements began to show as old inhibitions were shed.

Being a man of sensitivity as well as courage I think he must have found the building itself something of an affront. One of the first things that happened when Hood came was that the grey canyon-like corridor running from the Newsroom to the two studios was transformed by having its immensely high ceiling and half the walls painted a tomato red. Acres of blue carpet were then conjured up so there were no more pounding feet to be heard. As a final gesture he hung a gay impressionist print of a couple in a horse carriage riding along the front at Nice. It looked utterly lost against the vast expanses of wall, but it was at least a human touch.

Our lives at the Palace were also brightened about this time by the experimental colour transmissions carried out from Studio 'A'. Again, dancing girls trod the corridors and to be surrounded by lovelies in fish-net stockings when making my way to the News studio was mighty distracting. Momentarily, I began to feel I was in the wrong business. Even one of our more staid editors was frequently seen peering through the porthole window in the door of Studio 'A' – wistfully twisting his forelock, as normally he would only do when under the stress of deciding the lead story.

There were very few colour sets then, but one of the BBC's Governors was Mrs Thelma Cazalet-Keir and she invited Steve Bonarjee and myself to dinner at her London flat, where a set had recently been installed. The reception and picture were almost perfect and yet it was to be ten years before regular colour transmissions started because it was necessary first to wait for the change in line standards from 405 to 625.

Our lives were further brightened by the inclusion of the first woman television Newsreader. Nan Winton had a good voice and excellent presence. She also had an absence of irritating mannerisms and might in time have made the grade. Unfortunately one of the snags about this newsreading business is that it is necessary to know at least a little about an awful lot. Otherwise one is certain to be caught out.

First it was Sir Alec Douglas-Home who floored her. Being a nice straightforward girl Nan pronounced his name to rhyme with ROME. The editor on duty was, as it happened, a very senior type from Reith's day, Michael Balkwill, and he was shocked to the core. So, when Nan came out of the studio thinking she had really done rather a good bulletin, Michael was waiting for her. Struggling to compose himself, he said in somewhat strangulated tones, 'Nan dear, it's HEWM you know.' With which in righteous, if misplaced, indignation she retorted firmly, 'It's spelt HOME on my script.'

Another time, on a Royal occasion, Nan referred to the Queen as riding in an open landau making the last syllable rhyme with NOW instead of SAW. It was really just bad luck and nowadays probably no one would have minded a bit. The fact is that I think she really had rather a lucky escape in not getting the newsreading job as she has had a marvellous time ever since travelling all over the world with a quizz team for the BBC World Service.

Incidentally a BBC Audience Research poll came up recently with the findings that 41% of viewers were in favour of having a woman Newsreader and 45% were against with 13% undecided. It adds: 'not surprisingly perhaps, men were, on balance, in favour and women, on balance, against!' I predict that it won't be long before a woman Newsreader is heard again in the land.

At one time or another every Newsreader puts up a black. I certainly have and, in my case, it was one that practically every child over ten years spotted. I must be one of the few people in the country who hasn't seen a Western for about forty years. As a boy, it's true, I was nuts about Buck Jones, but by the time I was fifteen I had had enough. That was my undoing when an earthquake or something occurred in Arizona at a place called Tucson. It seems I was the only person in Britain who did not know it was pronounced TEWSON. I blush.

Then there was a Welsh place name which suddenly bristled

up in a News item one day. It was spelt LLANHILLETH. I had to say something, but what I said sounded more like a sneeze. In a day or two the letters started coming it. The first pointed out that when two l's appear in the middle of a Welsh word they are pronounced as a soft 'l'. I felt suitably cast down and went on to open another letter. This came from a man who lived near the place – in Flintshire. He said that he was not surprised I had had difficulty because the placename was wrongly spelt anyhow. It all went back to the time when the railway station was built. The Sassenachs put the name board up on the platform as LLANHILLETH, instead of the correct spelling which was LLANITHEL – meaning the chapel of Ithel – and no one had ever bothered to correct it. So, I felt a bit better after that. There's no doubt about it though, British placenames are never to be trusted. Mercifully the BBC has a Pronunciation Unit which has been compiling an index of place names and proper names for forty years or more. Each day a list is circulated of names that are liable to occur in the News, with recommended pronunciations. Unfortunately the staff of the Unit go home at 6.30 in the evening and so after that the Newsreader is on his own. The golden rule if not sure about a foreign word is at least to say something with conviction. Look fairly fierce as well and you may get away with it – that is as long as it's not a British placename, in which case – there is no escape.

Recently I motored to Scotland with a Yorkshire friend of mine. As we passed through a place marked as Kirk Deighton, I asked him whether it was pronounced DAYTON or DYTON. DEETON said he drily. He also confided that he knew a village spelt FUNZIE pronounced FINNIE. I got a little of my own back when we got over the border. Driving through Lanarkshire, I tried him out with Strathaven. STRATHAYVEN? – he ventured. 'Nuts,' said I, 'it's STRAYVEN.'

19 Hampstead and Suffolk

One of the most exacting aspects of the television News job is the need for consistency. No matter what the state of one's feelings or the time of day it is always necessary to be as near as possible on peak form. The cameras not only clinically show any tiredness or boredom, but traces of incipient debauchery are also instantly revealed. Nothing less than one hundred per cent concentration and co-ordination will serve. For this reason, a fairly ordered private life is really essential and, as far as I am concerned, the job would have been unthinkable had I not been blessed with a happy, stable marriage. Our children Miche and Alastair both went to London day schools so we were all united at home too.

Larry the poodle had always been left with a weakness after the terrible illness which had ravaged him as a puppy. Eventually, the Vet advised that the only answer was to have him put to sleep. At least he had had seven hilarious if neurotic years.

The big Hampstead house we'd moved to before Alastair was born, began to seem unbearably empty. There would have to be another dog, but, this time I was determined nothing should be left to chance. After research, we decided the breed best suited for us would be a Dalmatian. The Kennel Club provided the name of a breeder in Buckinghamshire, so Nan and I set off confidently in the car for the pleasant sounding address of 'Chestnut Farm', near Great Missenden.

We drove up the lane, to the sound of much excited barking and then a smallish Victorian house came into view. At nearly every window there appeared a happy Dalmatian. No wonder they were happy – the whole house was geared to their well-being and, inside, they had all the best armchairs. There were more of them in the garden. One splendid dog welcomed us with a horsey type of grin.

This particular dog had sired a litter of nine, so he obviously had something to smile about. The pup we liked best had a small black patch over his left eye. This would have told against him, if we had wanted him for showing, but, as he was to be more a member of the family, it just enhanced his individuality.

Grock, as we named him, because of his clownish patch, was peerless among dogs. His only failing – a terror of thunder or the sound of jet fighters. Unfortunately, in his time, there were many American and RAF fighters based near our cottage in Suffolk and, for some reason, they reduced him to a quivering jelly. His hearing was highly sensitive and he obviously picked up all sorts of horrible high frequencies, mercifully not heard by the human ear. Many a time, when out with me on the reed-beds, he would hear the whine of an approaching jet and streak off for home in uncontrollable panic. Apart from this and the fact that he perpetually shed short, white hairs all over us Grock had no imperfections and we were privileged to enjoy his company for thirteen and a half years.

When Grock was six he had a canine companion. Miche was then fifteen and struggling with adolescence, so Nan and I thought a puppy all of her own might help. For Christmas we gave her a Cairn terrier and she named him Quince. There was nothing sour about his disposition and he made it clear from the start that he loved the whole human race. Apart from his love affair with people, even as a small puppy, his chief mania was chasing sticks. This nearly led to disaster when he was about five months old. It was Easter Monday and Nan and I were taking Grock and Quince for a run on the Heath. In rushing headlong after a stick, Quince stumbled in a rut and turned a somersault. Then, with hysterical, high-pitched screams, he careered off madly, at a tangent, with us after him. The chase came to an end in a muddy brook. Quince kept up his uncontrollable screaming and so we, remembering the vet's advice over Larry and his fits, thought perhaps we ought to keep him away from the light. Nan was wearing a new, camel-hair coat but off it came, and the convulsive Quince was bundled up in it and thus borne, unceremoniously, home. All this to the intense curiosity of a wide-eyed, Bank Holiday crowd, as our sorry little party, covered in mud, made its way home, carrying a twitching bundle emitting muffled screams. Grock walked smugly and sedately behind trying to pretend he had nothing to do with us.

Although it was Easter Monday, we soon had a red-alert out for vets. We needn't really have bothered. The first one who came announced that it was a puppy-fit and that he would probably always have them and, in fact, he wouldn't give much for his chances. He departed gloomily to be followed shortly

224

by a second vet, we had also called. His diagnosis was – worms. As Quince was persisting in his screaming, we requested the vet to leave some bromides, so that we could all get some peace.

That night, we heard not another sound and since then Quince, who at the time of writing is a lively thirteen-year-old, has had scarcely a day's illness. We are both convinced that what he was in fact suffering from was a severely wrenched muscle. The only lasting effect was damage to his vocal chords and he has always had a falsetto rather than a proper bark. He has undoubtedly been top of the league for intelligence, gameness, walking to heel, and speaking, in his high-pitched, explosive squeak, on request.

These accomplishments have been of considerable assistance in training our latest acquisition – a highly strung, handsome Pointer we call Rollo for the simple reason that, as a puppy, he was all too apt to roll in gamey substances. We collected him from a Suffolk farmhouse one February afternoon. There were seven wriggling puppies in the large flag-stoned kitchen. Rollo was the one who bounced at us most insistently, and whose black and white markings gleamed like satin. I tucked him under my coat, because it was snowing, as we walked back to the car.

The next day, we took him to the London vet for his jabs. and were dismayed to learn he had an ingrowing upper lid on his right eye. This meant an operation. Our friend the vet rang through afterwards to warn us we might get a shock when we saw him. We did. His eye was a huge, blue-red plum, as though he'd gone ten rounds with Muhammad Ali. The eye was obviously paining him and we had to see he didn't bash it with his paw, in which case the stitches might have come out and a bloody mess would have got bloodier still. So, a mattress was laid beside him on the sitting-room floor and Nan and I took it in turns, night and day, to clutch at his paw every time he tried to raise it to his eye. This went on for a week, until the stitches came out and, after that, improvement was rapid. He now has just a slight droop in his right eye to show for it.

Perhaps because of this early experience, Rollo has always been very dependent on us and tremendously anxious to please. He walks to heel and, almost always, comes immediately he is called. Quince has a steadying effect on him and, when we are out and he gallops off into the distance, I just tell Quince to speak – and his falsetto squeak brings Rollo back from wherever he happens to be. We couldn't possibly wish for a nicer pair of dogs, although they look an oddly assorted couple. They remind me a little in their temperaments and contrasting size of Don Quixote and Sancho Panza.

Of course, it hasn't been all dogs. An old, stately, stiff-jointed black tom moved in on us, when we had the flat in West Hampstead. Two days later, at our front door there was a group of Irish children, asking for him back. We duly handed him over, but, in an hour or two, there was a black face at the window again and – in he came. Quite clearly, he had made up his mind to adopt us and that was that. Soon, the children tired of asking for him and Wiz was on the strength. I can't remember why we came to call him Wiz, perhaps it was because of the air of mystery surrounding him.

His teeth were a distinctive feature – they were long and brown: and if he was particularly pleased about something he would bare his fangs, work up a rusty purr, and dribble like mad. When we moved house, Wiz came too and settled down at once in his new quarters. Of course, we realised he would always suit himself and that if anything didn't meet with his entire approval – he'd be off. It was five years before that moment came. Miche was then about six and badly wanted a kitten of her own. We brought one back with us after a family holiday at Southwold. He was ginger and scrawny with pale yellow eyes and a pink nose. It's not often kittens contrive to be ugly, but this one undoubtedly was. He looked tough, a sort of spiv cat – if he'd been human, he would most likely have chewed gum. We called him Dexter.

Wiz took one look and that was enough. This time, we had gone too far. He left us for another billet two hundred yards further up the hill. I'm happy to say Dexter's looks improved with age. He became a reasonably distinguished marmalade job and, with the years, his pink nose turned quite black. Also, for some strange reason, he began delicately raising food and even milk to his mouth with his left paw. A fastidious touch this, which seemed totally out of character.

He had other characteristics, which were less engaging, like being sick in the car. This was unfortunate, as we made frequent visits to the Suffolk cottage. Our dogs have always been marvellous travellers but not so Dexter. Soon after leaving Hampstead, he used to start a rapid, uncontrollable panting; fearful caterwauling followed, and then, almost always at the same point – the Odeon at Edmonton – we would sadly become aware of a noisome stench pervading the whole car. Windows would be rapidly wound down, Miche giggling happily, while I steeled myself to keep on driving, until at the earliest possible moment a place could be found to park. Then mopping up operations, until some sort of order was restored. Once he had erupted, we knew we were safe and, thereafter, he would sleep peacefully all the way.

It was while on a visit to the Suffolk cottage that five kittens arrived at a house opposite. In no time, Nan was over there and I knew danger threatened. Sure enough, on the evening when we were returning to London, she came back from the house over the way with a kitten on her shoulder. It was the old story – the owner said this one was going to be destroyed in the morning, if no home could be found. It was wholly adorable – a tortoiseshell female with a black patch over one of her green eyes. The owner pointed out that she had seven toes on each foot and feared that his trees might suffer from the extra claws. Although only a few weeks old, her white paws were vast, as though she were wearing boxing gloves.

I said it was ridiculous: we already had two dogs and one cat and that was our lot. The car was loaded up in a heavy silence and we prepared to set out for the journey home. I drove the car down the lane and stopped:

'All right, go and get it.'

Nan was out of the car in a flash, returning a moment later, beaming and clasping the kitten to her bosom. We called her Mildred because she was so darn pretty and sweet. Perhaps Dexter thought so too, because he, now a dignified fourteen, also seemed to welcome her.

Both cats frequently came with us on our journeys to Suffolk and, once arrived there, settled down perfectly happily. The only difficulty was that Mildred, as a young cat, got up to some fearful escapades. One morning – it was about six o'clock – we heard plaintive, insistent mewing. It took me a little time to locate it, until I went up to the attic, looked out of the window, and saw Millie – swinging from the telephone wires, with a sheer drop of about twenty feet beneath her. Then I remembered there were sparrows nesting under the eaves and the temptation had obviously led her astray.

She seemed pleased to see me and, calling her as gently as possible, I managed to persuade her to swing along from the wires on to the white insulators near the roof. From there, she got on to the tiles, but that still left some eight feet of steeply slanting roof for her to negotiate, in order to reach me leaning out towards her from the attic window. Fortunately, she had good sense to flatten herself against the tiles, inching her way towards me and making good use of her extra toes. I grabbed a broom, and, by craning out of the window, managed to get the business end within a foot of her. Millie seemed to understand what I was trying to do and with great presence of mind clambered on to the broom and wrapped herself round it. Then, slowly and gingerly, I pulled her in.

As for Dexter, he lived for sixteen years. When he died his absence was keenly felt and, as Christmas came round, a new kitten became a top priority.

We were in London and, perhaps because it was near Christmas, kittens were in short supply, but Nan, ever resourceful, found some in a pet shop in Willesden. One of them in particular was determined to be bought. He was half Abyssinian, a tiny, wiry, grey bundle only six weeks old and he looked all ears. For some reason we called him Joseph. The vet said he was too young to have the necessary immunisation jabs, but to bring him back in a fortnight. On Boxing Day he started coughing and would take no food. Next day he was worse and, when the vet came, a diagnosis of the dreaded cat enteritis was announced. There was only a slight chance of saving him.

Twice a day for a week he had injections and Nan, who slept on a mattress beside him, fed him with calves'-foot jelly from a mustard spoon. It really seemed impossible that he could live. Then eight days later, at two o'clock one morning, Joseph suddenly started trying to struggle to his feet. He was too weak to stand up but kept on trying and even had a little milk. From that time on recovery was rapid – the injections and Nan's nursing had saved him.

Since then, Joe has practically taken over. He is, understandably, potty about Nan and does his best to boss the whole house. Mildred pretends to live in terror of him, though we suspect she rather enjoys his seemingly ferocious assaults. Rollo the Pointer loves him and, when younger, they used to play together for hours. Joe will still lick Rollo's face with his rough pink tongue, whenever he gets the chance. Quince the Cairn is the only member of the family who has totally resisted Joe's advances, and, from the word go, has tried to pretend he simply doesn't exist.

There was no doubt though that as I had started life in Surrey and spent all my younger days there it took a little time before I felt completely at home north of the Park. West Hampstead when we first settled there after the war had seemed to me characterless and alien. It was different for Nan – she had been born there. In time, the Heath itself, and the immense charm and fascination of Old Hampstead completely won me over.

Walking over the Heath one can still feel as did John Keats:

> To one who has been long in city pent,
> 'Tis very sweet to look into the fair
> And open face of heaven – to breathe a prayer
> Full in the smile of the blue firmament.

Having the Suffolk cottage as well we were never short of fresh air. Sometimes up on the east coast it was too darn fresh. One bright morning in early spring, I was walking back over the marsh after a visit to the Harbour Inn. There was a cutting north-easter, so cold that it hurt to breathe. That evening we were due to return to Hampstead but by then I was feeling grim. Nan had to go back because of the children and before leaving me she arranged for the doctor to call the following day.

He came about lunchtime and found my temperature was 105°. It was my third bout of pneumonia and, as I was alone, he rushed me into the tiny Southwold Cottage Hospital. I was there for nearly three weeks and pumped full of penicillin. My behind began to feel like a pincushion from perpetual jabs delivered by elderly rustic ladies who served as part-time nurses. They were marvellously kind, but more proficient perhaps with a harvest pitch-fork than a medical syringe.

Recuperating afterwards in the cottage, scarcely able to crawl, I made a great decision. No more smoking. It's one of my few achievements, but I haven't smoked since – not even one cigar. I was there quite on my own for about a fortnight so that helped. I laid in a supply of good burgundy and that helped too. A wonderfully kind neighbour, Mrs Coney, used to bring me a splendid lunch on a tray every day. What with the good food and wine and not being able to move much I got enormously fat. By the end of my convalescence I had gained sixteen pounds. One day, lying flat in the bath, I realised that instead of just seeing my feet there was a great mound in between. It was clear I was growing a pot. The doctor advised knocking off bread and potatoes and, mercifully, that soon did the trick.

We loved the cottage, but as the children grew bigger it became too small. Also, what with all the television I was doing, youngsters began coming up to me on the beach asking for autographs and people began to stare and nudge. It was clearly time for a move. For some time, on walks with the dogs I had tended to walk south across the common, over the Bailey bridge spanning the River Blyth to the next village.

There was a house just outside the village which Nan and I fell for. Two May trees heavy with red blossom arched over a white farm gate. Looking through one saw a small, pink-washed farmhouse which might have been there two hundred years or more. But it hadn't. On further enquiry, we learnt that it had in fact been moved from a site twenty miles inland. An abandoned seventeeth-century farmhouse, it was dismantled just before the war and shifted timber by timber to be reassembled on its present site with new brick foundations, a damp course, and an outer skin of lath and plaster. The old mellowed tiles were then spread like a patchwork quilt over the steeply sloping roof. The original doors and windows with leaded lights were fitted and no two window catches are the same. In fact it is a highly individual house created with loving care and a refreshing absence of straight lines. Wood, the kindliest of all building materials, has made here a living house.

When we first saw the house it had been up for sale for some time and we felt, in a curious way, it had been waiting for us. Luckily we got a quick sale for the Southwold cottage and were able to make the move of a few miles across the river with the minimum of difficulty.

It was a marvellous place for mooching. It was also a marvellous place for birds. From the garden at the back of the house a wooden wicket-gate opens straight on to a field of barley. I skirt round the field and down a rutted lane towards the sea which stretches high across the horizon and in some lights looks more like a long range of hills. The lane soon peters out, as the field ends, and the reed-beds take over, stretching away half a mile or so to the shallow dunes and the sea. To the right is a tangled covert where in May the nightingales sing.

My favourite walk is along a narrow track high in bracken along the edge of the wood. Almost always I hear the ringing laugh of the 'yaffle' bird, the green woodpecker and then glimpse his dipping flight. Soon I turn left along a dyke wall which winds down to the sea. On either side, nothing but reeds. As the wind sighs through them and over them they ripple and sway – like an extension of the ocean itself. It's good to stop here and listen to the silence.

Then from far off may come the repeated boom of a bittern. Usually I see a heron or two, either lumbering with slow, leg-trailing flight across the sky or standing rigid as a post beside the dyke. If I am patient and watch, suddenly I may see his long yellow bill flash down and there'll be one eel the less. Heading on towards the sea, the redshanks will be fluting over-head, their white wing-bars flashing. On either side in the reeds I can hear the metallic 'ching ching' of a family party of bearded tits. There's also the harsh, chattering sound of a sedge-warbler singing there somewhere in the reeds and sound-ing like a skylark with a sore throat. He is in fact a great mimic of other birds and I've often heard him singing after dark, although he is no nightingale. His colouring is dark-brown and russet with a paler underneath and a distinctive light eye-stripe.

Close by I may see a slightly larger bird with a black head and throat. The rest of him is greyish, streaked with brown and his tail is dark with white outer feathers. A cock reed-bunting. Nearing the sea, on the mudflats, are shelduck, oyster-catchers and a host of small waders. Sometimes, at the back of the dunes, I have seen a nightjar sitting snake-like in a shallow depression in the sand. Then overhead, along the empty shore-line, the graceful terns and ringed plovers.

The first sighting of a species is always exciting. There was the evening in late November when, walking along the deserted beach, I saw a pair of large, gull-like birds flying strongly to-wards me about thirty feet up over the edge of the sea. As they approached, in strong smooth flight, they showed dark-brown against the sky and there was about them a look of indefinable menace. When they were directly overhead I saw that two central feathers projected from their rounded tails in the form of a spike about three inches long. This distinctive feature told me they were arctic skuas.

As I watched, one of the birds suddenly peeled off at a sharp angle and in hawk-like flight set off in pursuit of a pair of terns.

He dived down viciously on one of them, and I saw a small fish fall away from the tern as it was forced in panic to disgorge. The 'pirate' bird then swooped on the fish in mid-air, swallowed it and rejoined its mate who had meantime continued along the shore-line in undeviating flight.

There was another afternoon I shall always remember. It was 3 September 1965. All the morning I had been slaving in the garden and so, after lunch, I thought I deserved a 'kip'. The weather had been stormy and unsettled, but whenever possible I prefer to be in the fresh air, so I put my deckchair in a sheltered place for a half-hour doze.

When I opened my eyes blearily, I could scarcely believe what I saw. The whole garden was alive with birds. First, I saw the fiery, quivering tails of the redstarts, whose name comes from the old English 'steort' meaning a tail. Everywhere I looked, these handsome little birds were fluttering from branch to branch in the hedgerows and some were feeding on the ground. As I looked, in bewilderment, I also noticed the distinctive black and white of pied flycatchers, there were wheatears too with the blue-grey backs, black on wings and buff colour underneath and the white rumps from which some say they get their names. The shepherds on the South Downs in olden days called them white arses, which became refined to wheatears. Normally on this part of the coast we see a few in early spring and summer, but nothing remotely like these numbers. Evidently something very odd had happened.

Then, a few yards away on the edge of a flowerbed I saw a bird that was new to me. He was obviously exhausted and the beige and grey mottled plumage bedraggled. There was a reptilian look about the way he moved his head. I realised it was a wryneck, sometimes called the snake-bird. As I watched him he twisted his flat head round, a black line on the back of his neck adding to his peculiar appearance.

I eased myself slowly out of my chair so as not to alarm him and took a look round. There were more wrynecks and other exhausted birds in the hedgerows and fields. I was witnessing a remarkable ornithological phenomenon; certainly the largest fall of migrant birds ever to be recorded on our coasts. While flying from Scandinavia and the far north to winter quarters in southern Spain and Africa they had flown into a great depression blowing up to the north-west from Italy. After battling against it for perhaps a night and half a day they had gratefully found a landfall on this twenty mile stretch of the Suffolk coastline from Lowestoft down to Minsmere.

At Minsmere, Herbert Axell, Eric Hosking and others recorded 52 species that afternoon, including 4,000 wheatears, 750 whinchats, 7,000 redstarts, 400 robins, 2,000 garden-warblers, 200 whitethroats, 500 willow-warblers, 300 spotted flycatchers, 1,500 pied flycatchers, 150 tree-pipits. It was quite an afternoon.

20 *Exorcising 'Auntie'*

A close contact with natural things has, I am sure, helped me over the years towards seeing life as a whole. Working in a medium like television it seems to me important to be able to place events in perspective. Those who only know the London scene sometimes can't see the facts for the fumes or the truth for the trivia. Certainly, throughout the traumatic sixties I found I needed a true sense of balance to cope with the daily communication of the News.

There can be few more impressive big city panoramas than the great sprawl of London as seen from Alexandra Palace on a clear summer night. The Newsroom windows in the south-east tower looked down on the grounds which sloped away darkly to Alexandra Park racecourse; and then, in brilliant contrast, myriad lights took over spreading out like some marvellous carpet of jewels. As News time approached, it was daunting to think that in those millions of homes out there one's face would soon be popping up on the screen in the corner of the room. Perhaps it was especially difficult for me because I am rather a reserved sort of person. On some evenings when the News was more than usually grim I would nip off to the dingy dressing room opposite the studio and make a quick prayer I had thought up to the mysterious God who pervades all life and in whom I put my trust:

> Dear Lord, may I become as unto an empty vessel,
> fit, in some small measure, to receive thy spirit,
> so that in my public and private life
> I may at least reflect the good
> and, in time, given courage and strength,
> may my actions come to be more pleasing
> in thy sight.

The Newsreader was still the main instrument for conveying the news although rapid progress was being made in introducing contributions from BBC correspondents in the capitals of the world. By 1960 there was not only Eurovision but also

234

Cablefilm devised by BBC engineers which sent television pictures either way across the Atlantic over the telephone cable. There were now ten million television sets in Britain, and, perhaps as a result, two ailing national newspapers, the *News Chronicle* and the *Star*, sadly ceased publication. In the battle of the ratings with the ITA the BBC was now on the march under its new Director-General, the first professional broadcaster to be appointed to the top job – Hugh Carleton Greene. I had known him when he worked in the European Service of the BBC at Bush House during the war. Before I joined the Navy I used to take part regularly in a magazine programme broadcast to Germany under the title *England diese Woche* (England this Week). The programme was produced by Leonard Miall; others who took part were German speaking actors Marius Goring and the late Stephen Haggard.

Afterwards, we used to cross the road to a pub in the Strand which became almost an extension of the BBC. The tall burly figure of Hugh Carleton Greene was often to be seen there raising a tankard with his colleagues from Bush House. A member of the East Anglian family brewery firm of Greene King of which he is now Chairman, Hugh was no mean drinker himself with a special liking for beer. It is rather odd that as head of the German Service he had a slightly Teutonic appearance himself. A large, bullet head, thick neck and close cut hair. His suits were rumpled in what seemed an almost cultivated untidiness. And he was nearly always grinning hugely, his eyes gleaming through metal rimmed spectacles. There was an air of impish mischief about him.

In the next decade he undoubtedly changed the face of the BBC and to a certain extent of the country. As he put it: 'broadcasting is no longer a profession for gentlemen; the players have taken over.'[1] Unlike his predecessor Sir Ian Jacob, Hugh Greene took pride in never having worn a bowler hat.

From the start his aim was to transform the BBC operating from 'his command post', as he put it, 'on the Third Floor of Broadcasting House'. He was indeed a formidable commander and had served a long and hard apprenticeship in psychological warfare. After being Head of the BBC German Service for

[1] *The Third Floor Front: A View of Broadcasting in the Sixties* by Sir Hugh Greene, published by The Bodley Head Ltd, 1969, page 11.

most of the war, he was appointed Head of the BBC Russian Service in 1949 and then spent a year as Head of Emergency Information Services in the struggle against the terrorists in the jungles of Malaya.

Two of his principles of the task of psychological warfare are perhaps worth noting: 'to impose your own view of the situation on the enemy and then to lead the enemy to behave in the way you desire.' And: 'It achieves its effects slowly and gradually.'

What were his objectives in 1960? First he knew he had to transform the BBC's 'Auntie' image. No longer was the Corporation to seem a pillar of the Establishment. Then, a liberated BBC would have to offer tough and stimulating competition to ITV who had captured nearly three-quarters of the television audience.

He had already taken over the News Division in 1958 which he called 'the Kremlin of the BBC'. In future News coverage was to be livelier, its presentation racier ; henceforth journalistic 'scoops' would not only be allowed but encouraged. The news and current affairs elements in broadcasting which had hitherto been in watertight compartments were to be welded together. This was all in character ; but apart from these reforms there was one experience above all which may provide a key to an understanding of Greene's attitude.

As a foreign correspondent for the *Daily Telegraph* in Germany immediately before the war he had learnt to loathe the intolerance and suppression of freedom which characterised the Right-wing Nazi dictatorship. For this reason he was determined to allow the maximum amount of latitude for discussion and for the exchange of ideas. His concern, it would seem, was to flush out any signs of incipient fascism in the national cupboard, even if in the meantime the odd anarchist or red was to slip under his bed.

As he put it in a speech in Rome to the International Catholic Association for Radio and Television, in February 1965:

I believe we have a duty to take account of the changes in society, to be ahead of public opinion rather than always to wait upon it. I believe that great broadcasting organisations, with their immense powers of patronage for writers and artists, should not neglect to cultivate young writers who may by many be considered 'too advanced', even 'shocking'.

236

[Later in the same speech he affirmed that] Provocation may be healthy and indeed socially imperative.[1]

Another factor which governed his attitude was I think his obsessive desire to demonstrate to the world that the BBC was in fact truly independent. It is of course almost impossible for most foreign nationals to comprehend the peculiarly British nature of the BBC's independence.

Clearly if the BBC were seen to be 'knocking' the Establishment of the day, he would be achieving two aims simultaneously. Hugh Greene had witnessed at first hand the effectiveness of satire as a weapon in Germany itself, where especially in Berlin there has always been a strong tradition of political satire in small cabarets and clubs.

It was just such a lively company which formed the nucleus of the first weekly satire programme on BBC television. 'That Was the Week That Was'. Until now this type of show had been only for the small West End theatres, but Greene gave it a nation wide platform and an audience of up to twelve million.

The programme had a strong team of waspish writers with Ned Sherrin as presiding genius behind the scenes and a young man from the Cambridge Footlights, called David Frost, out front. The targets were for the most part: all authority, religion, the monarchy, class, sex, and there was a deal of schoolboy fun thrown in based on words like bum and knickers.

In one programme when taking the mickey out of authority they compiled a sequence of talking heads and substituted voices totally at odds with the faces. De Gaulle and Lyndon Johnson were reasonably hilarious and then to my amazement up came a still picture of my own head speaking with a high-pitched 'scouser' accent.

Afterwards I wrote to Frost saying I thought it weird to include me as a figure of authority when I was only a BBC wage slave. I had a charming letter back from him, written with a flourish and a felt pen, in which he said how I was indeed an authoritative figure and an infinitely better Newscaster than the pale imitations on the other channel. That is something he presumably would not say today now that he is involved with the other channel himself.

Eventually in 1963 when the show was in any case running out of steam, Greene took it off. As he explained: 'It was in

[1] Ibid, page 101.

237

my capacity as a subversive anarchist that I yielded to the enormous pressure from my fellow subversives and put "TW3" on the air ; and it was as a pillar of the Establishment that I yielded to the fascist hyena-like howls to take it off again.'[1]

Take it off he did, but it had been a potent spearhead in his campaign and broadcasting has never been the same. The tone of 'TW3' has spilled over into plays, light entertainment and some aspects of current affairs. 'Till Death Us Do Part' and the egregious Alf Garnett for instance could not possibly have come about without 'TW3'.

If there were any one man who more than any other helped to shape and influence opinion in Britain in the sixties it must surely have been Hugh Greene. His operation was all the more effective because his anti-Establishment sallies were directed from a sure base. The BBC over the years had come to be regarded as a repository of truth and wisdom, so it followed for many folk that when they saw aspects of the Establishment and authority derided on BBC air then the shafts struck firmly home. It may not be just a coincidence that by the end of his nine and a half years in power this country was riven with doubts and anarchy was in the air.

On the other hand, the battle of the ratings had been won and the BBC with its lively new image had gained at least 50% of the viewers.

At the very outset of Hugh Greene's reign came a Government Inquiry into the future of broadcasting. He had to convince the Inquiry that not only should the BBC remain the national instrument of broadcasting, but that it should also be given permission to build the second TV channel. In July 1960 the industrialist Sir Harry Pilkington was appointed Chairman of the Inquiry Committee and Greene set about the job of organising the BBC evidence.

He himself described it typically as 'an exercise in psychological warfare and I confess that I found my experience as Head of Psychological Warfare in Malaya in the early 1950's extremely useful.'[2] So successful was he in the presentation of the BBC's case that the Report was a total triumph. In fact it was almost embarrassingly favourable and vindicated the Corporation at every point. The Report also recommended that the BBC should have the second network essential for a properly planned public service.

[1] Ibid, page 135.   [2] Ibid, page 131.

A member of the Conservative Government described it as 'washing the BBC whiter than white'. It was clear that both main political parties were swayed by one overriding fact: whatever Pilkington might say, two thirds of their constituents at that time preferred ITV to the BBC. So, in the event, only a few of the Report's recommendations were ever put into effect and although the BBC got the second channel there was no increase granted in the licence fee to pay for it. But Greene had won his first victory and flushed with confidence went on to plan his second campaign against the Establishment image and to increase the viewing figures. As he told the Parliamentary Press Gallery in February 1963: 'So it was no coincidence that "That Was the Week That Was" came into existence at this particular moment and no coincidence that our programmes generally, from one angle or another, are trying to take a harder, franker look at "This Island Now", trying to illuminate our national and international problems and our place in the world at this revolutionary time.'[1]

This was all in direct contrast to the BBC's traditional role as a stabilising factor in our national life. Voices were soon raised in the land claiming that 'Auntie' was now running a knocking shop. It is the old argument about the chicken and the egg. Greene's view was that the BBC was merely reflecting and fostering the spirit of the age.

Certainly from the start of the sixties every kind of ferment was in the air. Through the whole of this time I was involved at the television News desk. I saw the news sifted, then edited and finally it was my job to pass it on: the good and the bad, the trivial and the tragic. It was Harold Macmillan, the Conservative Prime Minister, fresh from his election victory in 1959, the first ever to be fully covered on television, who set the tone with his 'wind of change' speech in South Africa.

As he was leaving on his African tour, he heard that his Treasury ministers had resigned. At the airport he paused just long enough to give a memorable interview for television News. With his peculiar brand of seedy aplomb he dismissed the domestic crisis as 'one of those little local difficulties'. Already it was clear his eyes were firmly fixed on far horizons and the main goal of disentangling Britain from her imperial responsibilities.

Soon in Cape Town came that famous speech to an unsus-

[1] Ibid, page 63.

239

pecting Parliament. No longer would Britain support South Africa in her policy of Apartheid. As he put it: 'It is our earnest desire to give South Africa our support and encouragement but . . . there are some aspects of your policies which make it impossible for us to do this without being false to our own deep convictions about the political destinies of free men, to which in our own territories we are trying to give effect.'

Dr Verwoerd, the South African Prime Minister, made it clear that no wind of change was going to blow in his part of the continent and soon television News was carrying some of its most horrifying and unforgettable pictures. The shooting at Sharpeville of sixty-seven Africans and later the assassination attempt on Verwoerd himself.

At home, Macmillan's words although not leading to immediate bloody violence had nevertheless considerable effect: they spelt out the end of the Empire. The wind of change was now blowing Britain, however unsteadily, towards Europe and it wasn't long before the Common Market attempts were launched with Heath at the helm.

In May 1960 the Paris summit meeting between Khrushchev, Macmillan, Eisenhower and de Gaulle came to an untimely end – Khrushchev stalking out in a rage after the American U2 spy plane had been shot down over the Soviet Union. This gave television News more memorable pictures.

Ironically, with the big powers as nationalistic and stiff-necked as ever, the feats of exploration in space were inviting all men to raise their eyes to a higher plane. But viewers soon became accustomed to the bleeping of sputniks and less than enchanted with the pictures of dogs and monkeys trussed up with electrodes and sent orbiting in space. Then one event in the spring of the following year brought it home to everyone that man was really making a breakthrough.

Nan and I were spending a few days at the Suffolk cottage. It was April and a fresh, typically East Anglian day, bright and keen with clouds chasing each other across the sky. Yuri Gagarin had just become the first man to orbit the earth. I had been working alone in the garden, starting a tentative spring assault, when I remembered there was to be 'live' television coverage of Gagarin's arrival in Moscow. Paul Fox and other BBC men were in the Soviet capital preparing a 'live' relay of the May Day parade when this biggest television scoop of the year fell into their laps. Fox leapt into action and somehow managed to get television pictures relayed from Moscow to Helsinki. Finnish television then sent them on from there to the Eurovision network and to our British screens three thousand miles away. Seeing the pictures coming 'live' from Moscow with perfect clarity was a thrill.

The Russians stage-managed the welcome faultlessly. In fact it almost strained belief that the lone, slight figure walking across the airport in Moscow could only a short time before have been hurtling through space. Seeing it in that remote part of Suffolk made the event seem all the more incongruous. I looked through the lead panes of the window in that heavily beamed room to where a long disused farm wagon still stood at the foot of the garden – its simple shape outlined against the sky.

At this time in any case Russia was very much in my mind. The British Trade Fair was due to be held in Moscow the following month and the chief organiser of it, V. G. Sherren, had invited me to go out there and help with the language problem. The Fair was also to include a show of British fashions which I was asked to compère in Russian. Free travel and a good fee were offered; it all seemed perfect.

I had some difficulty with my editor who said I couldn't be spared from the bulletins but, on appealing to the Director-General, permission finally came through. I was granted three weeks' 'grace term' leave. Nan was keen to come too so it was arranged that I should fly direct to Moscow, stay there for ten days to do the Fair, Nan meantime making the trip by sea to Leningrad. We would then meet there, stay for a few days and return by sea calling *en route* at Copenhagen. I promptly busied myself with brushing up my Russian which I hadn't used much except for the occasional broadcast in the BBC Russian Service.

There was just one little thing we had overlooked. Alastair, now nine years old, had mumps. The glands on both sides of his neck had swollen up simultaneously so that his head merged straight into his shoulders. As curious a sight as ever I'd seen, when he came into our room one morning early and stood by the door in a dressing gown rather too big for him; he wasn't really ill, but just looked porcine and devilish funny. I was so busy getting visas and making all arrangements that I didn't have much time to think about it. That is not until, with only a few days to go, I sensed a very slight tenderness behind my left

241

ear. In fact I had been feeling a bit rough all day and must have looked on the glum side while reading the News.

Next morning I thought perhaps I'd better call in on my old Hampstead doctor friend Ian McAlley for a check-up. In a moment he was saying, 'Ever had mumps?' Just to confirm the diagnosis he called his partner in from the next room.

In a couple of days Nan and I both started swelling beauti-fully – I had a great bulge on the left of my neck, she had it on the right. There was not a hope of going to Russia or any-where else. Instead we sat in beds on opposite sides of the room making facetious remarks about each other's appearance. Alastair was not in the least sympathetic, but then I don't think he really wanted us to go to Moscow anyway.

As a fittingly ludicrous postscript to this episode, about six weeks later I was summoned to report to an office in White-hall. All very mysterious. The security official wished to know whether there had been any attempt on the part of the Russians to compromise me in any way when I was in Moscow? This I felt was the last straw and I told him so in no uncertain manner.

The Television News Editor was now Michael Peacock, Stuart Hood having become Controller of Television Pro-grammes. Peacock, who joined us from being editor of Pano-rama, was one of a group of young men in their thirties who rose like meteors to positions of authority in television. When I first saw him he was haranguing some of his junior staff in front of everybody in the bar at Television Centre.

At Alexandra Palace he seemed determined to leave his mark on the News. For months auditions were held almost daily in an effort to find new faces. Although it was unsettling at the time for us regulars, Peacock finally gave up the hunt. The only changes were that Kenneth Kendall, to our regret, suddenly decided to try his luck in other fields as a freelance; Barry McQueen, an experienced and engaging Australian News-caster, then joined us from Melbourne and the ebullient Michael Aspel came on our strength after a spell of programme announcing.

By the summer of 1962 the space age had begun paying divi-dends in world communications. The boffins discovered that if a satellite were put in orbit round the earth television signals could be bounced off it. On 10 July the Telstar satellite was launched from Cape Canaveral and the first 'live' pictures were transmitted across the Atlantic to the ground station at Goon-hilly Downs in Cornwall.

The Atlantic satellite meant a breakthrough for television News and satellite coverage was soon invaluable in tracing the breathtaking events of the greatest crisis to face the West since the end of the war. The great trial of strength between President Kennedy and the Soviet leader Khrushchev came dramatically to a head.

Already, they had confronted each other in Vienna the previous year, when like two fighters at a weigh-in they had sized each other up. Khrushchev made threatening noises about Berlin and in a month or two built his wall to fence in the people of East Germany. From then on rocket rattling was the order of the day and Nikita Khrushchev was soon telling a group of journalists from the United States that he had a missile that could hit a fly in outer space.

He evidently thought he had the measure of Kennedy and in the late autumn of 1962 tried as an ultimate throw to establish rocket bases in Castro's Cuba. This would have been like a gun stuck in America's ribs and Kennedy wasn't having any. With a world nuclear holocaust an eyelash away, Kennedy kept cool and made his great decision. In a broadcast he announced: 'All ships of any kind bound for Cuba, from whatever nation or port, where they are found to contain cargoes of offensive weapons, will be turned back.'

This was a tremendous running story by any standards and kept our Newsroom fully stretched. I tried to look and sound as calm as possible in front of the News cameras although heaven knows I wasn't feeling it. Then, the untold relief when we heard the Soviet ships loaded with missiles were in fact turning back. Kennedy had won his biggest gamble and we all breathed again.

Of all things it was the weather which made big news at the start of 1963. January and February were the coldest since 1740. As the freeze went on and on, into our Hampstead garden came a host of birds one would not normally expect to see near London. In addition to the regulars, there were fieldfares, redwings, bramblings, greenfinches, linnets, tree-pipits and, at one time or another, all three varieties of woodpecker. The two months' freeze killed birds in their tens of thousands and if it hadn't been for the food put out for them in gardens, the loss would have been very much greater. It was several years before some species were able to build up their numbers again; in particular – bearded tits, kingfishers, bitterns and wrens.

But in surveying the News scene, the editors had other things than the weather to consider. Hugh Gaitskell, the leader of the Labour Opposition, was still critically ill in London's Middlesex Hospital, with nine doctors in attendance. One of our reporters, Ronald Allison, was waiting there to give the latest bulletin on the struggle to save his life. That was to be our lead story, but the editor's main preoccupation was whether Mr Heath's plane would arrive at London airport from Brussels in time for us to go over for a 'live' interview on the latest twist in the Common Market negotiations. It was clearly going to be one of those tricky nights when a Newsreader feels he really earns his money. The main News time then was 9.15 p.m. In the studio with two minutes to go I was still trying to find out whether we were going over to the airport or not, when one of the editors stuck his head round the studio door and said in a frenzied sort of way, 'He's dead' – and rushed out again. I grabbed the telephone to try to get new instructions and was told, 'Carry on as arranged.'

With all the last minute activity before the News goes on the air, it is never easy suddenly to look calm and composed; that night I found it harder than most. Having been told Mr Gaitskell was dead, I had to open the News after the music and the film titles: 'Mr Gaitskell is still critically ill, said his doctors tonight.' There were then some details and I finished by saying: 'Ronald Allison recalls the background to this fifteenth day.'

In was the first time I had ever felt I was not telling the true facts in the News. Meantime, unbeknown to me, the editor of the day, Desmond Taylor, was getting confirmation of the death from Middlesex Hospital. We then duly went over to Brussels for a report on the Common Market talks and Mr Heath's plane obligingly arrived back right on cue for him to give a 'live' airport interview.

Furious activity must have been going on meanwhile in the Newsroom and I could hear feet pounding along the corridor. A chief sub-editor rushed into the studio with a flimsy copy of an obituary notice which he passed to me to read. As he did so, I noticed his hand was shaking and that put me on my guard. I spotted at a glance that it had been written by our radio unit, probably some years before, so I ignored it. It would have been deplorable if that had been broadcast then. Although a News-

244

reader has no editorial responsibility, there are times when he has to use his loaf. After all he is the man at the end of the line.

The next moment another item was handed to me. This was short and to the point: 'Since this bulletin began, the sad news has come to us that Mr Gaitskell had died.' And it ended 'Mr Gaitskell seemed to be resting and was quite peaceful, said a Labour Party spokesman making the announcement a few minutes ago.' We then went to 'black'. which is a way of saying we left a blank screen for ten seconds, as a mark of respect.

I continued with the next item of news of massive power cuts in London and the south-east. A sombre enough bulletin but to the viewer at least it appeared calm and collected. It could so easily have come apart at the seams.

If Hugh Greene aimed at exorcising the BBC's Establishment image, the Establishment itself in the spring of '63 seemed obligingly to be conniving at its own demise. No satirist in his wildest dreams could have improved on the Profumo fiasco, but then in the sixties life was constantly outstripping fiction. De Gaulle said 'NON' to our first Common Market application although few people seemed to care. We were becoming a nation of 'don't knows'; someone remarked that swinging Britain was in danger of sinking giggling into the sea.

CND marchers straggled hither and thither – the television News cameras assiduously dogging their steps. Indeed, it was even suggested that a number of the demos and sit-ins and punch-ups might not have occurred at all had the cameras not been present. The medium was in fact becoming the message, but, of course, from a producer's or an editor's viewpoint the more mayhem the better – it was all 'good television'. There were also those who felt that some of the more well-intentioned idealists on the marches ought to have realised that the mushroom cloud had now turned into an umbrella and that without it there would be precious little to prevent the Russians from sweeping through to the Channel ports.

Then, with the great, two and a half million pound, mail-train robbery at Cheddington in Buckinghamshire, thriller-writers also had to take a back seat.

In politics, Harold Wilson elbowed George Brown out of the way to become leader of the Labour Party and Britain's other Harold – Prime Minister Macmillan – retired on health grounds. There followed a situation P. G. Wodehouse himself might have dreamt up whereby the Earl of Home, a comparatively unknown Scottish peer who liked grouse shooting and cricket, was elevated to the leadership of the Conservative Party against the seemingly stronger claims of more experienced campaigners, 'Rab' Butler outstanding amongst them.

Also in '63 the popular Pope John died and Valentina Tereshkova became the first woman in space.

There was one evening that year I shall always remember. It was quite early, about half past five, when the telephone rang at home in Hampstead. Nan and I were just thinking about changing to go to the Society of Film and Television Arts Ball at the Dorchester Hotel. I could scarcely believe it when the Reporting Organiser from BBC TV News asked if he could send a camera crew round to the house to interview me on my award? He then explained that I had been voted Clearest Television Speaker of the Year, and was to receive a presentation at the ball from Lord Simon, President of the Royal National Institute for the Deaf. The interview was duly given in a tremendous rush while I was still tying my tie; it felt rather strange for me to be the one answering the questions.

One way and another Nan and I had had quite a day as it was also our son Alastair's eleventh birthday, but we managed to get to the Dorchester in a state of some excitement at about 7.20.

We had invited four personal guests to sit at our table, also my two colleagues Richard Baker and Michael Aspel with their wives. This is the big night of the year for Television when all the various Awards for the year are presented. The usual throng of people milled about in the foyer and there was much greeting of friends. Suddenly, a rumour went round that President Kennedy had been shot and wounded. Eamonn Andrews told me he had just heard a News flash over his transistor radio.

Minutes later as we were settling at our tables came the news that he was dead. The evening was shattered. Everyone was numb with shock and horror. The Kennedy magic was such that we all felt we had suffered a personal loss. As Cecil Day-Lewis, then the Poet Laureate, wrote afterwards:

One man stood for the hopefulness of youth
And fell by his generous vision. Those shots echoed across
The world. Blood ran out of us all. More than a President
Was blasted – a large pipe-line of the free spirit.

I and my two colleagues would have given anything to be on duty at Alexandra Palace, but all the telephone lines at the Dorchester were jammed. In any case the Newsreading duties were covered. John Roberts, a first reserve, was the duty boy that night. The function continued in a mechanical sort of way. We were all feeling like zombies. I had to walk what seemed about half a mile through the close-packed tables to collect my Award from Lord Simon. I remember Sybil Thorndike giving me one of her marvellous smiles and then Lord Simon shaking me by the hand. Camera lights flashed and, for some reason, he couldn't find the one foot high bronze trophy he was supposed to give me although it was on the table in front of him all the time. Afterwards he was most apologetic and explained that he thought it was a menu-holder.

In fact the trophy is a most elegant bronze abstract by the Polish sculptor Edward Ihnatowicz – and has something of the look of a bird soaring or perhaps a bittern with spear-like bill pointed to the sky. The artist probably had in mind the penetrative power of the spoken word to break through into that loneliness and isolation which besets the deaf.

I didn't realise it at the time but the receipt of this Award was to be the start of a long and happy association with the Royal National Institute for the Deaf. As my mother had herself always suffered from slight deafness, it was fitting that the RNID should become one of my favourite charities. There are about five million people in Britain with some kind of hearing defect ranging from those who are only slightly inconvenienced to those extreme cases who can hear nothing at all. If the hard of hearing find my voice today easy to follow it may be partly due to those years I spent in the BBC Empire Service before the war, when clear speech was essential to cut through the static and interference on the world short waves.

It was the opening of BBC 2 in April '64 which among many other innovations saw the start of a Sunday half-hour News programme with the deaf very much in mind. Bill Northwood, a News features producer, with whom I had often worked in the old 'Radio News Reel' days, was put in charge of it and still is to this day. He invited me to introduce it and this I did with pleasure and interest for several years. Once again the BBC was pioneering: 'News Review for the Deaf and Hard of Hearing' became the first programme of its kind in the world.

Bill, a genial and most likeable character, has shown a single-minded dedication to the programme over the years and with his production team has invented many new techniques for projecting explanatory captions on to the screen. He has also become a highly competent sign language translator himself and frequently appears in that role.

'News Review' was soon to build up a following among the general public as well. There are very many people who enjoy the more leisurely coverage which can be given to the best visual stories. It also gives a screening to a greater footage of the ten miles or so of newsfilm received each week from all over the world. 'News Review' is in fact one of television's 'naturals'.

By the time BBC 2 opened, television News had acquired a new top editor. Michael Peacock had been transferred to be Controller of the new channel and Waldo Maguire, a tough, energetic young Ulsterman, whom I remembered as a sub on radio's 'Yesterday in Parliament', was appointed as the fifth of the line.

No new television channel anywhere in the world can ever have had a less auspicious opening night. Minutes before the 'off' an explosion at Battersea Power Station blacked out a large area of south-west London including the Television Centre studios at Shepherd's Bush. There, journalists from all over the world had gathered for a launching party but all they got with the nosh-up was blank screens. Even a vast live kangaroo, which for some reason had been chosen as the symbol, got marooned in a studio with the lift out of action.

Then Ally Pally came to the rescue. The two News studios which had seen the start of the first television service in the world in 1936 again came into their own. In no time BBC 1 was back on the air and my colleague Richard Baker was able to announce the showing of a Western which had prudently been kept at Alexandra Palace as a stand-by. The new BBC 2 eventually got a programme of some sort. Mainly News from a tireless Gerald Priestland.

Even when the new channel got properly under way disaster dogged its opening months. Peacock's idea was to specialise each night of the week, so that, for instance, Sundays would be devoted to prestige plays and films, Monday was light entertainment night, Tuesday education, Wednesday 'repeat' programmes, Thursday hobbies, Friday was drama night and Saturday classic serials and documentaries.

It smacked too much of an academic time-table and not altogether surprisingly the public didn't like the arrangement. They certainly made no rush to buy the new 625 line sets and it was some years before BBC 2 began to make any impact. By then Peacock had been transferred to BBC 1 and David Attenborough had succeeded him. In the same reshuffle Huw Wheldon was elevated from Head of Documentaries and Music to become overall Controller of Programmes.

So, in fact, BBC 2, which the Corporation had worked so hard to get and which the Pilkington Committee had recommended they should have, brought, at first, nothing but problems. Auntie had to go running to 'Uncle' – insomuch that for the first time in its history the BBC had to borrow to finance its new channel. A whole range of new equipment was required, new studios and offices, cutting rooms and warehouses. At least a thousand new staff had to be hurriedly recruited and trained – production assistants, floor-managers, designers, costume and make-up assistants, film editors, cameramen, technicians and heaven knows what else. All this with no corresponding increase in the licence fee. Once again the politicians had put the BBC in a spot.

Anthony Jay, who at that time was Head of Talks Features, Television, explained in a thoughtful article[1] that this inevitably hasty recruitment may have been partly responsible for the consensus of anti-Establishment opinion which existed among the new wave of young producers. As he said:

We were appointing production staff and trainees for BBC 2 throughout 1963, the year of TW3 and Profumo and the Beatles and Macmillan's resignation, when authority was taking its biggest beating for a generation. It was a difficult time for finding intelligent and articulate graduates who identified with the established order.

[He went on to say:] It may be that the consequent rapid training and quick promotion resulted in some people reaching producer level before they had assimilated enough of the necessary BBC folk-wisdom, and occasional errors of policy have not helped the BBC in its relationships with the rest of the community.

[1] 'Public Words and Private Words', Society of Film and Television Arts, November 1972.

It would seem to me that as television is a young man's medium it is inevitable that the majority of new producers and trainees tend to have the same anti-authoritarian outlook that characterises some of the universities from which they are recruited.

The young have always rebelled against authority but never before have they wielded so much power. A few hundred television writers and producers can today influence the thinking of millions.

The problem is to assess the effect a comparatively new medium like television can have on a nation's behaviour. There are many who dismiss its influence as of little consequence but it would seem to me that it is difficult to exaggerate the power of the box in forming attitudes, ideas and behaviour. Its constant presence in the home makes it an incomparable psychological conditioner, especially for young minds.

21 The Beatles and Buckingham Palace

To offset the unease of trends and events I was lucky to have the continuity of my home life. The old house in Hampstead had become more comfortable with the installation of central heating, although nothing would make it easy to run. Most of the top part of the house we let, but as there was a separate front door approached by an iron staircase at the side, disturbance was minimal. Nan's mother, a formidable old lady in her eighties, who at one time had played hockey for Bedford, also lived in a large room up there.

Unfortunately Nan had never really liked the house and kept up a round of estate agents in search of her dream. I found this unsettling because as far as I was concerned it was fine and like most men the last thing I wanted was to move.

Alastair, by now an extrovert twelve-year-old, was nearing the end of his time at his first school, Arnold House, St John's Wood. If not outstanding academically he was a useful all-rounder. Under Jack Gutteridge's coaching (alias Jackie Pallo, the TV wrestler) he had become a handy boxer ; was captain of school cricket and in the football XI too. Soon it would be time to decide on his big school. He had been entered for Westminster almost at birth. Later, as second strings, we had put him down for Gresham's, Holt (Reith's old school in Norfolk) and Highgate which he would be able to attend as a day-boy. We let him decide for himself. Westminster – on inspection he pronounced rather dreary ; Gresham's – too far away ; so we agreed he should take the Highgate exam and, if he passed it, go there.

Miche after a difficult adolescence was discovering herself and Lord knows what else in Paris. My eldest sister was now based in the north of England for her buying job and she had also bought a cottage almost on the shingle beach at Kingsdown near Deal in Kent. There my two parents, now into their eighties, were also living. My other sister Moira and her husband Pat continued with their Army lives but, as they always seemed to be in Singapore or some inaccessible place we saw them all too seldom.

251

Nevertheless the number of places in the world where a British Army officer might be stationed was getting fewer and fewer as our Empire was hastily shed. India had gone, now Africa was going too. At the end of 1963 it was Kenya's turn to become independent. As a prominent American, Dean Acheson, put it: 'Great Britain has lost an empire and has not yet found a role.' Certainly our European Common Market hopes were being challenged at every turn by de Gaulle who had finally restored to the French some of their sense of greatness. It was small wonder that giving the News night after night I got the feeling Britain was withdrawing into herself; the country lacked any sense of identity or purpose.

For the young, of course, it was a great time. They had the money to spend without the responsibilities and it was they who called the tune. The pop group industry got off to a flying start with the Beatles, and later the Rolling Stones, and there were soon thousands of imitators. Many youngsters all over the land, even in the most distant villages, identified with the various groups which were seen nightly on television. In no time they began adopting the mop hair styles and cult of the shabby. They also took on much of the morbid outlook and slurred speech. Many of the older generation determined not to be thought 'square' heaped adulation on all the new boy-wonders. If television could have such a visible effect on the way people looked and the way they talked, it might also appear inevitable that it would be influencing their behaviour and their minds. Yet this notion was dismissed by many pundits because there was no positive proof.

One day on Hampstead Heath I met by chance one of the officials from the Soviet trade delegation house at nearby Highgate. He said somewhat loftily that he was disappointed with the appearance of British youth: he wanted to know 'Where are all those clean-limbed young Britishers I have heard about?' I countered by saying that in Britain people had total freedom to dress or behave as they pleased so long as they didn't break the law. He didn't seem impressed and no doubt put in his report that the country was now well on the slide.

In the autumn of 1964 for the first time ever a British General Election did not make the lead story in our bulletins. On the evening of 15 October I opened the main News by saying: 'Mr Khushchev steals the headlines from our own election with strong indications from Moscow that he is no longer the

252

Soviet leader. Mr Krushchev has been succeeded by Alexei Kosygin as Prime Minister and Leonid Brezhnev as Leader of the Party.' Then followed a background piece by Gerald Priestland after which I continued: 'And now our election. At the moment the last of Britain's thirty-six million electors are casting their votes.'

When all the results were in the following day Labour had 317 seats, the Conservatives 303 and the Liberals 9. Sir Alec Douglas-Home was out and Harold Wilson in. As Conservative supporters said wistfully, 'If only Sir Alec had come over better on television.' On that day too, China exploded her first atom bomb. The News that winter was bleak indeed. James Callaghan, the new Chancellor, brought in an economy Budget and increased taxes all round. Bank rate went up and money was borrowed from foreign bankers to save the pound.

As 1965 opened, the doctors were soon fighting to save the life of one of Britain's greatest men. Not long after his ninetieth birthday Sir Winston Churchill had yet another stroke and his last battle began. For a fortnight he clung to life against all odds. It wasn't just a man – an era was dying with him. On Sunday, 24 January when his last moment came there was a mighty sadness and there were few who did not feel in some way diminished.

Then came the lying in state in Westminster Hall – and the State funeral in St Paul's with representatives of 110 nations there to mourn him. On television throughout the world 350 million people shared our sorrow. With all the sobbing music and the poignancy of the trumpeter sounding the Last Post it was yet the last mute tribute which caught at the throat as the launch bearing the coffin up river to Waterloo slid past on the flood tide and the gaunt cranes of London dipped against the sky.

The grandeur and solemnity of the leave taking were matched by Richard Dimbleby's commentary: the last of his great national occasions. He must have known then that his own departure could not be long delayed. For five years he had been battling with cancer but continued with his commentaries and the weekly introduction of 'Panorama'.

I had known and admired Richard for many years, as had Nan ; he was, as I've written, Miche's godfather. I remember sitting with a party of BBC colleagues in the lounge of the Langham Hotel one evening in the early war years when

Richard came in, jauntily wearing his War Correspondent's uniform for the first time. He was so thrilled with it that he couldn't sit still for long. He bounced up looking very pink saying: 'I'm going to walk around outside to see how many salutes I get.'

It was a shock for us both when we saw him for the last time in that early summer of 1965. The occasion was pleasant enough – a VIP dinner at Television Centre for some of the principal members of Her Majesty's Household. Richard looked half the man he had been. His face was drawn and his suit seemed too big for him. We said goodbye for the last time in the courtyard at the Centre. He looked small and lonely as he waved to us from the back of his big chauffeur-driven Rolls.

The Queen was about to leave for her first State visit to Western Germany and that was to be Richard's last commentary. It must have been a desperately trying time for him coping with all the difficulties of broadcasting from strange studios. It was not surprising that for a few moments he lost his usual composure when, after being kept waiting through some technical delays and not realising he was on the air, the world famous voice was heard to say: 'Jesus wept!'

Shortly afterwards he was forced to give up the struggle and enter hospital. It was characteristic of his courage that he was among the first to remove 'cancer' from the list of taboo words. Before the year was out he was dead. The nation remembered him fittingly at a majestic Memorial Service in Westminster Abbey, which he had come to know so well.

One morning in the middle of that summer I was settling in for day duties at Alexandra Palace when there was a telephone call from Nan. She said a large, important looking envelope had arrived at home. It had 'On Her Majesty's Service', 'Urgent', 'Personal' all over it, and in the bottom left hand corner 'Prime Minister' – should she open it? 'OK,' I said, 'I expect it's only a summons.' There were muffled sounds the other end then a sort of throaty giggle of relief and Nan's voice saying: 'It's all right, they haven't found you out yet. The Prime Minister wants to know if you would like to be recommended to the Queen for an M.B.E. in the Birthday Honours?'

To say I was surprised would be an understatement. Wasn't it Evelyn Waugh who declined a C.B.E. saying he would rather wait until he won his spurs? In my case it was just astonishment at getting any official recognition at all. It's a curiously lonely job being a television Newsreader. Although it entails being a front man for an immense News organisation one's presence is taken for granted. After all one is just a member of a highly professional team. It is the letters from ordinary viewers which make the job so well worth while; it was a shock to think that official personages had also noticed me. But of course in those Birthday Honours it was not my M.B.E. that made the big news, it was the one awarded to – the Beatles.

The day of the Investiture was quite unforgettable. Nan, Miche and Alastair all came with me – the dogs were furious at being left behind. A super BBC car, I believe it was Hugh Greene's, called to waft the Dougalls to Buckingham Palace.

A big moment, especially for Alastair, when the sentry saluted as we went through the gates at about 10.15 a.m. As the headlines had it: 'Beatlemania at Buck House'. Hundreds of young folk were clinging madly to the railings waiting for their idols. When the Beatles' black Rolls finally swept through the gates the jostling fans broke the police barrier and surged after it like iron filings drawn by a magnet. It took a few minutes before they could be chased back again.

Inside the Palace, of course, perfect decorum reigned. The first thing that impressed me was the marvellous good manners of all the officials and staff. Nan and the children were wafted one way and I another. Handling a great throng of people feeling varying degrees of trepidation is no easy task and yet in a trice everyone was feeling calm and reasonably relaxed.

We were soon divided into categories: first the various Orders of Knighthood, then the C.B.E.S, O.B.E.S and lastly the M.B.E. mob. They ushered us into an ante-room to be briefed – all eighty of us. This meant a wait of just under an hour because we were last in the batting order. But, no matter, we had the Beatles to divert us.

They were still very much a group at that time. Four slim young men in dark lounge suits and dark ties. Nothing flamboyant about their dress although Ringo Starr's suit had eight buttons down the front and George Harrison's tailor had given him epaulettes and buttoned pockets. There they stood, all very well behaved, with their longish hair and pale green faces. I put this down to the amount of time they had spent in cellars and to the fact that even the Beatles, on this occasion, must surely have been feeling a modicum of awe.

Soon, inevitably, fellow M.B.E.s were asking them for autographs. Remembering Alastair I thought I had better join the queue. They signed away as nice as pie. Paul McCartney declared the Palace to be 'a keen pad' and John Lennon said he liked the carpets and especially the staff. He had expected them to be dukes and things but 'they are all just fellers'.

At that point, we middle-aged fans released the boys as one of the 'fellers' appeared to brief us. He was very tall and immensely elegant – the Comptroller, Lord Chamberlain's Office – Lt. Col Eric Penn.[1] I remembered meeting him at that dinner at Television Centre for members of Her Majesty's Household. The Colonel said we should shortly file into the ballroom in alphabetical order. As we neared the Queen we would see a Naval officer. At this point we should each stop and wait for our name to be called. The drill then was to walk forward, turn left, bow in front of the Queen and take four steps up to the dais where she would be standing. She would shake hands, perhaps say a few words, and we should then take four steps back, bow and move off to the right.

We waited in the ante-room a few minutes longer and I talked to the chap next to me whose name was Dr Robert Doig. He was a little pale-faced man who said he was Medical Officer of Health for the Isle of Lewis in the Outer Hebrides. He confided that he was seventy and had been kept on in his job because of his specialised knowledge of the area and his experience in tuberculosis which was prevalent there. Today was clearly the crowning moment of his long life of service and he was delighted to have got the Beatles' autographs too. He said he'd be murdered if he went back without them.

We then got the signal to move and filed out of the room into a seemingly endless corridor. There were miles of red carpet stretching into the distance which occasioned Ringo Starr to say: 'Cyril Lord could make a fortune in this place.' At the head of the procession were a dozen or so worthy, middle-aged lady M.B.E.s who had materialised mysteriously as if from nowhere followed closely, if somewhat incongruously, by the Beatles, who led the males not only in fame and fortune but more important on this occasion in alphabetical order. I came about six behind them with Doctor Doig from the Hebrides immediately in front of me.

We duly shuffled slowly along the corridor and it was all
[1] Now Lt-Col. Sir Eric Penn.

rather solemn. A special atmosphere – like nothing else. I was
almost certain that somehow I would do the wrong thing. That
is my kind of genius, so I told the little doctor that I should be
watching like a lynx when he went up and then I should try to
do the same as he did.

At that point he sank down gratefully upon a settee we had
come alongside. 'You may be feeling nervous,' he said, 'but I
don't expect you've got angina.' He was looking deathly pale
but got on his feet again in a moment as the file approached
where it was all happening – somewhere ahead on the right. We
could hear the discreet sounds of light music.

The Beatles were to go up as a group and when the chap
next to them asked if they were at all nervous John Lennon
said: 'Yes, we are a bit but we'll be all right when we go into
our routine.' How marvellous, I thought, to have a routine for
all occasions.

Then suddenly things began happening quickly. There on the
right was this vast cream and gold room and I thought I could
see a throne. Then sure enough the Naval officer we'd been
told to look out for hove into view; Dr Doig was already
doing his stuff and I was next. I watched him like mad.

As one walked into this great room with its chandeliers and
tapestries it was like walking on to a stage because all the rela-
tives were sitting there somewhere in the dim distance where
the soft music was coming from. It seemed totally unreal. Then,
I was shaking hands with the Queen. She looked very straight
and slim and was wearing a fabulous gold dress. The Queen
must have spoken to a few hundred people before me that
morning and yet she still showed charm and interest. Her voice
was tiny and seemed to be coming from miles away. I remember one of the things she asked me was what had I done before
television News? And my replying that I had started in the
BBC Empire Service in 1934. Then she smiled, I took four steps
back, moved my head and moved off, right.

It would seem to me that an Investiture is so supremely well
stage-managed, so dignified, well-mannered and serious in the
nicest possible way that even the hardest cynic or anti-
monarchist would be impressed.

The following day in one of the morning papers I was
shocked to read this: 'Dr R. S. Doig, Medical Officer of
Health for the Isle of Lewis, died yesterday in London shortly
after receiving the M.B.E. insignia from the Queen. Dr Doig,

I

aged seventy, was travelling with his wife from Buckingham Palace to his son's home at Kingston-upon-Thames when he had a heart attack. He died in hospital.' At least the little doctor had gone on the crest of a wave.

Earlier that year at Alexandra Palace there had been another change at the top in television News. Waldo Maguire had been appointed Controller, Northern Ireland and his assistant, Desmond Taylor, another Ulsterman, became our sixth editor. Barry McQueen had returned to Australia and in his place we recruited Corbet Woodall from radio Newsreading. At one time in the BBC Corbet would not have found it a handicap to have been at Eton but with the old snobberies reversed it was almost something to live down. Fortunately he was a great cricketer – and when in the annual match against ITN he hit five sixes off successive balls all was forgiven. Corbet when on form was also a first-class television Newsreader with the right blend of authority and mateyness. His radio experience was a great help because verbal fluency was at his command and he only had the visual techniques to master.

At this stage the type of teleprompter used for the News was fairly rudimentary. It looked like a small black metal box ; the front of it was a convex magnifying lens. The script was typed on a four-inch roll of paper which was wound on to a magazine and then fitted snugly into the box, mounted on an adjustable stand. The reading position was two and a half inches below the level of the camera lens.

The girl operator sat on a low stool beside this contraption and by pressing a button was able to control the speed at which the script rolled. It was a fairly rough and ready device and demanded a high degree of professional expertise on the part of the reader. It also demanded first-class eyesight. The operator's job was no sinecure either and she had a frenzied time trying to make the inevitable last minute changes to the script.

At best, the 'prompter' enabled the reader to look the viewer more or less in the eye. At worst, it was a nightmare. The instrument was not infallible and on occasion the speed at which the script rotated unaccountably changed. The danger then was that you suddenly found yourself reading like crazy or conversely sounding like a record player running slow.

It was to a large extent the difficulty of coping with this dodgy machine which made it so difficult to find replacement

Newsreaders. The secret was always to regard the foolscap pages of script on the desk as the mainstay and the 'prompter' merely as an occasional production aid.

The main reason why more faces are seen in the News nowadays is that there are sophisticated electronic 'prompters' in use which can be read with greater ease.

Another device which has taken much of the strain out of the job is a tiny plastic hearing piece moulded to the shape of one's inner ear. With this gadget the producer can talk direct to the Newsreader and keep him *au fait* with all developments during transmission. There are also fewer technical mishaps thanks to improved equipment and this means fewer occasions when the Newsreader is left with egg all over his face, which he then has to pretend is not there.

It was during the sixties that television News first became highly professional and also broadened its appeal. We were aiming at a mass family audience. Some of the heavier political and international news had to go and in its place came human interest stories, especially if there was good film to illustrate them. We were always conscious of the direct competition with ITN and so this trend was inevitable.

Some viewers accused the BBC of lowering its standards but news values after all cannot be measured with scientific precision. News is simply what the professional journalist in charge decides at the time. When I first .joined the BBC, murders were seldom reported and crime in general got barely a mention. The pendulum as in so many other matters swung perhaps too far, and I believe there are indications now that we are achieving a better balance. Certainly there were nights when our bulletins tended to become a catalogue of cataclysmic horror, crime and violence.

The war in Vietnam seemed to have been going on for ever. A war which through television had become part of the wallpaper in every home. One of the BBC's greatest reporters, the late James Mossman, described it as: 'a nightmare in which America stumbled and punched her way through humiliation and blunder to a growing acceptance that this was one war that could never be won.' Mossman was deeply affected by his experiences there and shortly before his own untimely death I took part in a programme in which he said his last bitter word on Vietnam: 'When I last left Vietnam I looked down at it out of the aircraft window. I think the hostess was bringing drinks

259

around at the time. And everywhere I looked I could see smoke rising, it rose from burning buildings, from cooking pots, from jungles. It rose towards our aircraft like an unheeded sacrifice.'

Then throughout the summer of 1968 that other unforgettable tragedy was played out on our television screens. In Czechloslovakia, could their new leader, the gentle-looking Dubcek, succeed in giving Communism a human face? For a brief moment, freedom flourished behind the Iron Curtain. This spelt deadly danger for the Soviets and they sent their tanks to crush it. Every move in that invasion was seen on television by a world aghast.

Thanks to Eurovision and one of our staff at Alexandra Palace the Soviets were caught red-handed. They had reckoned without world television coverage but this is how it happened. I quote from a BBC pamphlet *BBC Record* 61:

Members of the European Broadcasting Union have a daily exchange of news stories and each month one of the member organisations provides a co-ordinator. For August it was the BBC's turn with Luise Gutman, the news film co-ordinator at Alexandra Palace. When Miss Gutman heard the 6.30 a.m. news on Wednesday the 21st of August she telephoned the European Broadcasting Union in Geneva and asked for Austrian TV to monitor Czechoslovak TV via Bratislava. Austrian TV began to monitor at 9 a.m. and carried through the morning until Czechoslovak TV went off the air. This material was videotaped by Austrian TV and transmitted via the Eurovision link throughout Europe. Later these pictures were retransmitted to North America via satellite.

That gives some indication of the central role the BBC played in the television News coverage of the Czechoslovak Crisis. A closing comment came from the twenty-one-year-old student Jan Palach, who poured petrol over his clothes and set himself alight in Prague's Wenceslas Square.

There were many nights when my evident relief on reaching the cricket scores at the end of the News made viewers think I was potty about the game.

It came as a pleasant break from my duties when I was invited one evening to meet Princess Marina at a reception in

Television Centre. Like most people I had always greatly admired her dignity and charm which had never faltered, even after the air accident in the north of Scotland which killed her husband the Duke of Kent while on active service with the RAF in August 1942.

As she was particularly interested in the News and Current Affairs side of television, she had asked to meet certain members of staff. It was an informal occasion and the Princess was sitting on a settee in a corner of the room.

I was told that after being presented to her she liked people to sit beside her for a short talk. Robin Day spoke to her first and I followed him. Sitting beside her was to see that her features were now heavily lined and there was a sweet sadness about her.

She asked me many questions about the way we did the News and gave that famous endearing half smile. I recalled the time in 1940 when I had announced her late husband and how understanding he had been on hearing my appalling admission that I had overslept.

It was nearly a year before I saw her again and that was at a big inter-denominational service held in Westminster Abbey. The Dean of Westminster had invited me to be one of the five Readers at a service which was to be a thanksgiving for the achievements of the 'Feed the Minds' campaign. Once Her Royal Highness had arrived at the Great West Door, the procession of representatives from the various Bible Societies, the Salvation Army, the Baptists, the Methodists, the Presbyterians, the Congregationalists, the Church of Scotland, the Greek Orthodox, the Russian Orthodox and from the Roman Catholic Church moved eastwards through the Abbey. It was an impressive service with representatives from all over the world.

The first four readings were in foreign languages; Urdu, Japanese, Spanish and Swahili, the latter read at the grave of David Livingstone by a Mr Liwenga from Tanzania. When it came to my turn to read I left my seat and proceeded to the centre of one of the aisles under the lantern. I found it extremely difficult to see the print in this dim, religious light but thank heavens I had prepared the piece well beforehand and so was just able to cope.

The sermon was then preached by the Archbishop of York, Dr Coggan. Princess Marina looked very tired and indeed this was the last time I was ever to see her. In just under a year she had died from an inoperable brain tumour.

After the service the Dean invited Nan and myself to a supper party. As I was sitting next to the Archbishop I was able to have a long talk with him. Dr Coggan impressed me with the clarity of his mind and his grasp of world problems. Apart from his spiritual gifts he would have made a first class chairman of one of the big City companies.

On the subject of chairmen, earlier that same year an item in our main News nearly stopped me in my tracks. It was a late story handed to me while I was on the air. In fact, it seemed so unlikely that I paused for a few seconds before reading it. But there it was in black and white, so I took a deep breath, put on my po-faced expression and told the nation that Lord Hill, Chairman of the ITA, was to be the new Chairman of the Governors of the BBC.

David Attenborough was supposed to have said at the time that it was as improbable as putting Rommel in charge of the Eighth Army during the war.

In his great rich rumbling voice Charles Hill as the 'Radio Doctor' had first unforgettably made his mark by admonishing the nation, usually about breakfast time, to 'Open your bowels'. Was the BBC itself now to be purged?

22 Voice of Kenya

The Hampstead house was falling more and more into Nan's
disfavour. Her mother had died aged ninety-five and the two
top stories were usually let furnished, but it meant a lot of
work. In addition we had just had our fourth burglary and
what's more it happened in the middle of a spring afternoon.
Nan had been resting on the bed. At about four o'clock she
heard someone padding about in the corridor but thought the
footsteps must belong to a friend staying in the house. Perhaps,
thought Nan, she was even going to bring her a cup of tea. But
she wasn't.

When Nan tumbled downstairs half an hour later she found
three antique clocks missing, a new portable radio, and an iron.
To rub salt into the wound her handbag with thirty-five
pounds in it had taken flight too. Only that morning she had
drawn the money out of a savings bank to pay the local jeweller
who had just renovated two of the repeating carriage clocks.
Now she hadn't even got the money to pay for the clocks that
had been pinched anyway. And then the loot had been removed
in her favourite shopping basket which she had cherished since
the days we were in Singapore. That was the last straw.

When two days later a brochure arrived from an estate
agent with a photograph on the front of a small Georgian converted coach house situated in a cul-de-sac in the middle of the
Heath I knew I was in dead trouble. That was on a Thursday
morning. We went round to see it there and then. It was all the
brochure said it was and ensconced at the end of a small
walled garden. In other words the perfect set-up, irresistible –
this was it.

We moved fast and by the following Monday had had a
lightning survey carried out, and negotiated for a bridging
loan from the bank. As the house was being sold prior to auction
there were no complicated contracts ; all we had to do was sign
the brochure on the back and give the owner a cheque. This I
did that same morning. In the afternoon my friend the bank
manager, Mr Christian by name, rang to say he had just heard
from head office that they had agreed the loan and it would be

all right now for me to write a cheque. I told him I was a move ahead.

Then the solicitor tried to make our blood run cold by saying it was extremely rash to buy before we had sold our own house. Did we realise that if we failed to sell it quickly interest would be due to the bank at the rate of over five pounds per day? By this time Nan and I were feeling limp with exhaustion and rather lightheaded. Anyhow we had arranged to go on holiday to France in three weeks' time.

In a few days a charming couple called to look round the house. They had their two-year-old son with them and as soon as he was in our hall he made a bee line for the stairs and started clambering up them. This they took as a good omen. All went very smoothly except that the man's father who lived in Edinburgh read in a *Radio Times* article that we had had four burglaries. He promptly sat down and wrote to his son asking what sort of house did he think he was buying? That knocked a bit off the selling price because they then said steel grilles would have to be put over all the windows.

The final blow came the very night before we were to go on holiday. The estate agent had assured us that all was well and therefore he would not be sending anyone else round to look at the house. Nevertheless at about ten o'clock that night the prospective purchaser rang to knock another thousand or so off the agreed price. He must have known he had got us over a barrel and there was not much option for us but to agree. We did not spend a lot on that holiday ; but it had cost us a packet.

The move took place on a pouring wet day in June 1968. After sixteen years one had got rather rooted to the spot so it was a bit of a wrench. I felt a traitor deserting some clematis plants which I had been cosseting and was just getting established. I was sorry to leave the roses too. The ground elder was another matter.

The main complication was that we were changing eleven large rooms for five very small ones. A vast van full of furniture we airily sent to a Harrods sale but even so there was far too much left. The individual pieces were also overlarge for the rooms. This meant a lot more weeding out and then going in for a policy of miniaturisation. All the same it was months before we could move around freely in the cottage without barking our shins or bashing our elbows. The language was most foul.

On the other hand the Heath was just across the lane and, with no traffic to worry about, the two dogs, Rollo, the Pointer, Quince, the Cairn, and the cats, Joey and Millie, were in clover. The garden was full of roses and there were climbing plants everywhere – clematis, wisteria, jasmine and forsythia. In fact, the house and garden were so easy to run that we almost felt we were on holiday. Alastair was pleased too because it was easier for him to get to school at Highgate, which was only a mile or so along the road.

No sooner had we recovered from this move than out of the blue I was offered a trip to Kenya. It came about like this. When Kenya had gained independence five years earlier the broadcasting set-up had been Africanised more or less over-night. The key BBC staff headed by a former Empire Announcer colleague of mine Patrick Jubb, had been told to pack their bags and go. Junior, comparatively inexperienced, Africans were appointed in their place.

Not altogether surprisingly, standards soon nose-dived. American broadcasting advisers from Radio Television International were then called in but, after a few years, the Kenyans had become disenchanted with them. As Nairobi was becoming an important international tourist centre it was bad for the country's prestige to have sub-standard radio and television programmes and the News was of first importance. Accordingly, at the Commonwealth Broadcasting Conference which was held in New Zealand, the Kenyan representative put out feelers to the BBC boss Kenneth Adam to find out whether a BBC type could be sent to Nairobi to give some professional polish to their Newsreaders.

The information was passed on to the BBC Overseas and Foreign Relations Department and Tom Chalmers, a former Empire Service colleague, thought of me. This was how my editor, Desmond Taylor, came to buttonhole me in the corridor one afternoon at Alexandra Palace to get my reactions. The Kenyans wanted someone to go there for three months but Desmond said the most he could spare me for was one month. I would go under the auspices of the Ministry of Overseas Development.

Nan was naturally very keen to come but there was no hope of getting the Ministry, the BBC, or anyone else to pay her fare or keep. Fortunately, with the help of Mr Kenneth Meadows of the Kenya Tourist Office in London, a wand was waved which made it possible for her to come out without causing total financial ruin. The only snag was that she would be flying out two days after me and whereas I would lord it first-class on the Government she would have to fly tourist. There were all kinds of Ministry regulations which made it impossible to arrange it any other way.

This left the small matter as to what I was to do when I got there. As I would be the first BBC man to have a look at the News side of the Voice of Kenya since the takeover no one was able to give me much advice. 'You will just have to play it by ear, old boy' was about all anyone could tell me. Then on inspiration I arranged for the whole of one evening's output of television News to be filmed and to take that with me.

I left from Heathrow, London in an East African Airways VC10 at eight o'clock in the evening on the first Saturday in October. A very jolly aeroplane – more like something at Battersea Fun Fair, the interior decorated with highly coloured scenes of African animals – and soft jungly music throbbed all around. So relaxing was it that I found myself looking as though a flip to Nairobi was part of my daily routine. For my immediate neighbour I suspected this was very nearly the case. A slim, pleasant looking Asian aged about forty-five, he obviously knew the drill backwards. The air hostesses made a great fuss of him too and kept asking if we would like some more champagne.

There was a stop for forty-five minutes at Paris and my travelling companion and I wandered through a strangely deserted airport building and eventually found a bar. There was just time for a quick drink. We had a dry sherry apiece which I insisted on paying for and the French barman must have been skilled in his trade because he charged me just on two pounds. There was no time to argue as we had to get back to the plane.

The Asian was a Ugandan businessman with international interests and we talked a lot on that flight. He told me his son was at Charterhouse, his daughter at Benenden. It was clear that Uganda was jealous of the fact that Kenya got nearly all the tourists and he couldn't understand why the British and Americans seldom went to his country. He told me he lived near Jinja overlooking Lake Victoria and the headwaters of the Nile. When we parted at Nairobi airport at 7.40 the next morning he gave me his card and a pressing invitation to go

266

and stay with him when my broadcasting duties in Kenya were over.

I was promptly caught up in customs formalities and found that there were two cars to meet me. One with the VOK Pro-. gramme Controller James Kangwana and the other with BBC Correspondent Ronald Robson and his wife. As a result some of my luggage went in one car and some in another and my binoculars in no car at all. In the confusion I must have left them somewhere in the customs area.

I got in the Robson's car and arranged to call on Mr Kangwana at VOK headquarters the following morning. The Norfolk Hotel had no double rooms available so I had been booked into a newish hotel, The College Inn, on a main street near the University and the broadcasting studios. It was also immediately overlooking a police station. The room was on the third floor. Short on charm but large and functional with a balcony and an enormous bathroom. The Robsons showed me round and then drove me to their house outside Nairobi.

I was weary after the flight and everything seemed to be an awful effort. As this part of Kenya is 5,500 feet above sea level it takes quite a time to get used to the altitude. Ronnie raised an eyebrow when I told him about the Asian I had met in the plane and when I showed him his card he nearly took off. 'My dear Bob,' he said, 'this bloke is a millionaire six times over – why he owns half Uganda. Jayant Madhvani is the head of a huge family empire of factories and agricultural estates with an annual turnover of more than £25 million.' God! And I had insisted on paying for his drink.

Ronnie then went off to get the car to return me to my hotel. He was only gone a few moments before he was back and exploding with rage. His face was deep red and his moustache bristled: 'Those bastards have done it again – they've nicked my two rear wheels – clean gone!' I gathered that Ronnie had been having quite a bit of trouble with his African servants. Fortunately his wife Mary-Rose (or M-R as he always called her) had an old jalopy and so they trundled me back to my hotel in that.

By 9 a.m. one of the African administrative heads was waiting for me with a car at my disposal. My first call was at Barclays Bank in Queensway. When a man standing near the counter turned and saw me he nearly jumped out of his skin. He told me he was on holiday from Scotland: 'We see you on the box

nearly every night at home – and now here you are out here!'
Oh well, I thought, there is no escape.

After a call at the British High Commissioners' office I made
my first call at VOK headquarters, a long low complex of
white buildings in a sort of compound. I had to show my pass
to the sentry on the gate before I was allowed in.

As this was my first visit not only to VOK but also to Africa
it felt a little strange inside that broadcasting organisation to be
almost the only Britisher around, but it wasn't long before I
was made to feel welcome. There had been a lot of advance
publicity from London. An article about me had already
appeared in the *East African Standard* and the BBC had sent
out a whole lot of photographs. The result was that my own
face leered at me from the wall of nearly every office I entered.
Evidently they had faith and were expecting great things.

Kangwana then took me to the Director's office – a Mr
Koske. He pointed out my photograph on his wall too. It was
clear I had got to be good. They then took me over to the
Norfolk Hotel and gave me an excellent lunch. The Norfolk
retained the feel of the old days when it was the principal
settlers' hotel. Round the walls there were still some British
regimental prints and in the courtyard an aviary. I remembered
it was from this hotel that Theodore Roosevelt had set off on
one of his big safaris with a hundred African porters. White
faces predominated still but there were many Africans and
Indians as well.

After lunch Kangwana drove me out to the airport in search
of my binoculars. At the lost property office there they were
sitting in a pigeon-hole and I retrieved them with the minimum
of trouble. The efficiency at the airport impressed me so much
that I wrote a letter of thanks to the *East African Standard*,
which they published.

To have been in Kenya without my binoculars was unthinkable and I had to be firm with Kangwana in saying that I must
have three long weekends free to see something of the country.
I then made arrangements to open my training campaign with
a showing of the films I had brought with me.

The previous evening I took the precaution of getting an
operator to play them back for me. Thank heavens I did, because some unfortunate extraneous remarks of mine had been
left on the film which began with: 'Oh, let's get this bloody
thing done!' The operator had also failed to warm up the pro-

jector which was running at half speed. I got him to do the necessary editing and he also promised to have the machine running at correct speed in the morning.

At 9.30 a.m. about thirty of the staff were assembled in the large grey-walled studio – with Director Koske and Controller Kangwana in the front row. I opened with a half hour talk saying how glad I was to have been invited and how much I was looking forward to working with them. Then I spoke about BBC television News in general and ended by introducing the films. This went like a charm and they all seemed very impressed. At the end of it, Koske grasped my arm and said: 'I felt you were talking to us!' He also liked our opening sequence and the use of reporters and the varied maps, diagrams and stills. In fact he asked for a second showing on the spot and then insisted on taking me back to my hotel in his splendid black Mercedes.

That night Nan arrived and I collected her from the airport. She liked the hotel room so all was well. Owing to the advance publicity my visit had been given and an appearance on 'Here and There', a television chat show run by an African sophisticate called Oliver Lidondo, Nan and I were swamped with invitations from the British community, which I suppose gets bored with its own company.

On her first day I had been invited to be the guest speaker at a luncheon given by the SKAL Club of international travel operators at the Panafric Hotel. Before the lunch a bottle of champagne was raffled. Nan was invited to make the draw and – lo and behold – pulled out my ticket!

During our stay in Nairobi we were entertained by so many nice people that impressions became somewhat blurred, but we remembered best our visits to Dorothy Noad's delightful house overlooking the Ngong hills ten miles to the south of the city. She was the Headmistress of Hillcrest School and had lived there for many years. In her home there was quite an English atmosphere except that in each room there hung a cord which when pulled sounded a siren. There were still marauding gangs about, perhaps left over from the Mau Mau days, and every now and again they attacked isolated properties. She said leopards were also often seen in the grounds and she had once lost a dog to one.

So often in Kenya I was conscious of this dichotomy: one moment it was almost like being in England ; the next a chance

269

remark revealed the age old Africa just below the surface. Dorothy was worried and sad when we first visited her. On recently returning from a holiday she found that her servant had hanged himself while she was away. Witch-craft was suspected.

On another occasion Dorothy invited us to a small party. Her neighbour Leslie Brown, the famous ornithologist, was there and so was Michael Wood, a surgeon in the Flying Doctor Service. The talk was the normal kind of English chatter ; then it switched. Leslie Brown began complaining of the damage baboons had caused in his garden and went on to describe how he had seen a crowned hawk eagle neatly dissecting the rear leg of a buck. Michael Wood, who had a farm near Kilmanjaro, complained that an elephant had recently got into his wheat-fields with disastrous results.

Not to be outdone, I felt inclined to tell them one of my adventures when returning from Suffolk to London recently and I had run into a herd of cattle on the North Circular at Walthamstow. It was a murky evening and peering through the drizzle I suddenly saw these cows all over the road. They had strayed from Epping Forest where the farmers still have grazing rights. One heifer coming straight up the middle crashed into my near-side wing, collapsed and died.

Daily training sessions continued at VOK. I was asked to present the News myself but hastily declined. The Newsreaders had my sympathy. The editing and production gave them little chance. Even so most of them were inclined just to read the words but without necessarily communicating meaning. There were pronunciation difficulties too. On first arriving I was puzzled to hear much talk on television News about 'the fast lady' and then realised they were talking about President Kenyatta's wife.

I enjoyed the sessions because the staff were all so keen to learn and I got on very well with them. On the other hand I had to watch my use of language. Once in talking of the Rhodesian situation I found myself saying, 'some people think Ian Smith is the nigger in the woodpile.' Phrases like 'putting up a black' also died on my lips.

The senior Newsreader was a large, genial character called Norbert Okare. He had spent six months in London on a train-ing scheme and this gave him added authority. We became good friends and one evening he invited Nan and myself to dine with him at a top Nairobi restaurant, Bobbe's Bistro. Norbert said he thought we ought to wear dinner jackets but I had to reply, 'Sorry, I didn't bring one – it'll have to be a dark suit.' Norbert said all right but he would be wearing one. The reason perhaps was that his other guest turned out to be Kenya's Attorney General Mr Charles Njonjo.

A delightful dinner companion, he told us he had greatly enjoyed his time at chambers in London. To my relief he was dressed like a conventional English barrister with stiff cut-away collar, spotted tie and pin-stripe suit. When I asked him who his favourite English politician was, he replied with no hesitation: 'Duncan Sandys – one always knew where one was with him.' Throughout the excellent meal Norbert sat beaming and resplendent in his dinner jacket.

Clearly, the Kenyan top people are natty dressers. I was delighted recently to see a photograph in *The Times* captioned: Mr Charles Njonjo, the Attorney-General of Kenya and his British bride-to-be, Miss Margaret Bryson, the Kenya-born daughter of British missionaries.' The *Daily Mail* Diary added this note: 'It has just cost Kenya's dapper Attorney-General, Charles Njonjo, £350 to get a properly fitting pair of trousers for his wedding tomorrow to Margaret Bryson, the daughter of an English missionary. When his new morning suit arrived from Britain, he found the trousers a poor fit. So he took the next plane to London, rushed to his tailor, and went back to Nairobi the same day. I understand the amazed tailor didn't charge for the alteration.'

The astonishing thing about Nairobi is the speed of its growth. Just seventy years ago a wildlife authority Colonel Meinertzhagen wrote: 'The only shop is a small tin hut which sells everything. The only hotel here is a wood and tin shanty. It stands in the only "street".' Lions then roamed where now tower gleaming white hotels. To my mind the most delightful feature of the city is the miles of flowering trees and shrubs. Everywhere are stretches of red and purple bougainvillaea, the misty blue of jacaranda trees, the pink and white of hibiscus and frangipani, the vivid scarlet of the flame trees. They were originally planted by the British but the Kenyan Government lavishes great care on them. The refreshing thing is that in Nairobi there appears to be no vandalism. I saw not one tree snapped in two nor shrub despoiled.

To see the lions nowadays all you have to do is drive five

miles out to the forty-four square miles of Nairobi's National Park. This we did several times. It seemed strange to leave behind the gleaming white University and government buildings and in a flash to be among the 'whistling thorn' bushes of the primeval Athi plains. On our very first visit we came across a pride of lions gorged after a kill. They were sprawled out in the shade of a thorn tree – some looking thoroughly abandoned – lying on their backs with their great paws in the air. So cosy did they look that it was tempting to get out and tickle their stomachs, but notices admonished visitors on no account to leave their vehicles. The dirt roads over the reserve are good and the game has no fear whatever of the cars. It's an odd sensation lurching along in a Land-Rover being paced by a supercilious ostrich. Car windows are best kept wound up as baboons are apt to leap on to bonnets and roofs.

There were all the usual animals of the plains but so different from the ones in zoos. A glossiness of coat, alertness in every limb, twitching black noses and pricked ears. They were taut like elastic – no boredom here. Great giraffes flipping their ears about like signal flags. The family parties of wart-hogs were the funniest sight as they scuttled over the scrub – their tails pointing skywards. When feeding they really get down to it – kneeling and making sweeping movements with their tusks to tear up roots and tubers.

Along the River Athi where the hippos wallow it was safe to walk around and the grey vervet monkeys, their black faces ruffed with white, came down from the trees to inspect us. Here too were grotesque marabou storks with obscene red crops dangling. Like vultures they feast on carrion and also eat fish, frogs, insects and even young crocodiles. One of the many strange birds was the hammerkop. I saw one standing motionless in the middle of a shallow water-hole. A medium-sized dark brown bird with a long pointed crest and longish dagger-like bill. He probably had dark thoughts waiting to pounce on a frog. Another weird sight is the gawky-legged long-tailed, grey secretary bird as it bustles purposefully across the plain with long crest feathers streaming behind. Its tiny head and black plus-fours look comical enough but it is in fact a deadly killer of snakes and rodents.

For our first sight of elephants in the wild we had to wait for our visit to Tsavo. This is one of the biggest parks in the world, roughly the size of Wales. We planned the safari with

272

the Robsons so that we could spend a night there on our way to Mombasa and the coast.

It was early evening when we got to Kilaguni game lodge. We could just see the snow on Mount Kilimanjaro as we sat at small tables on a low wooden verandah. Looking out, Africa seemed to stretch away to infinity. Quite close I noticed salt-licks and farther away a group of water-holes. Nothing much to see – a lone hyena – a playful pack of eight jackals, some wart-hogs and circling vultures. Then concealed floodlights came on like soft moonlight. In a few moments majestically floating in from the wings came a massive pink elephant. The earth here is red and he had just had a dust bath. Others followed until there were ten of them, drinking, squirting water over each other, rooting about for salt and generally enjoying themselves in a most engaging manner. We felt privileged to be 'voyeurs' of their gentle games.

We had an excellent meal although interest was more in feasting our eyes. Then, with some annoyance, I realised I had left my binoculars in the thatched hut which was our sleeping quarters. On my way back to fetch them, I froze for a moment on seeing about twenty yards ahead of me the unmistakable silhouette of a hyena! Fortunately he was loping along the path away from me. Later I heard that the previous night a hyena had tried to break into the bar. There was a jagged hole down on the door bearing witness to the strength of his jaws.

We sat there until about 11 p.m. just looking and looking. A genet kept slinking to and fro in front of the verandah, ogling us with his great round eyes. Then before we called it a day, two rhino obligingly materialised by the water-hole. They were the black variety, slightly smaller than the rarer white rhino. Their upper lips have a finger-like point with which they can break off twigs or pluck leaves. Colour has nothing to do with their naming as both species of rhino are slate grey under the usual covering of dust.

And so to bed with the vastness and weird sounds of the African night all round – the chorus of frogs, cicada, waterfowl, baboons and other noises which might have been almost anything. I lay awake listening to something tobogganing all over the roof. What could it have been – a hyrax?

We surfaced for breakfast on the verandah at seven and left with the Robsons and one of the Rangers, in khaki with a foreign legion-like hat, for a drive in the area of the lodge. In a compound where the Rangers had their living quarters we saw a beautiful young girl with a six-month-old baby. They looked so perfect that Nan asked if she might take their photograph. The girl was standing all smiles when click went not the shutter but African dichotomy. A Ranger, presumably her husband, rushed up, waved his arms and bundled them away into a hut. We supposed he was afraid of the evil eye.

That morning we lurched around in the Land-Rover over a landscape of red earth, yellowing vegetation and outcrops of rock. We saw many elephant and all around signs of where they had been – trees uprooted, leaning drunkenly, others stripped of bark. Miles of devastation caused by the biggest and most chaotic feeder in the world.

After lunch at Kilaguni we set off to rejoin the Mombasa road. This turned out to be easier said than done. Having bumped over the trails for an hour or more to no avail I was beginning to think we might end our days there. No doubt in a week or so our bones would be found picked clean beside the car.

Just when all seemed lost we followed a track which really worked and once again we were on the road to the coast. Soon we were seeing the strange haobab trees with their swollen grey trunks and short, tormented branches. No wonder some say God made a mistake and planted the trees in a hurry with their roots in the air. The road cuts Tsavo in two and so game abounds. It's as well to keep a look-out for elephant and giraffe. A man we met said that one night to his amazement he had driven his car clean through the legs of a giant giraffe on this road.

Nearing Mombasa it was like being in a different country as we dropped from the plateau to the tropical coastal strip. Suddenly it was so hot and humid we found we were sticking to the car seats. We were among coconut palms. Moorish arches, narrow alleys and carved Arab doorways studded with brass. The Robsons were staying with friends in Mombasa, and so Nan and I took a taxi to the rather splendid Dolphin Hotel on Shanzu beach a few miles to the north. It was almost alongside President Kenyatta's coast residence. There was no mistaking that as the whole frontage was lined with giant sunflowers!

Hot and tired as we were, we got the perfect treatment. A large cool room and a low bed canopied with a mosquito net. Doors opened straight on to an empty beach of smooth white sand fringed with palm trees where the Indian Ocean rolled in. Rain cascaded down. After a light meal we slept and slept.

Next morning it was almost a relief to find the rain still there. A marvellous excuse to do nothing. Except that about tea time I had my first bathe in the Indian Ocean. It was quite rough, warm and soupy

Next morning at 6.45 the sun was shining and so I walked along that fantastic beach. The palm trees swayed in the breeze, their fronds rustling secrets. I swam out to a raft and there was no one to be seen. Just a pair of brilliantly coloured birds in the palm trees. They were green with brown heads, a band of yellow on breast and mantle and scarlet hooked beaks. I think they were yellow-collared lovebirds.

That day we had to leave after a look at the old quarters of Mombasa and an hour or so at Fort Jesus, built for the Portuguese by an Italian architect near the end of the sixteenth century. Under the British it became the coast prison for about sixty years and is now a historical museum.

We drove the 327 miles back to Nairobi at top speed pausing only to photograph elephants standing like hitch-hikers by the roadside. Finally to bed at the College Inn to the accompaniment of fire-crackers, as the Hindu population celebrated Dwahli.

I haven't said much about the birdlife of Kenya although in many ways it surpasses anything I could have imagined. Leslie Brown told me there are 1,035 known species and probably quite a few yet to be discovered. One of the best places is only an hour's drive from Nairobi – Lake Naivasha – and we were able to pay several visits. We were fortunate enough to be accompanied by another of East Africa's top birdmen John Williams, the author of *A Field Guide to the Birds of East and Central Africa*.[1] Nan and I rate him one of the pleasantest men we have ever met.

Naivasha is one of a chain of lakes in the Great Rift Valley. The Rift itself came about millions of years ago because of two almost parallel faults in the earth's surface. The land in between subsided. Dozens of volcanoes then erupted and major flows of lava streamed along the valley. One of these volcanoes over 9,000 feet high we saw on the road from Nairobi – Longonot with its unmistakable cone.

On approaching Naivasha for the first time we slowed the

[1] Published by Collins, 1963.

car by a field to the right of the road. The reason – a great con-course of marabou storks were gathered there, I should say about a thousand. As we watched, one of them slowly spread his wings. It seemed a signal for the others and one by one, as though by numbers, they all solemnly followed suit until the whole gathering stood stationary, their great wings at full stretch.

We lunched by the lake shore. Strange, exotic looking birds were all around and seemingly without fear. There was a kind of innocence. Then John took us out on the lake in his launch. Wherever we looked we saw something new. At least five kinds of heron – goliath, purple, night, squacco and grey. There were weird snake-like darters, glossy and sacred ibis and, perhaps most appealing of all, the jacanas or lily-trotters which with their spindly legs and immensely long toes stepped elegantly from lily pad to lily pad. Perched in trees we saw several fish eagles and heard their wild gull-like cries.

That day ended with a masterly sense of showmanship at Hell's Gate. Extraordinary volcanic formations of rock – it could have been the surface of the moon. John told us they had filmed part of *King Solomon's Mines* there. Circling above were augur buzzards and a harrier hawk. But that was not what we had come to see. About a hundred feet up on a ledge on the sheer side of the gorge was a lammergeyer's eyrie. Through our glasses we could make out a young bird on the nest. As we watched we heard his excited cries and then gliding down came the most impressive bird of prey we had ever seen. Half vulture, half eagle with a fantastic nine foot wing-spread. He is sometimes known as 'the bone-breaker', because of his pro-pensity for flying up with a large bone or carcase and dropping it on a rock. This enables him to gouge out the marrow from the splintered bone. No bird could have harmonised more per-fectly with its outlandish setting.

A few days later we made our last trip to one of the Rift lakes and this time with the Robsons to Nakuru. As we arrived it was early evening and the shores of the bitter soda lake were deserted except for the flamingoes which were everywhere. For once we could find nothing to say. A whole expanse of water was covered with what appeared at first to be a raft of pink flowers. Nearer the shore they were picking their way through the soft black mud with the elegance of courtiers. A peculiar stench and the murmuration of grunts and honks from these most unmusical birds did nothing to dampen our admiration. There must have been upwards of a million lesser and greater flamingoes to say nothing of pelicans in their thousands farther out on the lake. As we left the sun was going down. Looking back, long skeins of flamingoes stretched across the sky like pink vapour trails.

In between these short safaris I carried on with the training sessions at VOK. Soon I had to busy myself with writing my reports. I felt I had made some impact, but much still needed doing on the production and editing sides. It pleased me immensely that a short time after my return to London three BBC staff were seconded to VOK on longish contracts.

With only a few days to go an invitation came from Jayant Madhvani suggesting that Nan and I should now have a look at Uganda and stay at his home overlooking the Owen Falls – at Jinja. I sent a cable to Desmond Taylor in London but I couldn't be spared any longer from the News.

Before leaving we threw a farewell party at the College Inn. We were told that there was no point in asking VOK officials to bring their African wives because they never turned up. It was a great party and all the VOK heads from Director-General Koske downwards came ; what's more, so did their wives. I think that pleased us most of all.

23 The Move to the Centre

Back at Alexandra Palace there was much talk of the move to Television Centre. A new wing to be called 'the Spur' was being added for us at the northern end of the circular building at Shepherd's Bush. The date had been postponed so often that there was scepticism and many even thought that it would never happen at all. After fourteen years at Alexandra Palace and in spite of or because of all the building's disadvantages television News had developed a sturdy, professional independence from the main stream of programmes coming from elsewhere. A 'we'll show 'em' spirit had developed among all the staff which brought great results, especially in emergencies.

BBC 2 was now going out in full colour as was the five nights a week 'Newsroom' with Peter Woods and John Timpson from the reporting staff to introduce it. The idea was to give the two channels a completely different identity. An exception was made for the 'News Review' programme on Sunday afternoons and so this was where I had my introduction to colour. I found the studio lights hotter and the make-up messier. It was rather unpleasant having hands and even ears plastered with make-up. It was best not to look to healthy as red faces always had to be toned down. Clothes also had to be slightly modified. The best colour for a suit was found to be beige with a shirt of a lighter shade but not dead white. With a very dark suit and white shirt the picture was apt to be what the engineers called 'electronically noisy'. Ties on the other hand could be noisy or even loud, so long as they had no horizontal or diagonal patterns which caused 'strobing'. These two years of practical experience of colour were invaluable to the engineers and production staff when it came to launching colour on BBC 1 in November 1969.

Certainly 1968 had been another fantastic year for news: wars in Vietnam and Nigeria continuing with all the problems for the editors in deciding just how much horror the viewing audience could stand. The decisions they had to make nightly, under pressure, must have caused many an ulcer. There was a piece of film I remember from Nigeria. The Federal Commander, General Gowon, had been accused of allowing his officers to slaughter their Biafran prisoners. To convince the world's Press of the efforts he was making to prevent this, the General invited their representatives to witness the execution of one of his young officers who had been caught at it. All was prepared – rifles and cameras at the ready. The film showed the victim being led out, blindfolded and tied to the stake. At the last second a peevish voice was heard to say, 'Hold it! My camera isn't working.'

In this case that sequence was not included and we just saw the young officer being tied to the stake. More recently there was controversy when BBC television News showed public executions in Uganda. It was not news as the event had been widely reported in advance. Many thought that the scenes should not have been shown on a general programme seen in the home. It was argued that people already knew how bad the situation was in Uganda and that showing the executions was not an editorial necessity. On the other hand no acceptable alternative has been found to the judgement of responsible editors and *Ariel*, the BBC staff magazine, reminded its readers that Hugh Greene once said: 'The TV news editor has to make decisions from minute to minute. He has to balance what is true against what is tolerable. His decision must often be an agonising one and it will never satisfy everybody.'

Then back in '68 there were the protests – in Grosvenor Square against Vietnam, with two hundred arrests; in Paris battles between students and police – up to eight million workers on strike. That same year also saw the Soviet invasion of Czechoslovakia and France barring the door to Britain's Common Market entry. In America a liberal era died with the assassination of Dr Martin Luther King, the non-violent Negro leader, and the shooting in a Los Angeles hotel kitchen of Senator Robert Kennedy. Richard Nixon became the new President – when the names of his cabinet were announced some unkind person described the set-up as 'the bland leading the bland'. To close what *The Times* called 'this lunatic year' America's *Apollo* 8 successfully went ten times round the moon.

Lord Hill, the BBC's new Chairman, cherubic and owl-like, was at his blandest too. At Leeds University he spoke against those who blamed television for the gap between the generations. And he quoted these words: 'We are living in difficult and dangerous times. Youth has no regard for old age and the wisdom of centuries is looked down upon both as stupidity and foolishness. The young men are indolent and insolent, and the young women are indecent and indecorous in their speech, behaviour and dress.' He then pointed out with relish that those were the words of Peter the Hermit, 850 years ago.

On the other hand it was clear that his mind was not entirely at rest. Speaking to the Royal Television Society Convention at Cambridge, Lord Hill admitted there were problems posed by recent technical progress which had made exciting newsfilm from all over the world instantly available. As he said: 'You can fill an entire bulletin today with this kind of material, so giving an impression of even greater ferment than actually exists.'

Among the staff some thought that perhaps up on the bridge there had been a slight adjustment of course to ' 'midships' but, as with a giant tanker, it would be some time before it took effect. Speculation was general at BBC bars as to how long two such definite personalities as Sir Hugh Greene and Lord Hill would be able to run in double harness. The answer was about eighteen months. By the end of March 1969 the most controversial of all the Directors-General since Reith had departed - later - for a short time - to join the Board of Governors. Even his enemies had to agree that the television audience at least now divided itself more or less equally between BBC and ITV.

Greene's successor Charles Curran was a radio man and primarily an administrator, not widely known among the staff, although he had first joined as a talks producer soon after the war. The tight editorial control of those days he found irksome and so, being young and impatient, he resigned. There followed a year as assistant editor of a trade paper, *Fishing News,* and after that a term teaching. During this time he came to realise the advantages of working in a public service organisation and so applied for a job as a report writer in the BBC monitoring service which listens to the output of all foreign radio stations. Then he was selected as an administrative trainee and that led to his being appointed BBC representative in Canada. It was during his time there selling programmes to private radio and television stations that he impressed Sir Hugh Greene, then Controller of Overseas Services.

From that moment he was on the ladder upwards. By 1963 he was Secretary of the Corporation and coping among other things with all the complaints about 'TW3'. From there he moved up four years later to be Director of External Broadcasting and now here he was with all the problems of the top job.

In television hardly anyone knew anything about him apart from the fact that he was a Roman Catholic and a keen Rugby Union referee. On first hearing of his appointment Charles Curran hurried straight over from the headquarters of the External Services at Bush House to Television Centre. There, Kenneth Adam, the Director, had assembled some fifty of the senior staff. It cannot have been a cosy confrontation but as a former rugger man no doubt Curran's inclination was to put his head down and keep going. With all the scrummages and loose mauls still besetting the broadcasting world we can only hope the referee will never swallow his whistle.

The greatest television spectacular ever came that year at 3.56 a.m. our time when on Monday, 21 July 1969, man first set foot on the moon and six hundred million people were able to see him doing it. He was an American not a Russian, although Neil Armstrong studiously played this aspect of it down. As he stepped off the lunar module *Eagle*, his words will long be remembered: 'That's one small step for man, one giant leap for mankind.'

In Northern Ireland, Nigeria and Vietnam men of lesser vision still went on with the killing and August saw Chinese and Soviet forces at each other's throats on their frontiers.

Finally by the end of that summer we got a firm date for the move to the Centre – Saturday, 20 September. Earlier that week a farewell party was organised – not the first Alexandra Palace had seen. There had been the wartime close-down, the next when television programmes moved to the Centre and now the departure of the News after fifteen years beneath the famous mast. Two days after we left, the Open University moved in.

Seven hundred and eighty invitations were sent out but at least a thousand people turned up, among them the Chairman, Lord Hill, and Charles Curran, the new Director-General. Ted Studd, one of the top cameramen, shot a twenty minute film of some of the more hilarious moments in the history of television News and being something of an impresario hit upon the idea of Dicky Baker and myself winding up the party with a variation of the Dudley Moore and Peter Cook 'Goodbye' song. Dicky was Dudley at the piano and I did the Peter Cook bit. Most of us agreed the time had come to say goodbye even

281

if there were a moist eye or two at this final parting. The song went over a lot better than we'd expected and was even given an airing the next morning on the Radio 4 'Today' show.

So on Friday night, 19 September, it fell to me to give the last television News on BBC 1 from Alexandra Palace. Oddly enough the lead story was about one of our former editors. The bulletin opened: 'Six of London Weekend Television's senior executives are resigning in protest against the dismissal of the managing director, Mr Michael Peacock.'

It was difficult to believe this was the last night, but the removal men were standing around waiting to snatch the chair I was sitting in. So much had happened there, so many memories.

The move from the technical and operational viewpoint was the biggest of its kind ever undertaken by the BBC and it began at midnight. The first full News went out from the new quarters at the Centre at 6.15 p.m. the following day without a hitch, except that it was delayed ten minutes by the cliff-hanger finish in the Ryder Cup golf at Birkdale – the match ending in a tie on the last green in the final game between Tony Jacklin and Jack Nicklaus.

The first that viewers were told of the change was when at the end of that bulletin Richard Baker said: 'You might like to know that after a hectic overnight move from Alexandra Palace, we're now installed in our specially built headquarters at the Television Centre and this has been the first transmission from our new studios here.'

As far as I was concerned, unlike some staff, there was no great travel problem. All the same I made several dummy runs through the side streets of north-west London to find the quickest route. After the third effort and many wrong turnings I found I could get to the Centre from my home in Hampstead in twenty-five minutes door to door.

After all the discomforts and inconveniences of Alexandra Palace the Newsreaders had now been given two large dressing-rooms with divans and armchairs, shower and lavatory and also our own office with a television set. Kenneth Kendall after a long spell as a freelance had decided to come in out of the cold and rejoin the News team ; we were of course delighted to get him back. Corbet Woodall had left us through ill health and John Edmunds was acting as holiday relief.

At the end of that first evening Gerard Slessenger, the editor who had had most to do with the detailed planning of the new accommodation down to the last coat-hooks, felt well content when he heard complaints about the quality of pictures on the monitors in the Newsroom. If that was all they could find to moan about, he knew he was home and dry.

Television Centre itself is a highly functional building with everything purpose-built, but the endless circular corridors might have been thought up by Kafka and it is not the easiest place in which to find your way around. That is the trouble with a lot of contemporary buildings – they are so symmetrical that you never know quite where you are. In the case of the Spur everything is confusingly rectangular and in those first days it was nightmarish on the stairways because they had forgotten to number the seven landings.

In addition, at the end of my first night I got stuck between floors in the automatic lift. A marvellous start I thought – to spend the night all alone in a large cheerless box. On inspection I found a telephone in a metal recess and to my relief and astonishment someone answered it. In five minutes a bright and breezy fireman let me out.

It was weeks before I could find my way around with any confidence, but working conditions were undoubtedly much improved. The Newsroom up on the sixth floor at first looked vast – all 3,500 sq ft of it – everything purpose-built and open plan, on the lines of Marks and Spencer's. Unlike Alexandra Palace where we were scattered, all the main editorial work goes on here in this huge rectangular space with windows along two sides.

In the central area are the two teams who plan and prepare the national News programmes for Channels 1 and 2. At any one time they are each about ten strong. Between them is the Foreign Desk where you might find Sandy McCourt or one of the other editors nattering away casually to Charles Wheeler, Anthony Lawrence, or one of the dozen or more BBC correspondents in the capitals of the world – their voices come back loud and clear as though they were just the other side of the room.

Over on the right is what we call News Intake. This is where the organising of reporters and cameramen takes place. Here they are briefed before going out on stories and there is two-way radio contact with them while they are on the road – so there's plenty of nattering here too.

283

Intake also keep in constant touch with our Newsrooms from Plymouth to Aberdeen which offer coverage of regional events. Sometimes film comes direct to London or it may be processed in say Glasgow or Belfast and sent as television pictures by landline to be recorded here.

Near to Intake is Home Futures section. This is where they know the last word on all forthcoming events from a State visit to a race meeting.

In another part of the room the reporters have their headquarters. Martin Bell, Keith Graves, Clifford Luton, Michael Clayton,[1] or whoever, will be telephoning round to find an expert to interview on a big story of the day. Perhaps a colleague is frantically checking to see if all his jabs are up to date before flying to heaven knows where. Yet another may be studiously engrossed with the esoteric niceties of out-of-pocket expenses – than which, of course, nothing could be more absorbing.

And that's not all. In a rectangular alcove at the back a dozen teleprinters keep up a constant chatter with agency reports from home and abroad. Close by are wire photo machines receiving 'still' photographs perhaps taken only a few minutes before somewhere halfway across the world. This too is where the messengers wait to distribute the tape or the duplicated running orders of the bulletins.

You will notice also two banks of monitor screens so that editors on either channel by swivelling their chairs round can see what is going out on BBC 1 or 2 or ITV and they can also see the rushes of newsfilm as it is run on the machines in the viewing room below. Most of the listening is on headphones. Everything possible has been done to cut down noise and apart from the insulated ceiling there is carpeting from wall to wall, teleprinters are enclosed and telephones mostly work on lights. Even so, after an hour or two with all the activity in the room you can feel your head buzzing.

The Newsreader's desk is next to the copy-taster whose job it is to sift all the tape as it comes in and pass the important bits to the editors. Nearby is a colour camera used for News flashes. We can get on the air at a few minutes' notice and frequently do. The Newsreader just slings a microphone round his neck, sits on the edge of the desk and as soon as he sees himself come up on the monitor he knows he is in vision.

[1] Since appointed editor of *Horse and Hound*.

Sometimes it feels a bit odd to sit there spouting away with the normal racket of the Newsroom going on all round. The rest of the staff have to be on their guard too. Once a senior editor was caught doing the tango. At the end of the flash, the Newsreader unclips the microphone round his neck and as likely as not receives a sardonic round of applause.

As far as the scheduled News programmes are concerned, unlike Alexandra Palace, the two studios are not a hundreds yards' sprint away down a draughty corridor, but just a short walk from the Newsroom into the central part of the building. The two 1,200 sq ft studios N1 and N2 are side by side and each has its own production control room.

A few months after we arrived at the Centre, BBC 1 went into full colour, so 1969 was quite a year for television News. It was surprising how quickly the whole outfit settled down and I think we all now had a sense of belonging to the main stream of television programmes. I got a special kick one morning when to inaugurate the Pacific satellite it was arranged for a fifteen minute News to be broadcast 'live' from the Centre into the Australian networks. When I thought of all those years long ago that I had spent broadcasting to Australia on the short-wave radio frequencies this represented quite an advance. The round-the-globe chain of satellite and ground stations was now complete. All these technical developments fill me with total amazement. Apparently for this bulletin a satellite called Intelsat III in orbit 22,300 miles above the equator in the Indian Ocean was being used. The ground stations were Goonhilly in Cornwall and a new one at Ceduna in Australia.

A photograph appeared in the BBC staff magazine *Ariel* for March that year showing Len Woolard, our Australian Representative, sitting in his home watching a television set with my face clearly seen on it.

Another first-hand account came from Ian Chapman, the Collins Director, who told me that on the night he and his wife arrived from London at a Sydney hotel they went up to their suite, switched on the television and were staggered to find me giving the News from home. Several people wrote from different parts of Australia asking if we could possibly give the News from London every night, but unfortunately there was no question of our doing that because of the cost.

Since our move News and Current Affairs were in a position to co-operate on special projects. The June 1970 General

Election was covered on television by a joint unit under single editorial control and working in two of the Centre's biggest studios, TC1 and TC7. This brought together commentators, reporters, outside broadcasts units and camera teams. When the resources of BBC regional Newsrooms were added you had the largest News and Current Affairs organisation in Europe.

Harold Wilson and Labour seemed to be secure but as the campaign developed prospects began to look less rosy. With under a week to go to polling day three factors hit the Socialists hard: the latest strike figures, the monthly cost of living index and the numbers out of work which were all on the up and up. Then came a down-turn in the monthly trade figures of thirty-one millions. Wilson tried to explain the figures were distorted by the purchase of two jumbo jets but Heath continued to ram home his attack charging that under Labour we would have a further devaluation of the pound within four years. Finally, by midday on the nineteenth it was clear that, spitting in the eye of all the pollsters, 'The Grocer', as *Private Eye* insisted on calling him, or 'OGL' (Our Glorious Leader) – as Party followers affectionately know him – in other words the Rt Hon Edward Heath, M.B.E., M.P. – had done the trick with thirty-odd seats to the good.

No one could say how much the campaigns on television had influenced the voters but they were certainly the most sophisticated ever waged. As might have been expected the Conservatives had the edge in the new marketing techniques and Heath's appearances on the screen, invariably with the same halo-like backing, suggested that 'the selling of the Prime Minister' would henceforth be a feature of our own elections, as it is with the President in America.

The 'brand image' type of visual promotion even began to spill over into the News. At Alexandra Palace our own production staff had always decided on the look of the bulletins and the emphasis was on simplicity. We had after years of experiment come to the conclusion that for the News the fewer frills the better.

Once at the Centre it was, I suppose, inevitable that other specialists wanted to have their say. Thus it was that when the decision was made for the News on BBC 1 to be re-jigged as 'The Nine O'Clock News' the services of the Design Department were called on to devise a new set. It was decided that Monday, 14 September would be the launching date and that each Newsreader would be on for a week at a time. I was down for week one.

Over the weekend I was at home in Hampstead and kept ringing to find out if there was going to be a dummy run. The answer was always that the set wasn't finished. In fact, I got my first glimpse of the studio arrangement at about six o'clock on the first Monday evening. I didn't much like what I saw – even the desk surface was too small for all the sorting of the scripts. There was a backing of grey lavatorial-looking tiles and a huge round thing – a sort of futuristic symbol, which apparently was meant to suggest nine o'clock.

Dick Levin, Head of Design, was bustling about in the studio looking amiable. I didn't say very much. Then he plunged his hand in his jacket pocket and said, 'Oh Bob – here's your tie.' This shook me as I had always regarded ties as individual things. The colour was plain navy blue but right in the middle was a curious, circular white badge.

'What on earth's that?' I asked.

Dick looked rather injured.

'That's the logos,' he said. 'I had a terrible job getting it made – you can fasten it on any tie.'

I didn't know what he was on about until I realised it was a miniature of the huge, round, grey thing in the backing.

'If I wear that, I'll look like an Ovalteeny,' I said. The exchange was at an end.

This was one worry I could have done without. I banged into Desmond Taylor in the corridor and showed it to him: 'Paul Fox likes it,' he said. That didn't make my position any easier, but somehow I knew that I'd rather go to the stake than wear that tie. By this time I was heavily involved in trying to assimilate the stories of this opening Nine O'Clock News.

The floor manager called for silence, the count-down started, then came a weird electronic tinkle (I hadn't been warned about that) – and we were on the air. It was rather a jumpy bulletin and I felt more and more like a police horse with all the strange things going on. Near the end a late message was handed to the young floor-manager but for some reason he didn't pass it on to me. Afterwards he told me he had split his trousers and daren't move. I told him he must get his priorities right but fortunately the message wasn't important anyway.

We had a mixed Press. This is how *The Guardian* described the face-lift given to the News: 'It is now set in a sort of polystyrene padded cell and provided with a porthole which is occasionally flung open to show some topical scene. The impression is that they are sitting in a very clean coal hole and sometimes lifting the lid to see what is going on outside.'

The Tablet wrote: 'Poor Dougall was pushed down into the bottom right-hand corner, where he kept his end up looking rather wan ; most of the screen is filled with a wall which looks like pale grey imitation cheese briquettes.' The *Daily Telegraph* was disappointed too and said the huge symbol suggested the starting time and a plate half completed on a potter's wheel.

All the same our logos was looking brighter by the end of the week and the *Evening News* was able to report: 'The BBC's restyled nine o'clock news was today voted a hit with the viewers. It has got into the Top Ten chart in its first week.'

So perhaps Dick Levin got the last laugh after all.

24 The RSPB

Apart from the happenings reported daily in the News, the world was at last beginning to wake up to what it was doing to itself long term. Rachel Carson's book *Silent Spring* sounded the alarm back in the early sixties, warning about the destruction of wildlife and the danger to man from the indiscriminate use of persistent pesticides like DDT. Just as miners used to carry canaries down the pit and when the birds started choking they got out quick – so had vanishing wildlife acted as an indicator of trouble ahead for the world.

Conservation became a brave new banner and exhortations rang throughout the land until some wearied of the very words – pollution, environment and ecology. It was clear that man could have a cleaner, safer world but only if he were prepared to pay for it. Sir Frank Fraser Darling, the Scottish naturalist, in his Reith lectures put his finger on an important aspect of the problem when he said, 'most pollution comes from getting rid of wastes at the least possible cost.' Those lectures served as a curtain-raiser to European Conservation Year in 1970. My involvement with it came when I took over from Col. Sir Tufton Beamish, M.C., M.P., as President of the Royal Society for the Protection of Birds.

That is how one coldish, misty afternoon in November I came to be waiting in the grounds of the RSPB headquarters, at The Lodge, Sandy, Bedfordshire for the arrival, at any moment, of the Prince of Wales. With me were Major Simon Whitbread, Lord Lieutenant of the County, and Stanley Cramp, the Chairman of the Society. Bang on time, a red and blue helicopter of the Queen's Flight whirred over the tops of the trees and put down neatly about twenty yards away. In a moment the Prince was striding over towards us. He was paying his first visit to Sandy and I was carrying out my first official duty as President.

A pleasant, fresh-faced, brisk young man with a great sense of fun, the first thing he asked me was: 'Who's looking after the News today?'

The Director of the Society, Peter Conder, was in East

K

Africa, so the two Deputy Directors, David Lea and Cecil Winnington-Ingram, then joined me to conduct the Prince round the headquarters.

Over the front door of The Lodge, which is a mellow building in Bath stone, is the coat of arms of the Peel family. The house was built in 1870 for Viscount Peel of Sandy, a former Speaker of the House of Commons. It's rather odd that bird protection should now be organised from a house which once belonged to the descendants of the first Sir Robert Peel, the founder of the police force, who gave his name to the bobby on the beat. Curious too that the family motto should have been 'Industria' and that a bee is shown on the coat of arms. In fact our busy sales department so impressed the Prince that he cracked: 'The only time I have seen such frantic activity anywhere was in a men's underwear factory in Barbados.'

The department was then handling over three thousand orders every day at the height of the Christmas rush. GPO lorries were coming especially from Bedford every day to collect over two hundred mailbags full of cards, calendars, ties, identification charts, books, trays and all the other items in the Society's gift catalogues. One third of the year's turnover is crammed into November because that is when everyone starts thinking about Christmas. It takes upwards of eighty staff to cope with the rush and many of them stay until late at night.

The Prince joked with everybody and, somehow, at least feigned interest even in the most prosaic parts of the work. Many a young secretary will never forget his visit.

And how it would have pleased that dedicated group who founded the Society in the last decade of the Victorian era. Their President was that gracious beauty of her time – Winifred, Duchess of Portland. The main threat then to birdlife was women's hats – those massive winged creations for which countless thousands of egrets, herons, kingfishers and the rest were slaughtered for the elegance and colour of their plumes. When the parent birds were shot the fledglings were left to starve, so the loss in numbers was all the greater.

Happily the plumage trade more or less ended with legislation passed in 1921 and this was the first victory for the young Society ; but already another even more serious threat was beginning to cloud the waters – pollution from oil. Here again, largely thanks to agitation by members of the RSPB, Britain took the lead in prohibiting the discharge or escape of oil within the three-mile limit.

All this time tracts of countryside were being acquired as reserves and Royalty continued to support the Society's aims. In this connection *Bird Notes and News* for 1930 wrote portentously: 'The action of H.M. the King in declining to accept the early Plovers' eggs sent to him this spring has been received with general acclaim.' I don't suppose the populace actually danced in the streets, but still . . .

Another aspect of the Society's work was the campaign against the caging of British song birds which was helped by pamphlets, written by that great naturalist W. H. Hudson, the fight ending successfully in 1933 when an Act was passed to control the trade. As William Blake had written about a century and a half before:

> A Robin Redbreast in a Cage
> Puts all Heaven in a Rage.

Then, soon after the end of the Second World War, the avocets returned to breed in Suffolk – 1,500 acres of marsh and heath were leased at Minsmere and Havergate Island was purchased in Orfordness. Working ornithologists were now directing the Society and there was less reliance on aristocratic patronage.

Finally, after sixty-five years of service as President, which must surely be a record, the Duchess of Portland died in 1954. That same year saw one of the RSPB's greatest victories for which it had worked since its earliest days – the Protection of Birds Act. Since then progress has been rapid and five years later the now famous osprey hide at Loch Garten was set up where the public in their tens of thousands could see what was being done to protect the return of a rare species.

Ten years later the London headquarters at Eccleston Square was sold at a handsome profit and the move was made to The Lodge at Sandy. This became a springboard and the RSPB has now become the largest national voluntary conservation body in Europe with, at the time of writing, fifty reserves all over the country covering an area of 18,000 acres which are being added to all the time.

So the work goes on apace and pollution is fought in all its forms. We also have a Farming and Wildlife Advisory Group because the co-operation of farmers is so necessary. Many are keen to help conserve wildlife and we can tell them the best way to go about it. The legal department is kept busy investigating the trapping of wild birds and has brought many prosecutions against those who still use the cruel pole-traps. In general, our aim is to help people become more aware of the natural world around them and, once their interest has been sparked off, we hope they will start to care and then they will be half way to becoming conservationists.

The wonderful thing is the speed at which the RSPB's membership is growing. When I first joined over twenty years ago there were only about six thousand members, but by 1970 when I became President the numbers had grown to over fifty thousand. Then, just two years later at the Royal Festival Hall in London I presented, on behalf of the RSPB, the painting of an avocet by Robert Gillmor to the 100,000th member who had just popped out of our computer. Very charming she looked too.

Mrs Christine Bradley was a Derbyshire housewife married to a railway maintenance engineer. She was kept busy looking after her young daughter, but also found time to work three nights a week as a nurse. When I met her on the platform at the Festival Hall she said she didn't know a great deal about birds but thought their protection was important.

What a change in attitude there has been – not so long ago the main interest was in shooting birds or in taking their eggs, but now more and more people like Christine Bradley are finding pleasure in watching and studying the birds in their garden. Why should this be?

They are of course the most easily observed form of wildlife, but apart from obvious things like the variety and beauty of their song and plumage and the intricate craftsmanship of their nests, I think they also appeal to our sense of wonder because there is so much about them we still don't know. Take migration . . . What marvellous mechanism or instinct is it that enables a bird to navigate for thousands of miles across land and sea returning not just to the same country or district but to the very same tree or bush or even to the same corner of a garden shed or barn?

As an experiment some years ago, a Manx shearwater was collected from its breeding site on the Welsh island of Skokholm, taken across the Atlantic and released near Boston,

Massachusetts. This was well away from its normal range, as most of the British birds migrate to the eastern coast of South America. That shearwater found its way back over 3,000 miles of ocean to its nesting burrow and to its mate and chick in twelve days flat. Man can land on the moon, but he doesn't yet know the full answer to birds' migration and a little humility doesn't come amiss.

Perhaps the RSPB's soaring membership figures also stem in part from a growing unease over this technological age. Perhaps it is a form of protest against the monolithic tower blocks, the impersonal computers, the omnipresent motorcar, the mammoth oil tankers (bigger and better *Torrey Canyons*). Even without the major disasters thousands of tons of oil are spilt around our coasts each year. What future then for the seals and the sea birds – the clownish puffins, the razorbills, the divers and guillemots?

Mercifully there are brighter aspects and the Clean Air Act is one of them. What a marvellous difference that has made to many of our cities and London in particular. Charles Dickens wouldn't know the old place now and many foreigners are disappointed at not seeing the fogs they had read about in his books. The better atmosphere has meant among other things an increase in insect life and this, in turn, has brought back swallows, swifts, and martins to the London area. Fish are also returning to the Thames and other rivers and that may account for the fact that herons now nest in one of London's central parks. In fact, more than two hundred and fifty species of birds have been recorded within twenty miles of St Paul's and that is about half the British list.

I also have my interest in birdlife to thank for introducing me to many delightful people and places. One of the most stimulating and talented naturalists I know is James Alder who is also a gifted wildlife artist. I last met him on the stage of Newcastle City Hall on Guy Fawkes night 1970. The occasion was a Northumberland and Durham Naturalists' Trust programme. James showed his scenic slides and sketches while I did some of the talking. The Newcastle *Evening Chronicle* billed us as 'Alder and Dougall, double-act counter-attraction to the pyromaniac pleasures of Guy Fawkes Night'. In spite of all the rockets whizzing about outside we had a near capacity crowd in the City Hall.

It was an 'Exhibition of Bird and Wildlife Watercolours'

which led Nan and me to make our first visit to Woburn Abbey as guests of the Duke and Duchess of Bedford. We had been invited to a reception and private view of the paintings and then to dine and stay the night. Mist was gathering as we drove through the deserted deer park on an evening in late September. Deserted of people that is, because we saw several herds of deer: there are eleven different species roaming the 3,000 acres of Woburn. We also caught glimpses of black and albino squirrels among the trees and some crowned cranes and other exotic birds.

Our car seemed minute in this vast setting and as we approached the elegant eighteenth-century west front, built by Henry Flitcroft for the fourth Duke in 1747, we were wondering whether this really was the entrance meant for us. Somewhat tentatively we parked, then mounted the steps leading to the front door. Through one glass we could see the tall figure of the Duke standing in the hall and so we rang the bell.

Immediately the door opened to a smiling welcome from the Duchess. After the charm of her smile the first thing that impressed me was the engaging chuckle in her voice – and her distinctive French accent which reminded me of the late Yvonne Arnaud. The Duke is very tall – about 6 ft 5ins – and with a detached, faintly amused look about him. The Duchess explained they had only a few moments before arrived back from Turkey having stopped off in Paris for a wedding. They were just going to change and so we left our cases with our night things there and drove the short distance to the Art Gallery.

We saw a selection of the work of twelve leading wildlife artists which had been organised by Dr Eric Ennion, the bird painter and writer. The Duke and Duchess soon joined us and I heard her insisting that we must all dine by candlelight.

About thirty people sat down to a gourmet dinner at small tables in the refectory. Nan and I were seated separately – she on the Duke's left, while I sat at the Duchess's table on her left, Dr Ennion on her right. Looking down from the walls in the soft glow of candles were the faces and costumes of other ages.

Nicole de Bedford belongs firmly to the present. A plump, stylish power-house of energy, the driving force which keeps Woburn among the leaders in the stately home league – grossing something like £300,000 a year. No difficulty about conversation as she sustained a sparkling flow of anecdotes and reminiscence throughout dinner.

She was married at seventeen to a much older man but when they had had four children it ended in divorce. After a spell in the French Resistance movement during the war, she took up film production and it was while working on a series for television that she met the Duke of Bedford and became his third wife.

In the stately home stakes there is of course keen rivalry. Not purely by chance the kennels at Woburn bear the names of some of their competitors and once the Duke even went over to Blenheim Palace incognito and signed the visitors' book no doubt with a glint in his eye: 'Enjoyable – but not half as good as Woburn.'

The next moment I realised the Duchess was on her feet making a short speech, then Dr Ennion rose and said a few words handing to me as President of the RSPB a cheque for £100. This was totally unexpected, and I then had to get up and say something off-the-cuff. Lord knows what I said except something about the BBC canteen never seeming the same again. It really had been a fabulous meal.

After dinner, when everyone had left, the Duke and Duchess took us on a personal tour of the Abbey and its eight million pounds' worth of treasures. As this was their first night back after a trip abroad they made mental notes as we walked round of anything which didn't quite come up to their standard. Then at one point the Duke stopped in one of the corridors, unlocked a drink cabinet and so we finished our tour with brandy glasses in our hands. In was 1 a.m. when they wished us good night at the door of the Yellow Bedroom.

It turned out to be a suite with a vast old-fashioned bathroom as big as the sitting-room in our Hampstead cottage. We slept splendidly in brass bedsteads and woke to the sound of lions roaring – almost like Kilaguni – except that when I looked out of the window an English September mist was lying in swathes among the trees. And when we rang for breakfast the tea came up in gold pots – another Woburn speciality – and I think Nan liked that best of all.

RSPB occasions have also taken Nan and me to Scotland where I always get a feeling of being at home. In October 1971 there were two functions over one weekend. The first was at the Hydro, Dunblane, where I had been invited to reply for the guests at the Scottish Ornithologists' Conference. Although in conservation matters there were growing signs of awareness, I spoke of the tremendous job that remained to be done. By the year 2000 there will probably be another twelve million of us living in the UK. Unless we can educate people on a big enough scale to care about wildlife and the countryside now, then the future will be bleak indeed. That of course is why the RSPB places such importance on the setting up of Nature Centres.

I recalled meeting the Archbishop of Canterbury the week before with some of my colleagues at a small luncheon in Lambeth Palace. Sitting next to him, I was able to ask some questions. One of his answers seemed to me revealing. With all his world-wide responsibilities, I asked whether there was any one thing in particular that worried him. He was silent for a few moments – I thought perhaps he hadn't heard the question. Then with thoughtful deliberation as though talking to himself and looking straight ahead he said: 'Sometimes, I lie awake in the middle of the night and I wonder – am I acceptable to God?' That is the kind of humility many of us might feel faced with in this crucial decade of the seventies – so much to be done – so little time to do it in.

The following afternoon with the Chairman Charles Wilson, a genial hard-headed Yorkshireman, and Peter Conder, the RSPB's Director, I had the honour of opening the £30,000 Nature Centre on the shores of Loch Leven. It is housed in attractive grey stone buildings on the 300 acre Vane Farm bought by the Society as a reserve in 1967. The fact that it is set in farmland is itself important. There are children in city streets who have never even seen a cow let alone an osprey or a black-tailed godwit. Here cattle and sheep graze the hillside, while barley and potatoes grow in the fields. It is a first-class example of farming and conservation all in one and it came about through co-operation between a variety of different bodies. Support has come from five Scottish County Education Authorities and from the Carnegie United Kingdom Trust and the Countryside Commission. There have also been donations from the Wildfowl Trust, the World Wildlife Fund and the Helena Howden Trust.

Its success has already been overwhelming among the general public, who flock to it at weekends, and with the thousands of school children who make official visits during the week. The two principal rooms at the Nature Centre are fitted with display panels, relief models, a large tank containing wildlife from the loch and there are also facilities for showing slides and films. An eye-opener in every sense and we hope the first of many.

Another Scottish visit we made was to some of the reserves with a number of RSPB Council members in June 1972. First stop was Dunkeld in Perthshire. After dinner we drove out to the Loch of the Lowes owned by the Scottish Wildlife Trust. A smallish loch in a beautiful setting as so much of Scotland must have looked before the forests were felled for timber, and before the sheep came. It was scooped out by a glacier, just one of the features left by the ice which sculpted this landscape thousands of years ago. There are many theories about how it got its name – it may have come from the fact that this was the place where hounds were unleashed or 'lowsed' for hunting the boar.

It was very quiet in the wooden observation hide as we looked out across the grassy waters of the loch which are only sixteen to twenty feet deep. On the other shore at the top of a pine tree we could clearly see an osprey's eyrie with one of the parent birds and three young. How good to see this most persecuted of birds now breeding here in safety – protected by the eagle eyes of a former bank manager now a voluntary helper with the Scottish Wildlife Trust. Also in the hide was a fresh-faced lad of fourteen with tow coloured hair who had slept on site each night up to 3 a.m. until the eggs were hatched. Pellets below the nest showed that these ospreys fed mostly on perch, not the surface-basking pike as is more usually the case.

Next day we drove through splendid highland scenery up Glen Garry to Dalwhinnie on Loch Ericht – then by Glen Truim with the Cairngorms on our right. At Kingussie we turned right for Insh Fen – a new RSPB reserve. An excellent mixed habitat with many curlews making their liquid, bubbling cries, redshank and snipe.

A short distance away was the RSPB osprey site at Loch Garten near Aviemore on Speyside. At this, the best-known of the sites with a much greater pressure of visitors, the operation is organised each spring on semi-military lines. A forward post, barbed wire, electronic devices, round-the-clock watches by relays of volunteers, all are used to keep the eyrie free from harm. Here we saw the hen with two young on the nest. These must be the most observed birds in history. That year alone 50,000 saw them on site and millions more on television.

25 Golden Moments

At Television Centre, News Division had settled down as smoothly as could have been wished – not that we were standing still, especially at the top. Desmond Taylor, who had been editor longer than any of his predecessors, stepped up to become Editor, News and Current Affairs. The two departments were now drawing closer together as had always been intended from Sir Hugh Greene's time. In Desmond's place came an Assistant Head of Current Affairs – Derrick Amoore. Derrick, a Cambridge graduate and one-time paratrooper, had joined the BBC as a research assistant in 1959 working on the 'Tonight' programme and becoming its editor five years later. From there he went on to become editor of '24 Hours' and then devised and launched 'Nationwide'.

His appointment caused a fluttering in the dovecote because as a current affairs 'whizz-kid' it was thought he might bring gimmickry to the News. On the other hand, the bulletins were in any case becoming more like programmes and the Nine O'Clock News was being extended to run twenty-five minutes so that more emphasis on production was only to be expected. From the outset Derrick made it clear that he was not going to do anything in a hurry but wanted first to get a complete grasp of the News operation before making any changes. As he put it, 'all my options are open'.

Meantime, I found that one of the advantages of working in the mainstream of television at the Centre was the opportunity for taking part in programmes other than News. I have been lucky in being asked to do all kinds of things from educational programmes and documentaries to light entertainment.

Christmas is a time for letting hair down, so I was quite tickled when Producer Michael Hurl invited me to take part in a show called 'Christmas with the Stars'. The idea was that Cilla Black in the course of the programme would chat up some of the well-known faces on the box. There were Jack Warner, Cliff Michelmore and Geoffrey Keen, better known as Brian Stead of 'The Troubleshooters', and me. That is how the four of us came to be waiting in a dressing-room one evening in November 1970.

Television is to a large extent an exercise in illusion and the recording of all big shows well in advance means that the Christmas spirit has to come at least a month early to Television Theatre, the former Shepherd's Bush Empire. In our case we were all feeling rather dim. It might almost have been a dentist's waiting-room until Cliff, an inveterate golfer, came to the rescue and handed round the hip flask with which he normally consoles himself when landing in a bunker.

We each then had a preliminary natter with Cilla who was keeping remarkably cool as befits one of the real troupers in the business. A script had been prepared for my chat but I didn't like it much, so it was agreed that Cilla would feed me some questions and I would tell a story or two. Although the big show was being pre-recorded there was the feel of a 'live' performance with a packed house.

Once on stage I felt fine. Cilla may cultivate the look of the daft kid next door but she is in fact a steely professional and never fluffs a cue. She seems a really happy person and no doubt her marriage to manager Bobby Willis has a lot to do with it. She has come a long way since being discovered overnight when, as a Liverpool typist, she sang at a rock'n' roll club called the Iron Door. There she met the Beatles and through Brian Epstein landed her first recording contract. She still retains that look of faint surprise as though she can't really believe it has all happened and perhaps that's what her fans like about her best.

The following year, I was in two very different shows on Christmas day. At lunchtime there was 'Nature Spectacular' which consisted of a round-up of the best material from the year's wildlife films. The one and a half hour show opened with the Duke of Edinburgh and ended with Eric Morecambe. My extract had been filmed in one of the hides at Minsmere by Richard Brock of the BBC Natural History Unit.

Then in the evening I made a fleeting appearance in the Morecambe and Wise Show. Producer John Ammonds, or 'Big A' as the boys call him, rang to ask if I would take part in a 'Top-hat' dance routine. I said I was the worst dancer in the world but was told that did not matter. The other members of the male chorus were Cliff Michelmore, Eddie Waring, Frank Bough, Michael Parkinson and Patrick Moore. A right lot of charlies we looked too in our Moss Bros gear.

On going into the enormous hangar-like studio, the first thing I saw was Glenda Jackson and Ernie with linked arms advancing towards me grinning all over their faces. The two boys, apart from being tremendous pros, really are the nicest people which, of course, is why everyone in the entertainment business regards it almost as an accolade to appear on their show. This was also a special Christmas for them because it marked their thirtieth year as a double act. Glenda Jackson, fresh from playing Queen Elizabeth, seemed to enjoy the dance routines, although she said she had last had 'tap' lessons as a teenager.

Rehearsals had been held on and off for a fortnight and so the dancing was getting quite smooth. They made their entrance at the top of a great staircase flanked by candelabras and backed with flame-coloured drapes, Eric and Ernie resplendent in top-hats, white ties and tails, Glenda in a ginger wig and scarlet frock. Down the stairs they came singing the refrain of 'Let's face the Music'. On the words 'There may be trouble ahead' – Eric's collar burst open. That was not intended. They did another take

At the end of the 'Top-hat' sequence the camera panned along the chorus and when it reached me at the end of the line, I led them off with a tripping step and arms outstretched. What I didn't know was that, as I sang the refrain, some joker in the Control gallery had dubbed on a falsetto squeak. On play-back they decided they liked it, so that is how I came to sound as if I'd recently jumped over a five-bar gate.

Another pleasant Christmas duty has been the Appeal which I have made on six occasions for the 'Television for the Deaf Fund' run by the Royal National Institute for the Deaf. It was also at an RNID charity performance given by the great mime artiste, Marcel Marceau, that I was first presented to Princess Anne. She is tall and slim and was wearing a greenish-blue gown almost the colour of her eyes. Her elegance and charm are combined with a marvellous sense of humour, but she is rather more forthright than her brother.

She asked me whether I had ever got the pages of the News mixed up, because only the day before when she had presided as Commandant at the St John Ambulance Review in Hyde Park, they had handed her the three pages of her speech in the wrong order. Fortunately, she said no one had noticed.

We talked too about all the tragic news that had been coming from Northern Ireland. Even there though, a sense of fun is not unknown. I told her about an Army patrol which had marched down a certain street each afternoon for a week. Every day, an old man stood on the kerb outside his home and spat on them as they passed. By the end of the week they were distinctly bored with this so, to get even, one of the soldiers went up to him and presented a tray of empty cups shouting cheerily: 'Thanks for the tea, grandad.' The old boy was last seen being clobbered by his neighbours.

Nan and I have been in several programmes together. The first was 'Going for a Song' which is produced in the BBC Bristol Studios. Antiques are a considerable interest of ours although we have never had enough money to make a big collection. The programme we appeared in was the first of a new series and it was the first time a husband and wife had appeared as the guests.

Arthur Negus of the easy, knowledgeable manner we felt we had known all our lives and Max Robertson was an old friend of ours so that helped too. I felt relieved to be able to identify the first object correctly as a Georgian tea caddy, but the main subject was porcelain. When it came to pricing pieces Nan was much nearer the mark than I, although we were both foxed by a small Liverpool sauceboat which was officially said to be worth £850.

We hesitated a little before accepting an invitation to appear in 'He said – She said', but when we heard who the other husbands and wives were we felt happier about it. England cricketer, Ted Dexter and his wife Sue, James Villiers, fresh from playing Charles II, and his wife Patricia, and the other couple were Mr and Mrs Jimmy Perry who were both formerly on the stage. Jimmy is now the writer of 'Dad's Army'.

For this recording we went to the BBC's luxurious 'Pebble Mill' studios at Birmingham. David Jacobs was in the chair and we both knew him well so that made us feel at home. At one point the wives were asked whether there was any one thing about their husbands that they would like to change. I heard Nan saying how maddening it was when I washed my gumboots every morning in the sink. It gave the impression that I marched through the house with muddy boots and so for weeks afterwards I had to put up with a flood of letters. All most unfair because in fact I always take my boots off by the front door and then carry them through to the sink in the kitchen.

301

Apparently in the American version of the programme there are no holds barred at all and intense domestic dramas are played out on the box, resulting not infrequently in divorce. Thank heavens here the sting is removed and we all found it fairly innocuous fun.

The next time I was in Birmingham it was to appear on 'Pebble Mill at One' the lunchtime programme. This took place in the ground floor foyer of the building. Robert Langley, who had been a television Newsreader for a time at Alexandra Palace, did the compèring and I was interviewed standing against large plate-glass windows with the gardens on the other side. While we were in front of the cameras trying to discuss the pros and cons of caged birds I heard confused noises on the other side of the window and saw to my astonishment a whole lot of characters with their noses pressed against the glass holding up banners protesting about something or other. In these days of demos, the programme is perhaps a trifle too 'open-plan'.

One of the most prestigious shows I have taken part in was a two and three-quarter hour feature production to mark the end of the sixties. It was thought that such a traumatic decade should, on expiry, be given more than a passing nod so Robin Scott, head of BBC 2 commissioned Jeremy Murray-Brown to give it the full treatment. This was a formidable challenge which Jeremy took up with relish.

I was asked to provide the news-thread linking the programme and spent hours round the gas fires, drinking coffee and working on the script in those converted villas at Lime Grove – the think tank of Current Affairs. The main difficulty was that the whole programme had to be recorded in only two days of studio time.

Jeremy assembled quite a cast: Enoch Powell, John Peel, Sir Francis Chichester, the Archbishop of Canterbury, Cardinal Heenan, James Mossman, Susan Hampshire, Professor Day-Lewis, Arthur Schlesinger, Jun., Malcolm Muggeridge and Yehudi Menuhin to say nothing of the Biba fashion models, the Bonzo Dog Band and Jimmy Savile. It was almost like Madame Tussaud's come to life. The hospitality suite at the Centre was a stimulating place to be in and Jimmy Savile, as the interviewer, certainly had a fresh approach. Cardinal Heenan's face was quite a study as Jimmy asked him breezily: 'How're things with the Church now, business-wise as it were?'

302

Each of the pundits duly gave his impressions of the decade and even if the programme didn't make the Top Twenty it handsomely marked the passing of the sixties and was great fun to do.

An East Anglian documentary in which Nan and I took part was filmed on the River Deben in Suffolk. We followed it from near its beginnings as little more than a roadside ditch at Debenham down to Hollesley Bay, where it flows into the sea between Bawdsey and Felixstowe. At Woodbridge the river broadens out and becomes navigable, so there the producer Gordon Moseley with the cameraman, Nan and myself boarded a launch for the last section of the trip, stopping at various riverside pubs on the way. The filming took place in early May and we were blessed with perfect sunshine.

One of the radio programmes I most enjoyed making was 'A visit to Minsmere' which John Burton produced in stereo. Another wildlife series for the Bristol Natural History Unit was 'Sounds Natural' in which Derek Jones interviewed a number of well-known people on certain aspects of wildlife which interested them and the appropriate recordings of the birds or animals mentioned were then fed into the programme in a most natural way. It's amazing how many stage and television folk have this interest. My contribution opened a series which included Rolf Harris, Joyce Grenfell, Nigel Stock, Harry Secombe, Peter Cushing and jazz trumpeter Humphrey Lyttleton.

Throughout 1972 work in the Newsroom was governed by the thought that Derrick Amoore was planning a new format for the Nine O'Clock News. He would not commit himself to an exact date but it appeared that September would be the most likely month. That unfortunately was the month Nan and I had planned to visit Russia to see if by any chance the old place had changed, but obviously the visit had to be cancelled. In fact, I was asked not to be on leave at all for the last quarter of the year. This also meant we were unable to accept an invitation to fly to Hong-Kong to help launch a British Week there in November. Missing that hurt, because Hong-Kong is a place we have always been especially keen to see.

As the summer wore on it finally became clear that Derrick had not decided what form the new look should take and the date was then postponed until November. One of his main difficulties was that Studio N1 was too small by half. Really it was only intended for a simple, straightforward type of presentation. On the other hand there were many new electronic devices he was tempted to use.

Finally Monday, 13 November was chosen as the launching date and a busy time preceded it with many dummy-runs. On Friday 10th I signed off the single Newsreader style News for the last time. Some engineers came in afterwards and asked me to autograph a tile from the old backing as a memento. Not an eye was dry.

During that weekend the new set was hurriedly installed and so, on the night and not without misgivings, there I sat with Richard Whitmore from the reporting staff waiting for the off. The misgivings came not so much from having a twosome, as from the cramped space for the desks. Richard's was on my right at an angle of ninety degrees, then there was a desk for a correspondent at right angles to him and another reporter was situated behind my right ear. We looked like a bunch of kids kept after school. But – not to worry – the show must go on.

In the control gallery the production team were seated at the huge cockpit-like desk facing rows of monitor screens. Four gave the output from the cameras in the studio, a fifth showed the newsroom, another the BBC Parliamentary studio at Westminster. Other monitors were for the colour stills and the telecine and videotape machines. Incidentally, most people who visit the Centre are amazed to find that the News is not at all as simple as it might appear at home, but is, in fact, an intricate, electronic jig-saw puzzle.

In charge of production is a Director. At his right hand sits a secretary surrounded by stop-watches and coloured pens for marking scripts. However glamorous she may be, once the programme is on the air, she must become an icy calculator – timing each item to the second. On the left sits a long-haired youth in a pink shirt, his hand hovering above an array of press-buttons showing coloured lights. He is the vision-mixer and punches up the appropriate picture source, as required. Beside him – the all important senior television engineer. On the other side of a glass screen is the sound mixing panel and a bank of turntables and tape machines, which might be used to play a correspondent's despatch or add effects to a piece of silent film. More engineers across the room operate the cameras by remote control. Then, behind, at desks on a raised dais are

304

the two senior editors whose job it is to over-see and bear ultimate responsibility for the whole complex operation.

As transmission time drew near that night and the inevitable last minute cuts and alterations were communicated to the team, the air was edgy and the language blue.

That was the prevailing colour in the studio too, where Richard and I with a couple of minutes to go, were frenziedly checking through the sixty or more pages of script. Dark blue felt lined the walls. This was not for decor purposes but to appease the new god CSO or to give him his full title Colour Separation Overlay. It is not for me to attempt to explain this electronic wizardry but, roughly, CSO is a device which gets hooked on a certain colour. Ours is just mad about blue. So – sit a Newsreader or Correspondent in front of a blue background and – hey presto – CSO will project behind him a picture from a different source altogether. The Newsroom for instance. If one of us wore a blue suit or shirt or tie we'd get the Newsroom crawling all over that too. These background pictures are only communicated by CSO to TV monitor screens. The walls, as far as Richard and I were concerned, remained an inscrutable blue.

The adrenaline was beginning to flow now, heartbeats quickening, fingers crossing that the new, untried format wouldn't fall apart. Someone said 'good luck' and through my earpiece I heard the production secretary's voice intoning 'ten seconds to go'. Then the Director setting the machine in motion: 'Stand by tape' (that was for the opening music), 'stand by studio' (that was for us), 'stand by cameras'. The count-down was ending – four, three, two. The floor-manager's arm was raised to cue. A yellow light flashed on my desk and off I went with the new-look News. My voice was saying: 'Richard Whitmore will be joining me in the News studio from now on. Although, as you can see, we've changed the look of the Nine O'Clock News, we haven't changed our main aim of covering as much as we can in the time that we have. So, the main points tonight . . .'

From the studio viewpoint nothing came unstuck, except that handovers were awkward owing to our cramped situation. It also seemed strange just butting in with an item now and again, instead of giving the news in a consecutive flow. In homes throughout the land the new god found few worshippers – the moving figures which CSO was showing in the background tended in fact to drive viewers themselves up the wall. They

305

hastened to write and say so. It was a week before the Press pitched in and few papers pulled their punches: all disliked the new distractions.

After six weeks of this, it was decided to dispense with the moving background, except for the opening and closing headline shots. In between, the Newsreader would be shown against the backing of a Newsroom blind. A step had been taken in the right direction and an official BBC spokesman was quoted as saying: 'We are trying to improve the presentation all the time.'

These moves on the News were taking place as the BBC preened itself for its fiftieth anniversary. As far as Nan and I were concerned, the first celebration of 1972 had been in June, when we chalked up our twenty-five years. At least we were able to mark it in slightly better style than we had for our post-war utility wedding.

By November, BBC functions were falling thick and fast. Outstanding and unforgettable among them was the dinner at Guildhall to which we were lucky enough to be invited. It had a fantastic guest list and wherever one looked there were famous faces not only from the BBC but from Parliament, the professions, the stage, cinema, journalism and the arts. The Prime Minister was the principal guest and the ancient, grey stone walls were a dramatic setting for a glittering company.

Afterwards, the diners thronged down into the thirteenth-century crypt for drinks and informal talk. Mr Heath, in spite of a day conferring at Number Ten on critical industrial troubles, looked as calm, confident and self-contained as ever. I asked him how it felt making a speech in this austere, historic place and he recalled Lloyd-George's description in 1911: 'It was like speaking to a lot of penguins on an ice-floe.'

The other not to be forgotten occasion was the Royal Television Society Dinner at the Dorchester. Lord Hill was bowing out as BBC Chairman and in his speech the old campaigner was in scintillating reminiscent form. His term had been extended to cover the anniversary and no swansong could have been more effective. At its conclusion all critical assessment of him was suspended as the whole gathering of a thousand or so hardened professionals gave him a thundering, standing ovation.

It was inevitable perhaps that at the Variety Club Luncheon at Grosvenor House a week or two later Robin Day, in a sparkling speech, should say the BBC was now over the hill.

The new man to take on this top job, which must surely be one of the most difficult balancing acts in the country, was Sir Michael Swann, a fifty-two-year-old English academic who lives in Scotland. This prompted a London based producer to say of his appointment: 'A man from a far country of whom we know little.'

In fact, as a distinguished biologist, Sir Michael was no stranger to BBC microphones and cameras and just ten years ago even made the front cover of *Radio Times* as a contributor to Aubrey Singer's 'Science International'. He came to the BBC from Edinburgh University where since 1965 he had been Principal and Vice-Chancellor. There he had a reputation for standing up against student power and asserting university authority. On meeting the Press he said he thought the BBC was not wholly unlike a university, only jollier – 'it's the same lot of creative people with an independent turn of mind who have got to have freedom. But you have got to see that they do not clash with society outside.'

He does not wish to get bogged down in day to day administration but says he will be in the front seat alongside the driver reading the map and deciding which route to follow. A tall, grey, craggy man he certainly gives an impression of strength and decisiveness – two qualities of which the BBC always stands much in need.

Another key appointment came at about the same time as Sir Michael's; another Wykehamist, Alasdair Milne, took over from David Attenborough as Director of Programmes, Television. This meant a return to London for Milne after being Controller of BBC, Scotland. Originally appointed by that astonishing discerner of talent Mrs Grace Wyndham Goldie, he formed with Donald Baverstock a penetrating partnership which broke much new ground in 'Tonight'. Incidentally, to my mind it is not at all a bad thing that in these two new appointments there will again be some Scottish influence at the top.

From my fly on the wall viewpoint I would say that the BBC's unease is directly traceable to the start of commercial television back in 1955. Ever since then, the organisation has been turning itself inside out to stave off the competition. Perhaps, in some ways, there has been too much success and in overcoming its adversary the Corporation has been forced to adopt too many of his methods. As a result, some of the spirit of dedicated public service has gone.

Production staff and many others tend today to be on short-term contracts and, in a determination to make their mark, are perhaps more inclined to sensationalise. The physical or verbal 'punch-up' is not necessarily the best way of throwing light on a delicate industrial or political problem.

If one only knew of this country from what was seen or heard over the air, a somewhat sombre impression it would be. As through the media, sex tends to become erotica, so can news become 'newsrotica'.

This is not to say that the BBC is not the finest broadcasting service in the world bar none. But simply that in some respects I believe there has been an over-emphasis on the negative aspects of life. Perhaps the trouble was that in exorcising the 'Auntie' image 'knocking' as a habit became ingrained. But 'Auntie' is now no more. She was left as Peter Black[1] put it: 'standing on the corner outside Broadcasting House in her black bombasine wondering what was to become of her. (Some say that she was whisked away in a taxi to the ITA's headquarters in Knightsbridge.)'

As I write, the twitching of my news antennae suggests that Britain might just possibly be getting bored with being 'the sick man of Europe'. We have, of course, been given up for dead before and may yet again surprise the world and ourselves. Stranger things have happened and just as the BBC caught and reflected the mood of the abrasive, introspective sixties, so may it foster with equal success any positive signs of recovery in the seventies.

That is, of course, as long as its money troubles can be kept at bay. In this never-ending struggle, which the D-G has likened to running up an escalator for ever moving down, resource and initiative of a high order are shown. BBC Enterprises with Peter Dimmock at its head is in the forefront of the sales and marketing drive to help keep the Corporation from plunging too steeply into the red. Nevertheless, it was with a certain wry amusement that I received a telephone call one afternoon at home in Hampstead.

That exemplary canine, my near namesake 'Dougal' (but with only one 'l') of 'Magic Roundabout' fame had, it seems, lent his image to a new dog food to be marketed by Canada Packers. As BBC Enterprises would be receiving royalties on

[1] *The Biggest Aspidistra in the World*, by Peter Black, published by British Broadcasting Corporation, 1972.

the tins, how would Dougall like to help Dougal by attending the Press reception for the launching at a posh London hotel? There is, of course, nothing I wouldn't do for the dear old Beeb, so with eyebrows slightly raised, I said yes, sure, providing my editor agreed.

I hope there wasn't a departmental dog fight – but the answer was, not unexpectedly, 'no'. A small episode which perhaps stems from the Corporation's slightly schizophrenic stance.

Still reeling from the effects of the fiftieth anniversary celebrations, it was with a feeling of some dismay that I realised my own fortieth BBC anniversary was nigh. Although immensely proud and grateful to have played a small part in a large slice of broadcasting history, I did not feel in wildly celebratory mood. Nevertheless Derrick very kindly insisted on organising a splendid dinner for me at the VIP suite in the Centre. It did me great honour and Nan and I enjoyed it enormously.

There is another rather touching ceremony for BBC hands who have completed forty: the golden moment of the presentation of a watch I hied me to the Director-General's office after lunch that day. His office is up on the sixth floor in a grey-carpeted top people's section of the long corridor round the outer edge of the building. While I waited in the ante-room, I looked across at the space-age view of the inner side of this great, circular power-house. Below, in the middle, is a courtyard with a plot of grass and a fountain where two reclining figures represent Sound and Vision. Soaring up from it for forty feet is an obelisk topped by a gilded bronze figure of Helios, the Sun God. He looks exotic and pagan in silhouette against the great curve of white wall with tier upon tier of hutch-like office windows encircling him.

Owing to the fountain's position in the centre of this great well it was found that the sound of water reverberated so loudly that the office workers could scarcely hear themselves think. So now all is silent. Except for a curious soughing noise like distant ocean swell which apparently comes from the ventilators.

To me it all looks unreal, remote and ingrowing. The perfect setting for a big-brother boss. Fortunately, Charles Curran is not at all like that. A big man certainly, but in no way domineering. In fact, he is genuinely modest and kind. On his desk was a watch case.

We talked in general terms about broadcasting and then got

on to the pronunciation of proper names. It was very natural he said that people should get hot under the collar when they heard their home-towns being mangled. It was also annoying, the D-G continued, when people had their own names misspelt. I laughed and said it was always happening to me – I was used to it.

'Well now,' he said, 'I must give you this ... only I'm afraid it will have to go back – you see the engravers ...'

Inside was a jolly fine watch. The inscription read:

R. N. DOUGAL
B.B.C.
1933–1973

I swear I heard a little dog laugh.

Index

Abbey Manor, Evesham, 97-9
Abercrombie, Professor Lascelles, 47
Acheson, Dean, 252
Adam, Kenneth, 281
Akureyri, 121
Alder, James, 293
Alekseyev, Admiral, 154, 157
Allison, Ronald, 244
Amoore, Derrick, 298, 303-4, 309
Andersen, Hans Christian, 156
Anderson, Marjorie, 97
Andrews, Eamonn, 246
Anne, Princess, 300
Annison, Mrs, 22
Appleby, John, 200
Archangel, 140-1
Archer, Admiral, 126, 136-8
Armstrong, Neil, 281
Arnell, 'Skip', 106
Askey, Arthur, 60, 83
Aspel, Michael, 219, 242, 246
Astell, Betty (Mrs Cyril Fletcher), 21
Astor, Lady Nancy, 108
Astor, Viscount, 108
Athi, River, 272
Attenborough, David, 249, 307
Attlee, Clement, 149, 164, 192, 199
Axell, Herbert E., 204, 233

Baker, Raymond, 173
Baker, Richard, 217, 246, 248
Baldwin, Stanley, 77
Balkwill, Michael, 221
Barnet, Lady, 21
Baronova, 70
Bartlett, Vernon, 61
Basil, Colonel de, 70

Batten, Doctor, 202
Baverstock, Donald, 307
BBC: Empire Service, later Overseas Service, 50-114
  European Service, 167
  Listener Research Department, 190
  Natural History Unit, 299
  News Review for the Deaf and Hard of Hearing, 247
  Repertory Company, 190
BBC Television, Alexandra Palace, 73-84, 95, 163-4, 198-202, 234-5, 278, 281
  Outside Broadcasts, 163-7
  Television Centre, 282-8, 298
Beamish, Sir Tufton, 289
Beardsley, Aubrey, 30
Beatles, the, 191, 252, 255-7, 299
Beatty, Robert, 97-9, 101
Beckwith, Reginald, 97
Bedford, Duke and Duchess of, 294-5
Belfrage, Bruce, 96
Bell, Martin, 284
Bennett, Arnold, 37, 54
Berger, Joseph, 125
Berlin, 150-4, 158-9
Bermuda, HMS, 121
Bevin, Ernest, 184
Black, Cilla, 298-9
Black, Peter, 199, 308
Blake, William, 291
Bligh, Jasmine, 74
Blücher, 157
Bolshoi Theatre, 136
Bolshoi Zal, 136
Bonarjee, Stephen, 211, 217, 220
Bough, Frank, 299
Boult, Sir Adrian, 85, 190

Index

Index

Day, Robin, 213, 261, 306
Day-Lewis, Cecil, 246, 302
De L'Isle and Dudley, V.C., Lord, 39
Dean, Captain Dixie, 140-2
Deloitte, Plender Griffiths and Co., 39-41
Denbigh Castle, HMS, 146
Deodar, HMS, 101
Dexter, Ted, 301
Diadem, HMS, 139, 155-8
Diaghilev, Serge, 70
Dimbleby, Richard, 176, 198, 253-4
Dimmock, Peter, 163-4, 166, 198, 308
Dixon, Cecil (Sophie), 49
Djibouti, 180
Doig, Dr Robert, 256-8
Doran, Colin, 191
Dorté, Philip, 163-4, 200
'Dougal', 308-10
Dougall, Alastair (son), 197, 202, 241, 246, 251
Dougall, Moira (Mrs. Pat Sayers) (sister), 25-6, 50, 251
Dougall, Nan (Mrs. Robert Dougall), 9, 186-9, 192-5, 197, 209, 223-30, 240-2, 246, 251, 253-5, 262-5; marriage, 10, 168-9; in Singapore, 176-81; in Kenya, 269-77; at Woburn Abbey, 294-7; in 'Going for a Song', 301
Dougall, Nel l(sister), 25, 50, 251
Dougall, Robert (author's father), 25, 28-9, 36-7, 49-50, 161, 182, 192, 251
Dougall, Robert, at Bush House, 9; married to Nan, 10, 168-9; President of RSPB, 13; childhood and schooldays, 25-38; at Deloitte's, 39-40; enters BBC as accountant, 41; Announcer, BBC Empire Service and Over-Seas Service, 50-114; interest in Ballet, 69-70; in Germany,

77-81; at Abbey Manor, 97-9, 111; joins Navy, 115; training in Navy, 115-19; journey to Russia, 120-46; demobilization, 160; Staff Commentator, Outside Broadcasts, Television, 163-7; European Service, 167; British Far Eastern Broadcasting Service, 169-79; in Singapore, 170-81; the Light Programmer, 183; in West Hampstead, 186-8; and Southwold, 189; transferred to Presentation Department, 192; moving house, 193-4; interest in birdlife, 203; his cottage in Southwold, 209; family life in Hampstead, with Miche, Alastair and pets, 223; voted Clearest Television Speaker of the Year (1963), 246; association with Royal Institute for the Deaf, 247, 300; house and family, 251; awarded MBE, 254-7; moving house again, 263-5; in Kenya, 265-77; last news broadcast from Alexandra Palace, 282; as President of RSPB, 289-97; celebration party, forty years in the BBC, 309; presentation, and his name misspelt, 310
Dougall, Winifred (author's mother), 25, 28-9, 49, 161, 182, 192, 247, 251
Douglas-Home, Sir Alec, 221, 245, 253
Dower, A. V. Gandar, 52
Dubeck, Alexander, 260
Ducat, A., 36
Duff, Robin, 99-100, 103
Dunblane, 295
Dungeness, 204
Dunhill, David, 184
Dunkeld, 297

Edmunds, John, 282
Edward VIII, King, 72-3

313

Index

Edwards, Jimmy, 190
Eisenhower, Dwight D., 240
Elizabeth II, Queen, 22-3, 176, 185, 192-3, 254, 257
Elizabeth the Queen Mother, Queen, 22-3
Elliot, Colonel Walter, 94
Ellison, John, 97-8
Emergency Information Services 236
Empress of Scotland, SS, 176
Englemann, Franklin 'Jingle', 184-5, 191
Ennion, Dr Eric, 294-5
Epstein, Brian, 299
Everest, Mount, 211

Falls, Cyril, 61
'Family Favourites', 185-6
Farjeon, Herbert, 70
Farrer, 'Ajax', 57
Fender, Percy, 36
Festival of Britain, 192
Field Guide to the Birds of East and Central Africa, A, 275
Fletcher, Cyril, 21
Flitcroft, Henry, 294
Floyd, David, 118
Fogg, Eric, 59
Fonteyn, Dame Margot, 70
Foot, Sir Robert, 161
Fort Vérchères, SS, 140
Fox, Paul, 240-1, 287
Fraser, Peter, 109
Frost, David, 237
Fry, Lieutenant, 131
Furlong, Ronnie 169

Gagarin, Yuri, 240
Gaitskell, Hugh, 215, 244-5
Galle Face Hotel (Colombo), 180
Ganges, HMS, 115
Gaulle, General Charles de, 10, 110, 240, 245
Gedye, G. E. R., 83
Gee, Howard, 65
Genghis, Khan, 126

George V, King, 53-4; Jubilee, 67; funeral, 71
George VI, King, 73; death, 192-3
Georgic, SS, 169-70
Gibbons, Carroll, 40
Gill, Eric, 49
Gilliam, Laurence, 68
Gillmor, Robert, 292
Glen Garry, 297
Gloucester, Duke of, 61
Goering, Hermann, 95
'Going for a Song', 301
Goldie, Grace Wyndham, 307
Goonhilly Downs, 243
Gorham, Maurice, 46, 163
Goring, Marius, 235
Gorshkov, Admiral, 146
Goss, Mr, 212
Gowon, General, 278
Graves, Sir Cecil, 43, 51, 161
Graves, Keith, 284
Gray, Basil, 52, 58, 62, 168, 183
Gray, Sylvia, 22
Gray, Wendy, 168
Great Train Robbery, 245
Greenbaum, Hyam, 74
Greene, Sir Hugh Carlton, 219, 235-9, 245, 279-80
Greenslade, Wallace, 'Bill', 214
Grenfell, Joyce, 303
Grisewood, Freddie, 57-8, 69, 74
Grivas, Colonel, 215
Gutman, Luise, 260
Gutteridge, Jack (Jackie Pallo), 251

Haggard, Stephen, 235
Haley, Sir William, 161, 168, 191, 196
Halifax, Lord and Lady, 111
Hall, Henry, 53
Hamburg, 159
Hampshire, Susan, 302
Harding, Archie, 182
Harding, Sir John, 215
Harris, Robert, 97-8
Harris, Rolf, 303

314

Index

Index

Famous Animal Books in Fontana

Joy Adamson
Pippa's Challenge
    (Illus.)
The Spotted Sphinx
    (Illus.)

Born Free *(Illus.)*
Living Free *(Illus.)*
Forever Free *(Illus.)*

Gerald Durrell
**Birds, Beasts and
    Relatives**
Fillets of Plaice

Rosy is My Relative
Two in the Bush

Jacquie Durrell
Beasts in My Bed *(Illus.)*

Bruce Kinloch
Sauce for the Mongoose *(Illus.)*

Mary Chipperfield
Lions on the Lawn *(Illus.)*

Buster Lloyd-Jones
The Animals Came in One by One
Come Into My World

Harry Wolhuter
Memories of a Game Ranger

 Fontana Books